# Lecture Notes in Computer Science 11552

*Commenced Publication in 1973*
Founding and Former Series Editors:
Gerhard Goos, Juris Hartmanis, and Jan van Leeuwen

Brahim Hamid · Barbara Gallina ·
Asaf Shabtai · Yuval Elovici ·
Joaquin Garcia-Alfaro (Eds.)

# Security and Safety Interplay of Intelligent Software Systems

ESORICS 2018 International Workshops, ISSA 2018 and CSITS 2018
Barcelona, Spain, September 6–7, 2018
Revised Selected Papers

 Springer

*Editors*
Brahim Hamid
University of Toulouse
Toulouse, France

Barbara Gallina (iD)
Mälardalen University
Västerås, Sweden

Asaf Shabtai (iD)
Ben-Gurion University
Beer-Sheva, Israel

Yuval Elovici
Ben-Gurion University
Beer-Sheva, Israel

Joaquin Garcia-Alfaro (iD)
Télécom SudParis
Evry, France

ISSN 0302-9743          ISSN 1611-3349  (electronic)
Lecture Notes in Computer Science
ISBN 978-3-030-16873-5          ISBN 978-3-030-16874-2   (eBook)
https://doi.org/10.1007/978-3-030-16874-2

Library of Congress Control Number: 2019936518

LNCS Sublibrary: SL4 – Security and Cryptology

This Springer imprint is published by the registered company Springer Nature Switzerland AG
The registered company address is: Gewerbestrasse 11, 6330 Cham, Switzerland

# Foreword from the ISSA 2018 Program Chairs

Several frameworks have been proposed to help the designers of software system applications. However, we currently lack methodological tool support to take into account the interplay between security and safety and the other architecture properties. Just consider cyber-physical systems and the added complexity they offer. For example, the security of cars has been already compromised with the possibility to interact with different safety-related functionality like releasing the brakes while driving. Thus, security and safety in CPS can only be addressed holistically. Dealing with the complexity and connectivity of modern CPS can be challenging from a security and safety perspective because the architecture style can compromise security and safety, and vice versa.

This volume contains the proceedings of the International Workshop on Interplay of Security, Safety and System/Software Architecture (ISSA 2018), held in Barcelona, during September 6–7, 2018. The main focus of ISSA is on the topic of making security and safety expert knowledge available to system and software engineering processes. Special emphasis was devoted to promote discussion and interaction between researchers and practitioners focused on the particularly challenging task to efficiently integrate security and safety solutions within the restricted available design space for software systems.

The Program Committee of ISSA 2018 accepted for presentation three full papers and one short paper, out of ten submissions. Each submitted paper received at least three reviews. These proceedings contain the revised versions of these papers, covering topics such as software security engineering, domain-specific security and privacy architectures, and automative security. In addition, the program was complemented by an invited talk, by Gabriel Pedroza, from CEA France, on safety and security co-engineering intertwining.

We are grateful to the ESORICS Symposium Steering Committee and its chair, Sokratis Katsikas, for all the arrangements that made the satellite events possible, as well as Joaquin Garcia-Alfaro (ESORICS 2018 Workshop Chair), Miguel Soriano (ESORICS 2018 General Chair), and Josep Pegueroles (ESORICS 2018 Organization Chair) for their support in the workshop organization and logistics.

March 2019

Brahim Hamid
Barbara Gallina

# Organization

## International Workshop on Interplay of Security, Safety and System/Software Architecture—ISSA 2018

## Program Chairs

| | |
|---|---|
| Brahim Hamid | University of Toulouse, France |
| Barbara Gallina | Mälardalen University, Sweden |

## Program Committee

| | |
|---|---|
| Morayo Adedjouma | CEA LIST, France |
| Corinne Beider | ENAC, France |
| Julien Brunel | ONERA, France |
| Veronique Delebarre | SafeRiver, France |
| Raymond Feodoroff | Raytheon, Australia |
| Edouardo Fernandez | Florida Atlantic University, USA |
| Stefan Gruner | University of Pretoria, South Africa |
| Sigrid Gurgens | Fraunhofer SIT, Germany |
| Jason Jaskolka | Carleton University, Canada |
| Christophe Jouvray | Valeo, France |
| Jan Jurjens | University of Dortmund, Germany |
| Ferhat Khendek | University of Concordia, Canada |
| Thierry Lecomte | ClearSy, France |
| Antonio Mana | University of Malaga, Spain |
| Fabio Massacci | University of Trento, Italy |
| Anas Motii | Thales, France |
| Simin Nadjm-Tehrani | Linköping University, Sweden |
| Stéphane Paul | Thales, France |
| Genaina Rodrigues | University of Brasilia, Brazil |
| Carsten Rudolph | University of Monash, Australia |
| Jungwoo Ryoo | The Pennsylvania State University-Altoona, USA |
| Francesca Saglietti | University of Erlangen-Nuremberg, Germany |
| Christoph Schmittner | AIT Austrian Institute of Technology, Austria |
| Lionel Seinturier | University of Lille, France |
| Mark Strembeck | University fo Vienna, Austria |
| Matthias Tichy | University of ULM, Germany |
| Yanjun Wen | National University of Defense Technology, China |
| Godard Wenceslas | Airbus, France |
| Uwe Zdun | University of Vienna, Austria |

# Foreword from the CSITS 2018 Program Chairs

This volume contains the proceedings of the International Workshop on Cyber Security for Intelligent Transportation Systems (CSITS 2018), held in onjunction with the 23rd European Symposium on Research in Computer Security (ESORICS) in Barcelona, Spain.

Ever since humanity invented transportation systems, it has also introduced new problems, previously unknown. After inventing a boat, it was clear that a life-saving device must be invented as well. After inventing a car, it was clear that a safety belt as well as airbags were the new necessity. Today's boats and cars are being rapidly digitalized, thus introducing even more advanced problems. Similarly, today's digital life-saving devices and safety belts are digital, too. The physical problems that were affiliated for many decades with the transportation domain are now spilling out into the digital realm. It is therefore expected that the solutions to such new problems will emerge within the digital domain as well. Since modern vehicles, whether they drive, sail, or fly, are becoming more and more digitalized, they are also inheriting the cyber-security problems previously associated purely with the digital domain. The intersection between physical and digital is being blurred, and smart transportation is located at the center of this metamorphosis. Moreover, some of the security problems forged by the collision of digital and physical realms introduce cyber security phenomena, which are unique to intelligent transportation and may cost human lives. It is therefore critical to address the emerging cyber security-related problems, which may be inflicted upon the various phases of smart transportation.

The CSITS workshop attracted nine submissions from across 11 countries. All the papers were reviewed by at least three Program Committee members. Five full papers and one short paper were accepted, leading to a 66% acceptance rate. The accepted papers were organized into two thematic groups: car security and aviation security.

The keynote address was given by Prof. Ivan Martinovic, from the University of Oxford, with a talk entitled "Security and Privacy in a World of Safety: Analyzing Avionic Data Links and NextGen ATC Networks." In his talk, Prof. Martinovic presented insights into the various security and privacy challenges of next-generation air traffic surveillance technologies, shedding light on the practicability of different threats and the main factors that impact the success of realistic attacks. In addition, he described the OpenSky platform (https://opensky-network.org), which is a community-based receiver network collecting air traffic data. With over four trillion messages collected from more than 1000 sensors around the world, currently processing over 260K messages per second, the OpenSky Network exhibits the largest air traffic dataset of its kind. It is available to the research community for realistic and large-scale evaluation of various aspects of aviation systems and networks.

We wish to thank all of the people who made CSITS 2018 possible, including foremost the authors of all submissions for offering their work to this venue. We are grateful to the Program Committee for volunteering their time to review papers and engaging in a great deal of constructive discussion. Finally, we thank our colleagues at ESORICS for taking care of all of the logistics of this workshop. We thank the ESORICS Symposium Steering Committee and its chair, Sokratis Katsikas, for all the arrangements that made the satellite events possible as well as Joaquin Garcia-Alfaro (ESORICS 2018 Workshop Chair), Miguel Soriano (ESORICS 2018 General Chair), and Josep Pegueroles (ESORICS 2018 Organization Chair) for their support in the workshop organization and logistics.

March 2019                                                          Yuval Elovici
                                                                    Asaf Shabtai

# Organization

## International Workshop on Cyber Security for Intelligent Transportation Systems—CSITS 2018

### Program Chairs

Yuval Elovici        Ben-Gurion University of the Negev, Israel
Asaf Shabtai        Ben-Gurion University of the Negev, Israel

### Program Committee

| | |
|---|---|
| Martin Strohmeier | University of Oxford, UK |
| Nils Ole Tippenhauer | Singapore University of Technology and Design, Singapore |
| Rami Puzis | Ben-Gurion University of the Negev, Israel |
| Chris Johnson | Glasgow University, UK |
| Jianying Zhou | Singapore University of Technology and Design, Singapore |
| Anupam Chattopadhyay | Nanyang Technological University, Singapore |
| Ariel Stulman | Jerusalem College of Technology, Israel |
| Elisa Canzani | iABG Innovation Center, Germany |
| Masaki Hashimoto | Institute of Information Security, Japan |

# Contents

**Aviation Security**

**Invited Paper**

# Towards Safety and Security Co-engineering

## Challenging Aspects for a Consistent Intertwining

Gabriel Pedroza[(✉)]

CEA, LIST, Point Courrier 174, 91191 Gif-sur-Yvette, France
`gabriel.pedroza@cea.fr`

**Abstract.** The emergence of systems identified as both safety and security critical has motivated research and industry to search for novel approaches to conduct multi-concern engineering (co-engineering). But several aspects and issues have arisen during the process what has limited the advances. Among them, there are the specificities found in concepts, methods and development cycles, the current standalone practices of safety and security, and the lack of consolidated metrics for safety-security assessment. This paper presents synthetic discussions on referred topics along with some suggestions for solutions and perspectives.

**Keywords:** Safety · Security · Development cycle · Co-engineering · MDE · Safety-security metrics

## 1 Introduction

Safety and security are topics often referred in the literature as major concerns to be addressed in systems engineering. Along with the difficulties found in the practice of safety and security in their usual standalone mode, research and industry should also face new challenges arisen from the need of a common practice. The referred need does not only obey to a mere optimization of resources, but it is essentially generated by the emergence - or evolution - of application domains which are identified as both safety and security critical. Indeed, the observed dependencies between safety and security aspects in different use cases, the potential conflicts between proposed solutions, the variety of development and analysis methods, and the growing number of exigencies to improve systems' trustworthiness lead to a singular problematics. Structuring the aspects for a seamless co-engineering process is a vast, complex and, thus, very tough task. This short paper aims to describe, in a non-exhaustive manner, some aspects to move forward, highlight identified issues and perspectives for solutions, and, finally, address some questions that may enrich the ongoing discussions. In particular, it aims to raise attention on the need for a common practice of safety and security via the consistent integration of known techniques.

The rest of the paper is structured as follows. The Sect. 2 presents a conceptual positioning of safety and security. The Sect. 3 gives an overview of the

© Springer Nature Switzerland AG 2019
B. Hamid et al. (Eds.): ISSA 2018/CSITS 2018, LNCS 11552, pp. 3–16, 2019.
https://doi.org/10.1007/978-3-030-16874-2_1

standards ecosystem. A MDE approach that can be leveraged for safety-security co-engineering is explained in Sect. 4. Some difficulties to achieve integration and adoption of safety and security development cycles comes in Sect. 5. A discussion on the consistent integration of safety and security techniques is given in Sect. 6. Finally, the overall perspectives come in Sect. 7.

## 2    Positioning Safety and Security

This section introduces a minimal background to make explicit what safety and security stand for in this paper. To do so, some application domains are recalled including representative use cases which are recognized by the community as both safety and security critical. Afterwards, a conceptual positioning of safety w.r.t. security (or conversely) is given. This positioning helps to highlight commonalities and also specificities of both areas.

### 2.1    Application Domains Positioning w.r.t. Safety and Security

Industry application domains are defined by categories of problematics and by the technology applied/developed to tackle them. A wide variety of systems are developed within each application domain. They include software and hardware artifacts structured by an architecture which is often networked. Despite there is no consensus on metrics to assess criticality, the systems are labeled as critical regarding the goals and missions they should/must accomplish and the potential unwanted impacts of not succeeding in doing so. Several instances of critical systems can be found in aerospace, railway, automotive, health, and nuclear domains but also in other sectors like e-commerce, e-voting, and social-network based systems. The operation of systems in the different domains has been impacted by the evolution of Information and Communication Technology (ICT), and by the progress in autonomy, automation and - more recently - in artificial intelligence techniques. Despite these evolutions, it is likely that the emerging systems will lead to a handful of new relevant risks which have not been foreseen nor already faced by human-beings. If that occurs, our current paradigms to perceive systems' criticality will remain valid across time irrespective of the type of concern. However, what is changing for sure is the increasing gain in (1) usage of ICT over formerly manual works and missions, (2) systems automation, smartness, and complexity, and (3) physical and virtual accessibility of systems. All in all, the main stake is the trustworthiness that human-beings have on those systems, *i.e.*, the proven reliability, safety, security, etc. of those highly automated-networked-complex systems. By definition, catastrophic risks related to a safety critical system endanger human-being lives [1]. As long as those systems exhibit the three features previously listed, they will also become security critical. Thus for instance, a railway system including ICT artifacts, mostly automated, and physically and virtually accessible will certainly face critical security risks. On the contrary, certain security critical systems will be in no way safety-related, *e.g.*, e-voting, e-commerce, social network, mobile-communication systems (see Fig. 1).

This difference implies that certain application domains have technical specificities. The identification, assessment and management of risks may demand a clear understanding of them.

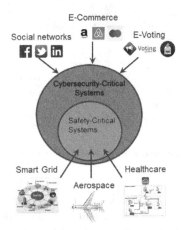

**Fig. 1.** Relationship between safety and security critical systems

## 2.2   Conceptual Positioning of Safety and Security

The current standalone practices of safety and security consists in separately integrate aspects to an engineering development cycle. The outcome is a couple of concern-oriented cycles that allow engineers to separately perform the different development phases up to the system disposal. Figure 2 roughly depicts the current state of safety and security engineering processes and their fundamental elements. Regarding the intersection between safety and security engineering processes, we can highlight the existence of commonalities between both processes. More specifically, there are conceptually similar terms and notions in both areas, like for instance, *risk, severity, likelihood*, etc.  As long as those terms and notions are proven to be semantically related, they constitute a basis for a common safety-security engineering process. But constitute such common basis is rather bulky, in particular, due to the variability of terms and notions found in standards, methods, guides and other technical documents. Some aspects to consider when determining notions similarity are:

*Syntactically Similar Terms with Different Meanings.* It refers to syntactically similar terms used in both safety and security having different meanings. For instance, even if the term *Feared Event* is used in both safety and security risks analyses, it does not necessarily have the same meaning nor structural form. A *Feared Event* in safety can be considered as a combination of a *hazard* and an *operational situation* [2] whereas a *Feared Event* in security can be the violation of a *security goal* [3] which is structured by a set of requirements, typed by a criterion or property (confidentiality, integrity, authenticity).

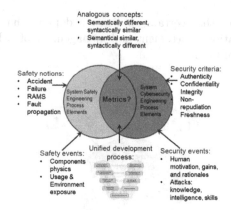

**Fig. 2.** Conceptual positioning of safety and security elements

*Syntactically Different Terms with Equivalent Meanings.* In this case, two different terms respectively used in safety and security stand for the same notion. For instance, the term *Threat Condition* introduced in the standards ED202 [5], ED-203 [6] mostly correspond to the notion of *Feared Event* found in standards like ISO-27005 [3] and also in methods like EBIOS [4].

It is expected that a common engineering process shall include metrics useful to evaluate both safety and security risks. Referred metrics are necessary when a path to a risk combines both safety and security events, and their likelihood of occurrence and severity of impact need to be evaluated. Along with previous commonalities, several specificities have been already identified:

*Specific Criteria for Evaluation.* The technical criteria for evaluation of safety and security are almost specific to each area. Known security criteria are for instance *authenticity, integrity, confidentiality, non-repudiation, freshness, controlled access,* etc. On the other side, relevant safety criteria are for instance *reliability, availability, maintainability,* etc. Despite for some cases certain criteria become common to both areas, for instance *availability*), to our knowledge, most of the criteria remain specific either to security or to safety.

*Different Nature of Events.* Safety and security analyses aim to asses the robustness of a system w.r.t. certain unwanted events. However, the nature of those events is rather different for each analysis. As for safety events, we can mention accidents, system failures and functions faults. As for security events, we can mention cyber or physical attacks, intrusions, and intentional damages and failures. Therefore, the physics of components, the system usage and its exposure to an environment are the root causes of safety events. On the contrary, security events are mostly determined by human-related factors like the motivations, gains and opportunities of attackers. In addition, successful events may require for an attacker to acquire certain knowledge, skills, and resources.

# 3   Standards, Development Cycles and Methods

## 3.1   Standards Ecosystem

A wide variety of standards have been published targeting safety or security aspects. The Fig. 3 shows some of them. Most standards are elaborated not only targeting a given problematics but also considering the particularities of an application domain. In the safety area, the standard IEC-61508 [7] is a generic reference to conduct functional safety analyses of so called Electrical-Electronic-Electronically Programmable (E/E/EP) systems. This generic standard has been taken as a reference in order to adapt and specialize the safety analyses for different application domains. An analogous pattern can be found in the development of standards pertaining to the security area (*e.g.*, assuming ISO-27005 [3] as a generic standard). However, the level of maturity, consensus and/or adoption of security standards is still questionable and many discussions and work are in progress. This disparity can be partially explained by the "delay" in the emergence of security as a strategic topic in the industry-research landscape. In addition, the identified security specificities introduce new elements and raise questions which increase the complexity of discussions.

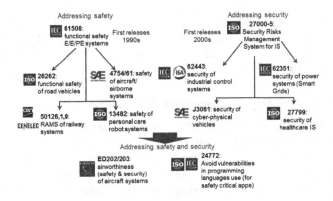

**Fig. 3.** Overview of some relevant standards for safety and security

Standards not only provide a conceptual basis but also guidelines for the integration of concerns in the development cycle. Thus, typically functional development cycles can be completed via the integration of safety and security aspects. A representative instance of such integrated process can be found in the ISO-26262 standard [2] (safety of road vehicles). A common practice of safety and security engineering will demand and integration of both safety and security aspects.

## 3.2   Towards an Unified Development Cycle

If a development process integrating safety and security aspects is required, such integration does not suffice to achieve an effective safety-security co-engineering.

For instance, typical standalone instances of safety and security development cycles include a requirements elicitation phase. A direct integration into a single cycle is to first conduct safety requirements elicitation and afterwards the security requirements phase (or conversely). This rather simple integration is largely inefficient and may even become ineffective, since it does not address potential conflicts between requirements. Moreover, conflicts may not only appear during the problem space phases but also during the solution phases in the development cycle, *e.g.*, a cypher mechanism deployed to protect frames confidentiality impacts system's performance and violates real-time safety constraints. Therefore, an unified development cycle should not only consider the integration of development processes and phases, but also the methods and techniques used in safety and security - in addition to the specificities of the application domains. The achievement of such unified development cycle shall be a milestone of industry-research working groups. However its definition is limited by: (1) the observed disparity between security vs. safety standards (maturity, consensus and adoption), and (2) the complexity of ensuring coherence between safety and security methods and techniques.

## 4   Model-Driven Approaches for Co-engineering

The importance of integrating not only processes but also methods for safety and security analyses was highlighted in previous section. This section provides insights on model-driven engineering (MDE) techniques for achieving co-engineering of safety and security.

### 4.1   Standalone Safety and Security Engineerings

The current state of practice shows that safety and security engineering are conducted in standalone mode and guided by independent processes and methods. Figure 4 shows an overview of two instances of processes to conduct safety and security activities in the development cycle. To tackle the structural complexity and integrate both processes into a single one, the following high level commonalities are observed:

- The usage of evaluation criteria is present in both processes and some criteria rely upon discrete evaluation scales (qualitative and quantitative).
- Both processes demand the definition of metrics or scales to evaluate *risks*, *likelihood*, and *severity*.
- Both processes are risk oriented and the evaluation of *risks* is based upon *likelihood* and *severity* scales.
- A function to classify the acceptability of *risks* exists in both processes.
- The elicitation of *Feared Events* is targeted in both processes.

Regarding the last item, notice that *Feared Events* identified during the safety analysis might be also targeted by attackers. Conversely, some *Feared Events*, unveiled during the security analysis, might also be caused by purely accidental functional failures. In such cases, common or interdependent *Feared Events* can be the basis to conduct the expected co-engineering.

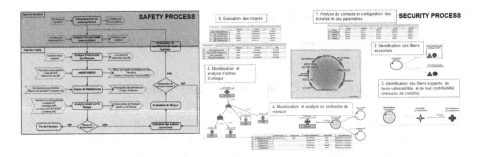

**Fig. 4.** Overview of standalone safety and security development processes

## 4.2   Model-Driven Approaches for Multi-concern Analyses

It is assumed that the reader is familiar with MDE principles and techniques. Even so, non-savvy readers can consult these references [16,17]. Model Driven Engineering (MDE) has been applied to support engineers during several phases of the development cycle, *e.g.*, design and verification [8,9]. In particular, during the design phases a model of the target system is usually constructed.   The

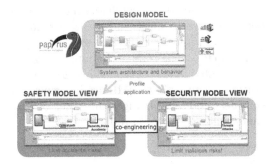

**Fig. 5.** View of safety and security models obtained after annotations

model is based upon standardized languages like UML [10] and SysML [11] which facilitate typical design tasks like system structuring, refinement, decomposition, extension, and/or transformation. MDE languages are flexible enough to be extended and specialized so as to capture the elements necessary to conduct safety and security analyses. Indeed, fundamental concepts, the relationships between them, and analyses steps can also be represented and implemented. Following typical MDE approaches, the system model can be enriched either with the elements related to safety or security. Annotating finally yields two models suitable to -separately- conduct safety or security analyses (see Fig. 5); the annotated models are insufficient to support joint safety-security analyses. However, they provide a basis to construct the co-engineering framework as explained in next subsection.

### 4.3   Joint Safety-Security Engineering

To support joint safety-security analyses (co-engineering), the MDE framework can be leveraged in the following way:

**Integration of meta-models.** Safety and security annotations are defined in separated meta-models. The meta-models allow to capture the fundamental notions, principles associated to the concern and also capture their relationships. The conceptual alignment necessary to achieve joint safety-security analyses can be started by the identification of common elements and the subsequent integration of meta-models. The Fig. 6 shows an excerpt of a diagram used to approach concepts pertaining to different standards.

**Solving conflicts.** Once meta-models are aligned and common parts linked, the dependencies can be observed and the potential conflicts along methods phases can be better identified and solved. Recall that conflicts can appear from the application of safety and security methods and techniques and also between their outcomes. In particular, when a technique is applied over modeling instances that are out of the common metamodel part.

**Integration of processes and phases.** Once method phases are supposed to be "free of conflicts", the processes can be integrated. When conflicts can not be identified in advance, the integrated development cycle should be enriched with new phases to identify and solve conflicts over concrete model instances. For instance, conflicts between safety and security requirements elicited at different phases, are solved upon specific case studies.

**Framework implementation.** The framework supporting joint safety-security analyses can be implemented following typical MDE development steps: meta-model implementation via an UML/SysML profile, generation of profile code, implementation of safety and security algorithms, customization of the framework front-end, and building the tool product.

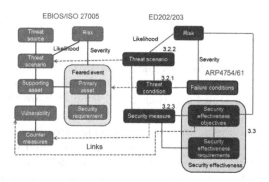

**Fig. 6.** Excerpt of a diagram showing meta-models integration

# 5   Difficulties to Achieve Integration of Safety and Security Processes and Their Adoption

In previous section, a generic, coarse description was provided about leveraging MDE techniques in order to achieve safety-security co-engineering. Our involvement in several academy-industry projects (AMASS, SESNA, ModSécAéro) allows us to prove the effectiveness of those MDE techniques. By doing so, several technical and non technical difficulties have been identified which may limit the scope of ongoing work. Regarding the current state of standalone safety and security development processes, they are in general complex, costly and mostly human based (few support to automate tasks). Despite there exist development processes that show certain integration of safety and security aspects (e.g., [5]), they are mostly specific to an application domain. Generally speaking, a low level of maturity is observed in aspects like integration, tool support and automation. Other aspects impacting the dissemination and progress of safety-security co-engineering are related to current field practices. Globally, conduct joint safety-security analyses is a quite recent research and engineering area. To our knowledge, information about case studies showing co-engineering in practice are rare. In addition, there is almost no feedback from industry on the effectiveness of applied methods and techniques. It is reasonable to believe that some years are still necessary to consolidate our understanding on the topic. For many industry sectors and several application domains, cyber-security is almost an emerging concern. In those cases, a posteriori reaction to cyber-security threats is observed; the lack of a cyber-security risks management culture often leads to underestimate, misunderstand or believe not concerned by the potential threats. Last but not least, some market, organizational and engineers practices may facilitate the adoption of new engineering processes. In particular, certification is a powerful mechanism to align technical criteria and ensure trustworthiness which finally shapes markets. However today, no certification process for safety-security critical systems exists so far. The impact of safety and security concerns in current organizations and engineers practices should be clearly identified in order to better understand it and disseminate their importance.

# 6   Integration of Safety and Security Techniques

This section is dedicated to explain an instance of integration of techniques which are usually applied in safety and security. The instance is relevant since it helps to highlight some challenges for a consistent safety-security intertwining.

## 6.1   Combined Attack-Fault Trees

Fault and attack trees are known techniques respectively used in safety and security areas. They are means to structure and evaluate unwanted events impacting a target system. On one side, fault trees are often composed by nodes representing system failures as boolean variables. The fault nodes are linked by logical gates AND, OR and can be assigned with a probability of occurrence. On the other side attack trees can be composed by nodes representing vulnerable states of the system, attacker actions, or conditions for attack progression. They are also linked by logical gates AND, OR. Despite the assignation of probabilities to attack nodes has been suggested, the estimation and interpretation of outcomes are still arguable (more details in Subsect. 6.4). Several approaches have been proposed to integrate (merge) fault and attack trees, *e.g.*, [13]. However, the integration is mostly structural and, in general, several issues still remain unsolved. Some pros and cons observed in approaches for tree merging are described in the following items:

**Pros:** Most algorithms for integration of fault and attack trees have a polynomial complexity on the number of nodes. Those algorithms can be implemented thus providing support for trees merging automation. In certain cases, the attack tree is transformed towards the fault tree what yields a merged tree with a simpler structure. It is also observed that safety metrics and functions are often reused for evaluating certain properties of attacks. In particular, failure rate, and Mean Time to Failure inspire their security counterparts, namely, Attack rate, and Mean Time to Attack. These metrics and functions are useful to estimate the probability of attacks occurrence.

**Cons:** The variety of attack tree nodes semantics is higher than their safety counterparts. Indeed, irrespective of the reference considered, the definition of fault trees remains mostly equivalent. On the contrary, there is no common definition for attack trees and consequently an heterogeneous variety of definitions exist; there is no common semantic for attack tree nodes. As a consequence, nodes describing attack steps or actions, can be specified at different levels of abstraction and granularity. Since vulnerabilities can be present at different system levels (HW/SW) and caused by different types of flaws, nodes representing them are also heterogeneous. Attack nodes representing the conditions for attack progression show similar characteristics. Referred specificities suggest that, to be consistent, fault and attack trees merging shall mostly remain a human-based task. Since the semantics and nature of nodes (safety and security events) are different, reusing safety metrics and functions to evaluate security aspects should be more thoroughly considered.

### 6.2    Discussion on Metrics for Safety Assessment

The so called Mean Time Before Failure (MTBF) is a central metrics applied in safety to estimate systems life and other related features. The MTBF is computed by obtaining the mathematical mean of a probability distribution function (*pdf*) with exponential basis (see Fig. 7). The exponential *pdf* measures the probability of occurrence of failures and is characterized by its parameter $\lambda$; $\lambda$ is a failure rate which measures the failures of a component (or system) per unit of time. However, as shown in Fig. 7, the exponential-based *pdf* is not the only probability distribution available.

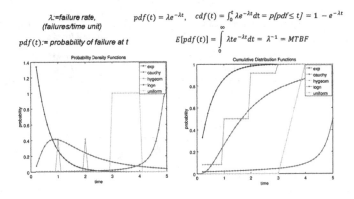

**Fig. 7.** Some metrics and functions used for systems safety assessment

The exponential *pdf* is currently adopted as a valid metric thanks to (1) the experiments that can be conducted to compute $\lambda$ and (2) the effectiveness of MTBF predictions w.r.t. systems life observed at field. This means that a suitable correspondence between the mathematical model and the physical phenomenon (systems ageing) has been settled. One of the main hypothesis for the estimation of the MTBF is that the failure rate $\lambda$ remains constant but this hypothesis has a limited validity. The Fig. 8 depicts the actual evolution of components failure rate across their life time. It is observed that the failure rate is mostly constant during the normal life interval, but rapidly changes during youth and ageing stages. All in all, even if the mathematical model reflects the essence of a phenomenon, the model remains limited by the validity of its hypotheses. Recent experimental results show that certain MTBF predictions may differ from real life time of systems observed at field [14]. According to this study, the failure rate $\lambda$ is not only determined by the physics of components, their nominal usage, and exposure to a given environment. It also depends upon the quality of the process for components (and subcomponents) development. In addition, accidental damages occurred during manufacturing over-stress components and finally increase their failure rate. A more precise calculation of $\lambda$ shall require to consider previous factors.

## 6.3 Discussion on Metrics for Security Assessment

Many approaches found in the literature rely upon variants of the exponential-based *pdf* to estimate the probability of an attack. But not all of them address the question on the adequacy of this choice w.r.t. the modeled phenomenon; attack progression. The work in [12] follows a pragmatic approach and provides experimental measures on the time to compromise a large informatics system. The proposed metrics is named Mean Time to First Attack (MTFA) and is calculated from data gathered from intrusions at field. The collected data are used to compute attacks frequency and afterwards to compute parameters of several *pdf*'s (and in particular $\lambda$). The predictions of the MTFA relying upon different

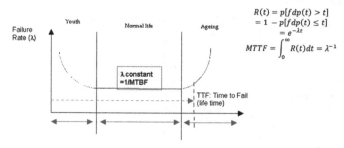

- *Youth phase:* precocious failures
- *Normal life:* failure rates almost constant
- *Ageing:* wear out, wear failures

Survival function:

$$R(t) = p[fdp(t) > t]$$
$$= 1 - p[fdp(t) \leq t]$$
$$= e^{-\lambda t}$$
$$MTTF = \int_0^\infty R(t)dt = \lambda^{-1}$$

**Fig. 8.** Typical evolution of failure rate across time. The graph is borrowed from [14]

*pdf*'s are then compared to the real periods of attacks' occurrence. The results of the comparison show that the best fitted model is not the exponential one but the Pareto based *pdf* [12]. Thus, it is reasonable to question about other potential issues like the ones identified for the safety assessment metrics. For instance, whether the attack rate may remain constant along a given period during the systems life. More specifically, whether the use of the attack rate suffices to characterize the whole phenomenon (including threats and vulnerabilities). A first element to answer these questions is that, along with factors affecting elements manufacturing (quality of development process, accidental damages), the attack rate is likely also impacted by other factors appearing before and during attack execution. Those factors can be observed and analyzed by studying phases of attack preparation and deployment. The so called *intrusion kill chain* [15] (see Fig. 9) defines several attack phases which can be useful for that purpose.

### 6.4    Perspectives for Consistent Assessment of Safety and Security

The use of field data to feed a mathematical model for attack prediction seems a quite consistent approach. However, the metrics used for security assessment may need to be validated in larger case studies and for other kind of systems. The *pdf*'s for predicting safety and security events occurrence might be better rely upon other basis than the exponential. Further studies may help to unveil the accuracy of predictions already obtained with the exponential model. To gain representativeness in the security assessment, larger and more diversified field data are necessary, for instance, data from different attack categories, known vulnerabilities, and application domains. To improve the computation of attack rates, factors related to attack preparation and deployment phases need to be introduced, for instance, attacker resources, skills, smartness, and motivations. Nonetheless, increasing the accuracy of a mathematical model also increases its complexity, and the cost and complexity of the prediction method. Consequently, more guidance and support will be necessary to bring forward these suggestions.

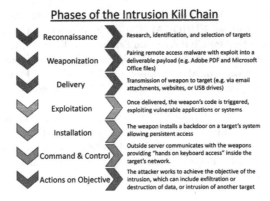

**Fig. 9.** Phases of the so named *intrusion kill chain*. Image borrowed from [15]

## 7    Overall Perspectives

Safety and security co-engineering is rather a young area and further works and progress are expected to gain in maturity. Regarding the conceptual and processes integration, certain engineering techniques (like MDE) will contribute to enlarge the intersection between safety and security. However, certain specificities of each area will remain and it is likely that standalone development practices will prevail for a while. The choice of an unified safety-security development cycle seems feasible but its deployment and adoption remains, for now, complex and costly to achieve. Further methodological and tool support are needed to help concerned communities to overcome these issues. Regarding the metrics for safety-security assessment, the consistency and representativity of metrics need to be ensured so as to achieve more accurate predictions. For that, the application of mathematical models in security assessment still waits for further validations.

## References

1. SAE International : ARP4754A - Guidelines for Development of Civil Aircraft and Systems. SAE International (2010). https://www.sae.org/standards/content/arp4754a/
2. International Organization for Standardization: ISO 26262 - Road vehicles - Functional safety. ISO (2011). https://www.iso.org/standard/43464.html
3. International Organization for Standardization: ISO 27005 - Information technology - Security techniques - Information security risk management. ISO (2018). https://www.iso.org/standard/75281.html
4. Agence Nationale de la Sécurité des Systèmes d'Information: EBIOS - Expression des Besoins et Identification des Objectifs de Sécurité. ANSSI (2010). https://www.ssi.gouv.fr/guide/ebios-2010-expression-des-besoins-et-identification-des-objectifs-de-securite/

5. European Organization for Civil Aviation Equipment: ED202 - Airworthiness Security Process Specification. EUROCAE (2014). https://eurocae.net/
6. European Organization for Civil Aviation Equipment: ED203 - Airworthiness Security Methods and Considerations. EUROCAE (2018). https://eurocae.net/
7. International Electrotechnical Commission: IEC 61508 - Functional safety of electrical/electronic/programmable electronic safety-related systems. IEC (2010). https://webstore.iec.ch/publication/22273
8. Pedroza, G., Idrees, M.S., Apvrille, L., Roudier, Y.: A formal methodology applied to secure over-the-air automotive applications. In: Proceedings on Vehicular Technology Conference (VTC Fall), pp. 1–5. IEEE, San Francisco (2011)
9. Hamid, B., Gürgens, S., Fuchs, A.: Security patterns modeling and formalization for pattern-based development of secure software systems. J. Innov. Syst. Softw. Eng. **12**(2), 109–140 (2016)
10. Object Management Group: Unified Modeling Language Specification. OMG (2017). https://www.omg.org/spec/UML/About-UML/
11. Object Management Group: System Modeling Language Specification. OMG (2017). https://www.omg.org/spec/SysML/About-SysML/
12. Holm, H.: A large-scale study of the time required to compromise a computer system. In: IEEE Proceedings of Transactions on Dependable and Secure Computing, vol. 11, no. 1, pp. 2–15, January–February 2014
13. Fovino, I.N., Masera, M., De Cian, A.: Integrating cyber attacks within fault trees. Reliab. Eng. Syst. Saf. **94**(9), 1394–1402 (2009). ScienceDirect, LNCS Elsevier
14. Institut pour la Maîtrise des Risques: Experimentation of the new reliability prediction method FIDES. IMDR (2017). https://eeepitnl.tksc.jaxa.jp/mews/en/20th/data/1_10.pdf
15. U.S. Senate-Committee on Commerce, Science, and Transportation: A "Kill Chain" Analysis of the 2013 Target Data Breach-March 26 2013. USA (2014). https://www.commerce.senate.gov/public/
16. Object Management Group (2019). https://www.omg.org
17. The Eclipse Foundation: Papyrus (2019). https://www.eclipse.org/papyrus/

# Safety and Security Interplay

# Understanding Common Automotive Security Issues and Their Implications

Aljoscha Lautenbach$^{(\boxtimes)}$ , Magnus Almgren , and Tomas Olovsson

Chalmers University of Technology, Gothenburg, Sweden
{aljoscha,magnus.almgren,tomas.olovsson}@chalmers.se

**Abstract.** With increased connectivity of safety-critical systems such as vehicles and industrial control systems, the importance of secure software rises in lock-step. Even systems that are traditionally considered to be non safety-critical can become safety-critical if they are willfully manipulated. In this paper, we identify 8 important security issues of automotive software based on a conceptually simple yet interesting example. The issues encompass problems from the design phase, including requirements engineering, to the choice of concrete parameters for an API. We then investigate how these issues are perceived by automotive security experts through a survey.

The survey results indicate that the identified issues are indeed problematic in real industry use-cases. Based on the collected data, we draw conclusions which problems deserve further attention and how the problems can be addressed. In particular, we find that key distribution is a major issue. Finally, many of the identified issues can be addressed by improved documentation and access to security experts.

**Keywords:** Automotive application development ·
Automotive security · Expert survey

## 1 Introduction

Imagine that, while driving on the highway, the driver seat suddenly starts to slide back and forth, and the seat adjustment controls are not responding. Clearly, the driver will have problems to drive the car safely: she may be unable to reach the brakes in a critical moment, or her movement may be so restricted that it is impossible to steer correctly. Perhaps the driver would be able to handle the situation for a short time, but after a while she would become fatigued from having to constantly adjust her body to the changing seat position, which can lead to dangerous situations. There are many safety-critical systems in a car, but as this example shows, even not directly safety-critical systems such as the seat adjustment system can have a negative impact on safety when attacked.

In the last few years, a growing number of cyber security problems have been discovered in automotive systems. The first systematic security investigations started early this millennium [24], but only the more recent works by Checkoway

© Springer Nature Switzerland AG 2019
B. Hamid et al. (Eds.): ISSA 2018/CSITS 2018, LNCS 11552, pp. 19–34, 2019.
https://doi.org/10.1007/978-3-030-16874-2_2

et al. [4,10], Miller and Valasek [13] and others brought the problem to the attention of a wider audience. Automotive systems face the same challenge as all embedded systems in the wake of ubiquitous connectivity: their technology was designed when connectivity was limited, and malicious attackers were not seen as a serious threat since local access was required to do any damage [9]. Therefore, security mechanisms are missing and must now be added in retrospect [24]. A first step to help remedy this situation is the "SAE J3061 Cybersecurity Guidebook for Cyber-Physical Vehicle Systems" [17].

In general, automotive software engineers are well trained in the safety aspects of their work, but few have security training. This is complicated by the fact that, depending on the context, the same terms may have different meanings across disciplines [3,6,8,12,16]. Without security training, even cyclic redundancy checks (CRCs) can easily be misconstrued as sufficient for security [25]. More generally, there is a broad consensus among security experts that implementing secure systems and using cryptographic libraries correctly requires finesse and training [2,11]. A recent study by Acar et al. [1] showed that the API of cryptographic libraries has a significant impact on the security of the resulting application code.

In this paper, we have used a conceptually simple example of a seat control application and enumerate issues that may arise or questions that need to be answered in the course of the development. This resulted in eight issues a developer faces, ranging from the open-ended act of understanding the threats to the much more concrete choice of key length for encrypted or authenticated data. These eight issues form the basis for a survey sent to automotive security experts, and the data is further analyzed before we present our recommendations and conclusions.

## 2 Methodology

Considering the design of a simple automotive control application, such as a seat control application, there are several security issues which arise naturally during the development process. We chose this simple use-case to capture the most common issues, and more elaborate use-cases will almost certainly unearth additional issues. In order to investigate to what extent the identified security issues are perceived to be problematic, we surveyed automotive security experts. We also questioned the experts to what extent some given recommendations address the issues. The survey was distributed to several contacts at seven automotive original equipment manufacturers (OEMs) and a small number of consultancy companies. Participation was voluntary and anonymous, and company affiliations were not tracked to preserve anonymity. This implies that participant distribution among the companies is unknown. The survey was roughly structured into four main parts: (a) background questions, (b) introduction of the contexts, (c) questions for each issue and (d) questions on the recommendations.

In part (a), we asked some demographic questions about the participants' background. This included questions on their number of years of experience with automotive systems, security, and safety respectively, and what their primary work task is (requirements engineering, software development, etc).

In part (b), we explicitly introduced three contexts, since some of the questions about the security issues can be understood slightly differently depending on each participant's interpretation of the context. The presented contexts were: (1) an independent context (i.e., "in a general sense"), (2) in the context of the participants' own work and (3) in the context of a scenario we called "simple automotive control application (SACA)". The scenario was described as follows.

> You are developing a simple automotive control application (SACA) that operates on two electronic control units (ECUs), which are connected via a CAN bus (max bandwidth of 1 Mbit/s). The two ECUs exchange messages periodically.

In part (c), the questions for each issue were presented. At this point it is important to point out that the issues were phrased in a neutral way as *activities* to avoid leading the subjects. For the same reason, illustrating examples and elaborations were avoided, with the assumptions that security experts would be familiar with the various difficulties that accompany each of the chosen issues. The issues were roughly grouped into the categories of "Design and architecture", "Programming" and "Parameters". The questions for each issue followed a fixed pattern. There were four questions per issue that can be paraphrased as follows:

1. Importance: How important is "activity X"?
2. Difficulty: To what extent do you agree that "X" is a difficult activity?
3. Frequency: How often do you perform "activity X" in your own work?
4. Comments: Do you have recommendations how to simplify/improve "activity or situation X"? Do you have any other comments? (optional free text)

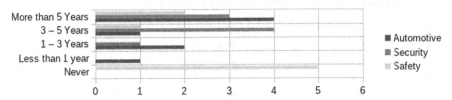

(a) Participants' experience with automotive systems, security and safety

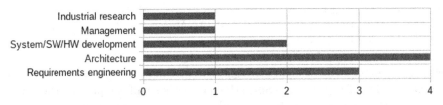

(b) Participants' primary work tasks (multiple choice)

**Fig. 1.** Survey participants' background

The questions on importance and difficulty were asked for all three contexts, while the frequency question was only asked in the context of the person's own work. The particularly interesting activities are those which are both important and difficult. An activity that is both frequent and difficult might also be of some interest, even if it is not perceived to be important.

## 3   Survey Participants

In total, eight industry professionals completed the survey.[1] Even though this is a rather low number of participants for a general survey, we argue that given the very specific target group of automotive security experts, eight is still a good number in this highly specific context. These are people with considerable expertise and knowledge of the area (see Fig. 1a). We considered to include non-experts in the survey, but felt that it would not benefit the quality of the results, and so it was deemed better to have relevant answers from a small but targeted group.

One demographic question was about the participants' experience with automotive systems, security and safety, and the results are shown in Fig. 1a, emphasizing that our target group has significant experience with security.

Figure 1b shows the distribution of the primary work tasks, which was a multiple choice question. Nobody answered that they primarily work with "Testing", "Academic research" or "Other", so these options are not shown in Fig. 1b. It is notable that seven out of eight respondents work with either architecture or requirements engineering, which may introduce a certain bias. Furthermore, only two respondents indicated that they primarily work with system, hardware or software development. Much system development happens at suppliers, so this makes sense.

## 4   Common Automotive Security Issues

As outlined in Sect. 2, we identified eight common automotive security issues by considering the security needs of a simple networked control application, and we designed a survey with the aim to identify which of these issues may warrant deeper investigation.

For the *importance* and *difficulty* related questions of the survey, we will only present the answers for the person's own context, the answers for the other two contexts are typically similar. In fact, there is a general trend that the importance of the issues is rated highest for the person's own work, and importance in the general context is rated lower than in the SACA scenario. The exact same trend can be observed for difficulty.

In the following subsections we present the eight identified issues together with the aggregated survey data, roughly grouped into *Design and architecture*, *Parameters* and *Programming*. Since the dataset is small, we present the survey answers per participant in the final subsection, and make some observations about possible correlations.

---

[1] As stated earlier, we did not track company affiliations to preserve anonymity.

## 4.1    Design and Architecture

Designing secure systems involves several steps, the first of which is to identify the threats to the system. The next steps are to choose security measures to counter the identified threats and to implement those security measures. Without identifying the threats first it is difficult to choose appropriate countermeasures.

**D1 Identification of Threats.** There are many different ways to gather the security requirements of an application, but they all require some experience and training. The identification of threats is typically paired with a risk assessment procedure, similar to the way hazard analysis is paired with risk assessment in safety engineering [7]. Therefore the identification of threats is the first issue to consider.

Once the threats have been identified and the security measures have been chosen, it is time to implement them. Many, if not most, security measures use cryptography in some form. For in-vehicle communication, the question of symmetric versus asymmetric cryptography is relatively simple to answer: symmetric cryptography is strongly preferred due to much better performance. Asymmetric cryptography still has a place in the vehicle for functions where speed is not

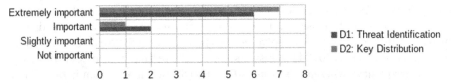

(a) The number of answers to how important the investigated design issues are

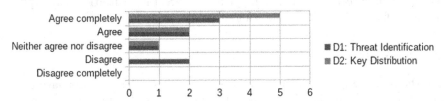

(b) The number of answers to whether the investigated design issues are difficult

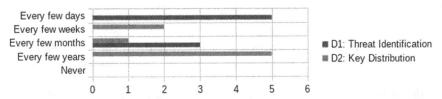

(c) The number of answers to how frequent the participants encounter the investigated design issues in their own work

**Fig. 2.** Survey results for the design related issues

critical, e.g., signatures for remote software updates, or when pre-shared keys are impractical, e.g., when communicating over the internet.

**D2 Choice of a Key Distribution Mechanism.** When symmetric cryptography is used, the keys must be available at both communication ends before communication starts. There are several ways key distribution can be done. One possibility is to use an out-of-band channel (pre-shared keys). This is usually done during production. Alternatives are public key schemes such as the Diffie-Hellman key exchange protocol or certificates.

The choice of the key distribution mechanism has both practical and security implications. For instance, repair and maintenance is an important criteria to consider [15]. If an electronic control unit (ECU) breaks, maybe due to an accident, and keys on that ECU become inaccessible, there must be a way to handle this. Additionally, the automotive ecosystem includes many multi-tiered suppliers, and some ECUs that arrive at the vehicle manufacturer for assembly are essentially black boxes, developed to precise specifications. This raises the questions, who installs the pre-shared key, and how is it installed on other ECUs that need to communicate with the ECU?

**Survey Results.** Figures 2a to c depict the survey results for design and architecture issues. As Fig. 2a shows, there is strong agreement among the experts that these are important issues. There is also strong agreement that key distribution is a difficult problem to solve, while the opinions on threat identification are slightly split (Fig. 2b). The answers also indicate that threat identification happens frequently, whereas choosing a key distribution mechanism is rare. This somewhat reflects that many of the participants work with requirements engineering and architecture. The high frequency of threat identification may explain why some disagree that it is a difficult task.

## 4.2   Parameters

Once the basic design decisions have been made, several parameters have to be chosen to implement the chosen security mechanisms. Parameter choices can include the choice of a cryptographic algorithm, choosing an appropriate key length and choosing a mechanism to ensure *freshness*.

**Pa1 Choice of Suitable Cryptographic Algorithms.** The choice of a cryptographic algorithm is not always straightforward. Cryptographers constantly try to find weaknesses in published algorithms, and an algorithm which was considered secure five years ago may not be so today, although this is often a gradual process. A good example for gradual deprecation is the SHA-1 cryptographic hash algorithm: first attacks have already been discovered in 2005 [23], and it has been considered weak for many years, but the first collision was only publicized in 2017 [19]. Since automotive products have a lifetime of 10 to

20 years, the algorithms must be chosen with care. Apart from pure security considerations, automotive systems have strict requirements for performance, and trade-offs must be considered.

**Pa2 Choosing a Suitable Key Length.** Once an algorithm has been chosen, another parameter must be considered: the length of the key (also known as *secret*), which is also a factor in the security of the scheme. Once again, the main consideration is the trade-off between security and overhead: in general, longer keys offer greater security, but they also require higher processing power which can be very limited on a microcontroller. However, in order to judge which key size is sufficient for what level of security requires a basic understanding of the algorithm and its weaknesses.

**Pa3 How to Implement a Freshness Mechanism.** In replay attacks, an attacker records a previous message which is encrypted or authenticated and resends it to achieve a particular goal. In order to avoid replay attacks, a *freshness*

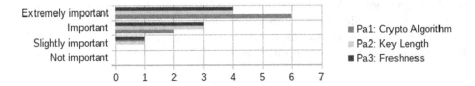

(a) The number of answers to how important the investigated parameter issues are

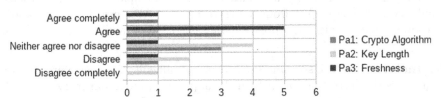

(b) The number of answers to whether the investigated parameter issues are difficult

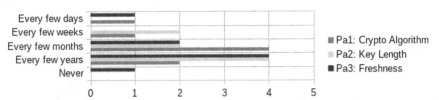

(c) The number of answers to how frequent the participants encounter the investigated parameter issues in their own work

**Fig. 3.** Survey results for the parameter related issues

mechanism is used. This can be a monotonic counter or a timestamp added to the message, so that two otherwise identical messages will be different. There are several practical difficulties with freshness counters or timestamps. For one, a counter must be chosen appropriately large: once the counter wraps around, a new key must be used. It is also important that the counters are synchronized so that only particular counter values are accepted at particular times. Clock synchronization is a particularly tricky subject.

**Survey Results.** Figures 3a to c show the survey results for the parameter issues. In general, there is consensus that these are important issues (Fig. 3a), but the responses on the difficulty are more nuanced. There is only slight agreement that choosing a suitable cryptographic algorithm is difficult, and there is strong disagreement that choosing a suitable key length is difficult (Fig. 3b). One participant remarked that for choosing parameters such as key length there are recommendations from NIST and AUTOSAR which simplify the process, a point we will return to in the recommendations in Sect. 5. We assume the availability of documented recommendations by trusted organizations is the reason for the perception of key length choice as an easy problem, and to a lesser extent for the algorithm choice. Another participant pointed out that the possibility for software updates, which are not universally supported in embedded systems, are of paramount importance to ensure continued security. For the most part, all three parameter choices happen rather infrequently (Fig. 3c).

### 4.3   Programming

At some point, the chosen security measures must be implemented, and various pitfalls await the developer: from the correct use of APIs over implementation of cryptographic primitives to programming language pitfalls.

**Pr1 Incorrect API Use.** One such source of difficulty for developing secure programs is the correct use of APIs. If the application programmer uses an API incorrectly, this may lead to insecure programs [1,2,5,11,14]. For instance, if programmers do not understand why an initialization vector is necessary, they may pass NULL for it, which may be allowed by the API but is semantically incorrect.

**Pr2 Writing Secure C Code.** In addition to API specific problems, there are also typical development pitfalls that apply to any program written in the C programming language. It is easy to write insecure code, e.g., due to faulty memory management, pointer handling or lack of input validation [18]. These problems are well known and well documented, and yet they still occur in practice [21,22]. Since most automotive software is developed in C, writing secure C code is another programming issue.

**Pr3 Implementing Cryptographic Primitives or Libraries.** In order to implement security measures that use cryptography, cryptographic libraries or primitives must be available. However, since automotive systems are highly heterogeneous and often use minimal libraries, there is a chance developers may be tempted to implement their own cryptographic primitives. Consider for example the AUTOSAR standard for automotive software: AUTOSAR defines interfaces to access cryptographic libraries, but the standard also clearly states that the underlying implementation is the responsibility of the software vendor. Cryptographic libraries should always be written by cryptographers or security experts, otherwise there is a high probability that they are insecure [2,11]. If this is not immediately obvious, consider the Debian SSL bug discovered in 2008: two small, superficially harmless changes by the Debian maintainers significantly lowered the entropy during SSL key generation, which led to a huge number of insecure keys. Thus, the implementation of cryptographic primitives or libraries is the final programming issue we consider.

**Survey Results.** Figures 4a to c show the survey results for the programming related issues, some of which are surprising. Figure 4a shows an outlier for the importance of correct cryptographic implementations. However, since the con-

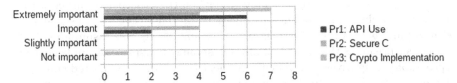

(a) The number of answers to how important the investigated programming issues are

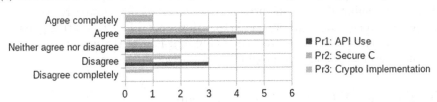

(b) The number of answers to whether the investigated programming issues are difficult

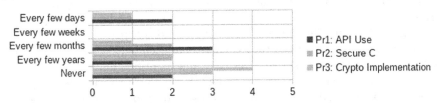

(c) The number of answers to how frequent the participants encounter the investigated programming issues in their own work

**Fig. 4.** Survey results for the programming related issues

**Table 1.** Responses per survey participant (see legend below), in the context of their own work

| | Primary work tasks | Experience[a] (Auto., Security, Safety) | D1[b] D2[b] Pa1[b] Pa2[b] Pa3[b] Pr1[b] Pr2[b] Pr3[b] |
|---|---|---|---|
| Participant 1 | Management | 5,4,5 | 5,4,3 5,3,2 4,4,2 4,4,2 4,3,2 4,4,3 5,4,3 4,4,2 |
| Participant 2 | Industrial Research | 5,4,1 | 3,3,3 3,4,2 2,3,2 1,3,2 4,4,2 2,4,2 4,3,2 2,4,2 |
| Participant 3 | Architecture | 5,4,4 | 2,4,3 5,4,2 4,4,3 3,3,2 3,3,1 4,4,1 2,3,1 3,4,1 |
| Participant 4 | Architecture | 4,5,1 | 5,4,5 5,4,2 3,4,4 3,4,3 2,3,2 2,3,5 4,3,1 5,4,1 |
| Participant 5 | Requirements Eng. | 5,4,1 | 5,3,5 5,4,2 3,3,3 2,2,2 4,2,2 3,3,3 3,3,2 1,1,1 |
| Participant 6 | Req. Eng., Arch. | 3,5,5 | 2,4,5 4,4,3 4,4,3 2,4,3 4,4,3 2,4,1 4,4,1 2,4,1 |
| Participant 7 | Req.   Eng,   Arch., Dev. | 3,5,1 | 4,4,5 5,4,4 5,4,5 3,3,4 5,4,5 4,4,5 4,4,5 4,4,5 |
| Participant 8 | Development | 2,3,1 | 4,4,5 4,4,4 3,4,3 3,4,4 4,4,3 4,4,3 4,4,3 4,4,3 |

| | Experience | Difficulty | Importance | Frequency |
|---|---|---|---|---|
| | 1 Never | Disagree completely | Not important | Never |
| | 2 Less than 1 year | Disagree | Slightly important | Every few years |
| Legend | 3 1–3 years | Neither agree nor disagree | Important | Every few months |
| | 4 3–5 years | Agree | Extremely important | Every few weeks |
| | 5 More than 5 years | Agree completely | | Every few days |

[a]Triplets in the order: Automotive, Security, Safety
[b]Triplets in the order: Difficulty, Importance, Frequency

text is the person's own work, it may simply be that the person never works with cryptography, and thus finds it unimportant. There is consensus that it is an important issue in the other contexts, thus supporting this assumption.

Most surprising is that only half of the respondents agree that implementing cryptographic primitives is a difficult problem (Fig. 4b). We expected complete agreement here. Two people strongly stated in the comments that you should never implement your own "crypto", which may be a hint for the reasoning behind the results: if you outsource it, it is not difficult. However, even in a general context several people answered that this is not difficult. Another possible reason may be hidden in the frequency (Fig. 4c): half of the experts answered that they never implement cryptographic primitives in their own work.

### 4.4   Intra and Inter Question Correlations

So far we have only considered aggregate survey results, but it may also be of interest to look at the participants' individual answers to investigate possible correlations. We will only highlight a few observations here.

Table 1 presents the dataset (in the context of each person's own work) in a codified form, and Table 2 summarizes the eight identified issues for easy cross reference with Table 1. Each row in Table 1 corresponds to the answer of one survey participant, and each answer is represented by one number, grouped in triplets. For experience, the triplet represent the answers for automotive, security and safety experience, respectively. For the eight issues, the triplet represents the answers for difficulty, importance and frequency, respectively. For instance, participant 1, who primarily works with management, has more than 5 years of experience with both automotive systems and safety, and 3–5 years of experience with security.

**Table 2.** Identified issues

| D1 | Identification of threats |
|----|----|
| D2 | Choice of a key distribution mechanism |
| Pa1 | Choice of suitable cryptographic algorithms |
| Pa2 | Choosing a suitable key length |
| Pa3 | How to implement a freshness mechanism |
| Pr1 | Incorrect API use |
| Pr2 | Writing secure C code |
| Pr3 | Implementing cryptographic primitives or libraries |

Studying this data, several interesting observations can be made. For instance, not one participant has more than 5 years of experience with both automotive systems *and* security, hinting at the fact that security is still relatively new in the automotive industry. It is also worth pointing out that the three participants with the most security experience collectively answered 20 times that the issues are extremely important, and 4 times that they are important, indicating a strong agreement with our claims, averaging at 3.835. For the remaining five participants, the average is 3.5, still a high level of agreement. Another, perhaps unexpected, observation is that, compared to the participants with less automotive experience, more experience in the automotive industry is negatively correlated to the importance participants ascribe the issues. This may be a side effect of the first observation, i.e., that participants with less automotive experience have more experience with security. Either way, the averages are still high, 3.375 for the group with extensive automotive experience ($auto\_exp = 5$), and 3.875 for the group without ($auto\_exp < 5$). Similar analysis shows that the more frequently a person is involved in a particular activity, the more difficult and important they rate that activity.

## 5    Recommendations

As we have seen, security is a pervasive design issue which affects every level of the development process, and even trivial systems can be dangerous when exploited by an attacker. Consequently, security must be included in all development steps. Based on the previously identified issues, we give four recommendations how automotive software development can be made more secure.

**R1.** *Improve documentation, for instance by adding look-up tables for recommended key lengths, algorithms, MAC length and freshness parameters.*

**Rationale:** Software developers in the automotive industry are usually well trained in safety, but they often have little or no training in security. As a result, they may inadvertently introduce security relevant bugs into their code. Therefore, it should be made as easy as possible for automotive software developers to write secure code. This can in part be achieved through improved documentation. For instance, the difficulties in choosing the right key length, choosing the right cryptographic algorithm and choosing good parameters to guarantee freshness can be alleviated by adding more security related documentation.

**R2.** *The vehicle manufacturer should develop a process for key management.*

**Rationale:** The topic of key management deserves special attention, because of its wide ranging implications. If symmetric keys or a public key infrastructure setup are chosen, the vehicle manufacturer must maintain a central infrastructure to store and retrieve those keys on demand in a secure manner. The key management also needs to be coordinated with suppliers to clarify how and when the keys are installed. Furthermore, the keys must be accessible to licensed workshops for repair and maintenance.

**R3.** *Every development team should have access to at least one security expert and every team should have at least one developer who is trained in security.*

**Rationale:** Some of the identified issues can be alleviated by providing developer training or by providing access to security or cryptography experts. For example, for identifying threats at the architectural stage, a security expert should be available to provide an analysis. For the implementation of cryptographic libraries, cryptographers should be used, and developers should confirm that the library they use was developed by experts. Finally, API misuse can obviously be limited through developer training, too.

**R4.** *Adhere to the MISRA C guidelines.*

**Rationale:** The MISRA C guidelines were developed specifically to make the C programming language safer to use in critical systems.[2] One effective result of requiring conformance to MISRA C is that all unsafe C library functions are implicitly forbidden to be used in production code. There are several commercial compilers which check MISRA C code compliance, but MISRA C contains many items which can not be checked automatically, or which require additional formal verification tools. Moreover, bugs which lead to security vulnerabilities can still

---

[2] There are several other coding guidelines for embedded, safety-critical or secure software, such as the *JPL C Coding Standard*, the *SEI CERT C Coding Standard*, or *The Power of 10 - Rules for Developing Safety Critical Code*, but a more detailed discussion is out of scope for this paper.

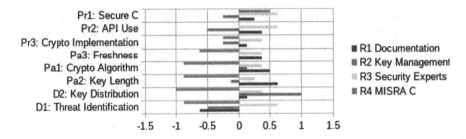

**Fig. 5.** Answers to what extent the recommendations address or mitigate the various issues: positive values indicate a high extent of mitigation, whereas negative values indicate a low extent of mitigation

happen. For example, it is possible to allocate a fixed-size buffer and accidentally write beyond its boundaries due to missing or insufficient run-time checks. Nevertheless, adherence to the MISRA C guidelines strengthens the security of the code considerably, even more so in combination with formal verification tools.

**Survey Results:** In order to validate the recommendations, for each recommendation the survey also included the question to which extent it addresses the issues discussed earlier. The results are summarized in aggregated form in Fig. 5: if a majority answered "Not at all" or "Slightly", the issue is depicted with a negative value, and if a majority answered "Significantly" or "Completely", the issue is depicted with a positive value. The results are not surprising. Since R2 (key management) and R4 (MISRA C adherence) address very specific issues, they are only of value in those particular circumstances, whereas R1 (improve documentation) and R3 (security experts) help with almost all of the issues. This also echoes some of the findings of Acar et al. [1].

## 6    Related Work

As outlined in the introduction, interest in automotive security has been slowly on the rise for the last 15 years. Wolf, Weimerskirch and Paar [24] pioneered an initial analysis, and Koscher et al. [10], Checkoway et al. [4], and Miller and Valasek [13] demonstrated practical attacks, both local and remote. An added difficulty stems from the safety-critical nature of automotive engineering and the necessary integration of safety and security [3,6,8,12,16,25]. Studnia et al. [20] wrote a survey summarizing many automotive security issues. Similarly, we highlight commonly encountered security issues, but we additionally investigate how security experts perceive them.

## 7    Conclusion

With the increased communication of cyber-physical systems, securing software is of ever-increasing importance. Even systems which are generally perceived to have no safety-critical components can pose dangers when exploited by an attacker. An implication is that the interplay of safety and security must be examined closer; traditional views of safety may no longer be adequate.

The results of our survey with automotive security experts indicate that three of the eight issues we discussed are of particular interest. According to our survey, key distribution is a very important problem that is also very complex and it should be further investigated. Similarly, the choice and implementation of a mechanism for freshness is also an important and challenging problem. Both of these problems have been very well covered by academic research in the last 30 years, so it may be slightly counter-intuitive that they are still difficult to solve in the automotive context. However, this can be explained with the strongly constrained requirements for such systems. Threat identification on the other hand is an interesting problem because it is both an important and a frequent activity. Since it is a very dynamic activity that is strongly dependent on the concrete system under review, it will likely remain very important.

Some of the results may not be particularly surprising, but we believe it is still of value to formally document them in form of this survey. Conversely, some results were surprising, e.g., that several experts did not consider cryptographic implementations difficult.

Automotive software developers are typically well trained in addressing safety requirements, but writing secure software requires additional knowledge and skills. Consequently, new frameworks, platforms and standards should make it easier to write secure code, and they should foster an environment which supports secure development. As the survey results indicate, this can be partially achieved with supporting documentation to facilitate informed choices about security measures. However, improved documentation alone is not enough. In order to integrate security into the entire development process, cultural and organizational changes are needed. For instance, as the survey results illustrate, having ready access to security experts should alleviate many of the issues.

In order to achieve such a security conducive environment, several aspects must come together. First and foremost, there must be organizational support. Secure development can not be done without a security budget. Then there are the complex interactions of OEMs and suppliers which must be coordinated. More documentation how to securely use existing security functions should be added. Moreover, development processes must be adapted to include security reviews and security testing. All of the above entails a cultural change, so a concerted effort of all involved partners in the automotive industry is needed to secure future vehicles. Finally it can be noted that much of this discussion probably extends to embedded system development in other domains as well.

**Acknowledgments.** We would like to thank all survey participants for their valuable time and input. We would also like to thank all anonymous reviewers for their constructive feedback. The research leading to these results has been partially supported by VINNOVA, the Swedish Governmental Agency for Innovation Systems, through the project "HoliSec" (2015-06894), and by the Swedish Civil Contingencies Agency (MSB) through the project "RICS".

# References

1. Acar, Y., et al.: Comparing the usability of cryptographic APIs. In: Proceedings of the 38th IEEE Symposium on Security and Privacy (2017)
2. Anderson, R.: Why cryptosystems fail. In: Proceedings of the 1st ACM Conference on Computer and Communications Security, CCS 1993, pp. 215–227. ACM, New York (1993)
3. Avizienis, A., Laprie, J.C., Randell, B., Landwehr, C.: Basic concepts and taxonomy of dependable and secure computing. IEEE Trans. Dependable Secure Comput. **1**(1), 11–33 (2004)
4. Checkoway, S., et al.: Comprehensive experimental analyses of automotive attack surfaces. In: Proceedings of the 20th USENIX Security Symposium, San Francisco, CA, USA, pp. 77–92, August 2011
5. Fahl, S., Harbach, M., Perl, H., Koetter, M., Smith, M.: Rethinking SSL development in an appified world. In: Proceedings of the 2013 ACM SIGSAC Conference on Computer and Communications Security (CCS), pp. 49–60. ACM (2013)
6. Firesmith, D.G.: Common concepts underlying safety security and survivability engineering. Technical report CMU/SEI-2003-TN-033, Software Engineering Institute - Carnegie Mellon University, December 2003
7. Islam, M.M., Lautenbach, A., Sandberg, C., Olovsson, T.: A risk assessment framework for automotive embedded systems. In: Proceedings of the 2nd ACM International Workshop on Cyber-Physical System Security, pp. 3–14. ACM (2016)
8. Jonsson, E.: Towards an integrated conceptual model of security and dependability. In: The First International Conference on Availability, Reliability and Security, ARES 2006, pp. 646–653. IEEE (2006)
9. Koopman, P.: Embedded system security. Computer **37**(7), 95–97 (2004)
10. Koscher, K., et al.: Experimental security analysis of a modern automobile. In: 2010 IEEE Symposium on Security and Privacy (SP), pp. 447–462, May 2010
11. Lazar, D., Chen, H., Wang, X., Zeldovich, N.: Why does cryptographic software fail? A case study and open problems. In: Proceedings of 5th Asia-Pacific Workshop on Systems, APSys 2014, pp. 1–7. ACM, New York (2014)
12. Line, M., Nordland, O., Røstad, L., Tøndel, I.: Safety vs. security. In: Proceedings of the 8th International Conference on Probabilistic Safety Assessment and Management (PSAM), pp. 685–699. IAPSAM (2006)
13. Miller, C., Valasek, C.: Remote exploitation of an unaltered passenger vehicle. Technical report, Defcon 23, August 2015. http://illmatics.com/Remote%20Car%20Hacking.pdf
14. Myers, B.A., Stylos, J.: Improving API usability. Commun. ACM **59**(6), 62–69 (2016)
15. Nowdehi, N., Lautenbach, A., Olovsson, T.: In-vehicle CAN message authentication: an evaluation based on industrial criteria. In: 2017 IEEE 86th Vehicular Technology Conference (VTC-Fall), pp. 1–7. IEEE (2017)
16. Piètre-Cambacédès, L., Chaudet, C.: The SEMA referential framework: avoiding ambiguities in the terms "security" and "safety". Int. J. Crit. Infrastruct. Prot. **3**(2), 55–66 (2010)
17. SAE International: SAE J3061_201601 - Cybersecurity Guidebook for Cyber-Physical Vehicle Systems, January 2016
18. Seacord, R.C.: Secure Coding in C and C++. Pearson Education, London (2005)
19. Stevens, M., et al.: Announcing the first SHA1 collision, February 2017. https://security.googleblog.com/2017/02/announcing-first-sha1-collision.html

20. Studnia, I., Nicomette, V., Alata, E., Deswarte, Y., Kaaniche, M., Laarouchi, Y.: Survey on security threats and protection mechanisms in embedded automotive networks. In: 2013 43rd Annual IEEE/IFIP Conference on Dependable Systems and Networks Workshop (DSN-W), pp. 1–12 (2013)
21. Szekeres, L., Payer, M., Wei, T., Song, D.: SoK: eternal war in memory. In: 2013 IEEE Symposium on Security and Privacy (SP), pp. 48–62, May 2013
22. van der Veen, V., dutt-Sharma, N., Cavallaro, L., Bos, H.: Memory errors: the past, the present, and the future. In: Balzarotti, D., Stolfo, S.J., Cova, M. (eds.) RAID 2012. LNCS, vol. 7462, pp. 86–106. Springer, Heidelberg (2012). https://doi.org/10.1007/978-3-642-33338-5_5
23. Wang, X., Yin, Y.L., Yu, H.: Finding collisions in the full SHA-1. In: Shoup, V. (ed.) CRYPTO 2005. LNCS, vol. 3621, pp. 17–36. Springer, Heidelberg (2005). https://doi.org/10.1007/11535218_2
24. Wolf, M., Weimerskirch, A., Paar, C.: Security in automotive bus systems. In: Proceedings of the Workshop on Embedded Security in Cars (ESCAR), November 2004
25. Zalman, R., Mayer, A.: A secure but still safe and low cost automotive communication technique. In: Proceedings of the 51st Annual Design Automation Conference, DAC 2014, pp. 1–5. ACM, New York (2014)

# SysML Model Transformation for Safety and Security Analysis

Rabéa Ameur-Boulifa[1]([✉]), Florian Lugou[2], and Ludovic Apvrille[1]

[1] LTCI, Télécom ParisTech, Université Paris-Saclay, Paris, France
Rabea.Ameur-Boulifa@telecom-paristech.fr
[2] Prove & Run, Paris, France

**Abstract.** While the awareness toward the security and safety of embedded systems has recently improved due to various significant attacks, the issue of building a practical but accurate methodology for designing such safe and secure systems still remains unsolved. Where test coverage is dissatisfying, formal analysis grants much higher potential to discover security vulnerabilities during the design phase of a system. Yet, formal verification methods often require a strong technical background that limits their usage. In this paper, we formally describe a verification process that enables us to prove security-oriented properties such as confidentiality on block and state machine diagrams of SysML. The mathematical description of the translation of these formally defined diagrams into a ProVerif specification enables us to prove the correctness of the verification method.

**Keywords:** Model-Driven Engineering · Verification · Safety ·
Security · Embedded systems

## 1 Introduction

In our increasingly connected world, security is a growing concern for embedded systems. This remark firstly applies to critical systems such as connected vehicles or industrial systems. There are already many approaches (i.e. methods, models and tools) to evaluate critical aspects of these systems independently from their security: real-time schedulability, formal verification techniques based e.g. on model-checking or correct-by-construction techniques. Model-Driven Engineering often considers safety aspects with coherence checks between diagrams or with model-to-formal-specification algorithms in order to evaluate safety properties from e.g. UML diagrams. Concerning security aspects, a usual practice is to rely on dedicated models and tools that are focused on the security aspect e.g. ProVerif [1] and Avispa [6], and are thus not compatible with safety-related models and tools. As a result, security is often seen as *the right way to use the right tools*, if not totally ignored. This however leads to more subtle bugs when out-of-the-box cryptographic solutions are not suitable, and in particular when the importance of an asset or communication is misunderstood. Such a security

© Springer Nature Switzerland AG 2019
B. Hamid et al. (Eds.): ISSA 2018/CSITS 2018, LNCS 11552, pp. 35–49, 2019.
https://doi.org/10.1007/978-3-030-16874-2_3

issue can be minor when the number of devices affected is small and when the vulnerability can be fixed easily, e.g. with a software patch. However, this is typically not the case for embedded systems where design flaws can be impossible to fix and can affect a whole range of products. Even when a security vulnerability is discovered before the product is released, the amount of work needed to rethink the whole architecture may be prohibitive.

To facilitate the design of critical systems with security requirements, we suggest enhancing safety-related models with security mechanisms, and to offer, from the same model, safety-to-formal-specification and in addition, security-to-formal-specification transformations. In the paper, we present the SysML-Sec environment that supports both safety and security. Then, we elaborate on the SysML-Sec-model-to-security-formal-specification that was first sketched in [16]. This transformation algorithm is valuable as it enables us to perform security verification on general-purpose design models and thus avoids error-prone duplication of models. However, the transformation algorithm had not been formally described yet. This paper gives a formal description of the transformation algorithm in order to prove the correctness of the method. Throughout the paper, we will illustrate our explanation of the different phases of modeling and verification on a pedagogical example. Although the example has purposely been kept to its bare minimum so that the reader can easily refer to it, it could still be used as a sub-part of a greater real-life design. In the presented scenario, two participants (called Alice and Bob) communicate through an unsafe (public) channel. Alice repeatedly sends sensitive data to Bob. The messages are encrypted by Alice before being transmitted over the public channel. The two participants have beforehand shared a cryptographic key and we assume the way the sharing was performed does not need to be modeled. In practice, the key could have been physically shared, built from asymmetric key material (through a Diffie-Hellman protocol for instance) or it could have been provided to Alice and Bob by a trusted third party. The key used by Alice to encrypt her communications periodically changes, and thus a new key is created. So each time Alice sends a new message, she attaches the newly created key so that Bob is able to decrypt the next message. We typically want to verify that the data sent by Alice can not be retrieved by a potential attacker eavesdropping and manipulating messages on the public channel. Other more complex security protocols and systems have been modeled and verified using the method described in this paper.

The verification method enables us to prove confidentiality and authenticity properties on these models within an acceptable time (less than 5 min on a general-purpose computer). We will not detail these case studies in the current paper but refer the interested reader to the SysML-Sec website[1] where the corresponding models are freely accessible.

The paper is organised as follows: in Sect. 2, we present the methodology chosen here and give a formal description of the modeling language (a SysML profile). Section 3 presents the basic model ProVerif language and we give a translation of SysML model to ProVerif model. Section 4 acts as a validation of

---

[1] http://sysml-sec.telecom-paristech.fr/.

our approach that can be used to assert the validity of our translation. Section 5 surveys related work before concluding in Sect. 6.

## 2   SysML-Sec Language

SysML-Sec [5] is a modeling language following a model-driven approach to design embedded systems with safety, security and performance constraints. This modeling language was chosen as it enables the user to analyze behaviors that will be implemented by the system and specifically targets embedded systems. Moreover, it is supported by a free and open-source tool to which the presented algorithm was added.

*Designing an Application:* Basically, SysML-Sec supports two main modeling phases:

1. The **system-level HW/SW partitioning** phase includes capturing functional elements of the target application, modeling candidate architectures and finally mapping functional elements—including communications between functions—to candidate architectures. Then a verification sub-phase follows in which safety, security and performance constraints are evaluated in order to select the "best" HW/SW partition.
2. A **software design** phase follows a successful partitioning phase. Software components are first built from high-level functions mapped onto processor nodes at the previous phase. Then, they are progressively refined. Refinement typically concerns the accurate description of algorithms and protocols, including security protocols.

Design elements of the two phases are built from (safety and security) requirements. Verification is supported in all modeling stages in order to assess the security and safety requirements. Attack trees also help capture potential attacks that are feasible in the considered mapping models.

   TTool is a free and open-source tool that supports the different phases and models of SysML-Sec. It offers a press-button approach for safety, security and performance verification, and can backtrace verification results to modeling views.

*Software Design Verification:* As formalized below, a software design is built upon communicating blocks whose behaviors are described with state machine diagrams. Software design verification intends to evaluate the fulfillment of safety and security properties. Safety verification checks a large set of properties including safety (e.g. deadlock-free) and liveness (e.g. reachability) properties. Properties can be modeled either with a subset of temporal logic language e.g. CTL, or with the use of observers in the model that are expressed with state machine diagrams. TTool relies on UPPAAL model checking tool for verification.

## 2.1  Syntax

In the software design phase, the SysML-Sec diagrams intend to describe a software *design*. This section provides a formal definition of software designs.

**Definition 1 Design.** *A design is defined by a network of blocks interconnected by links and a set of pragmas:*
$\mathcal{D} = \langle \mathcal{B}, \mathcal{C}, \mathcal{P} \rangle$ *where $\mathcal{B}$ is a set of blocks, $\mathcal{C}$ is a set of channels, and $\mathcal{P}$ is a set of pragmas.*

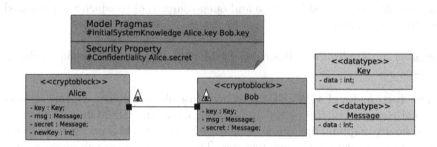

**Fig. 1.** A graphical representation of SysML-Sec design example

Figure 1 displays two blocks *Alice* and *Bob* as well as a public link—as denoted by the illuminati symbol—between the two. In this paper, we don't mention data types as they only act as syntactic sugar as far as security analysis is concerned.

SysML blocks consist of a set of methods and attributes. Communication ports can be attached to a block, and to each port are attached interfaces and signals [12]. For simplicity, we directly attach signals to SysML blocks.

**Definition 2 Block.** *A block is a tuple:*
block $= \langle ident, \mathcal{A}, \mathcal{M}, \mathcal{S}, \text{behav} \rangle$ *where*

- *ident is a block name.*
- *$\mathcal{A}$ is a set of attributes.*
- *$\mathcal{M}$ is a set of methods.*
- *$\mathcal{S}$ is a set of directed signals. For each $s \in \mathcal{S}$, type(s) $\in \{in, out\}$.*
- behav *is a state machine diagram.*

We define a function *block* that, for a given design $\mathcal{D}$, returns the set of its blocks; and functions *sig* and *att* that $b$ return the set of signals and attributes for a given block respectively.

**Definition 3 Channel.** *A channel connects signals between blocks:* channel $=$ $\langle \text{type}, \mathcal{R} \rangle$ *where* type *is a physical property which can be either* private *or* public, *and $\mathcal{R}$ is one-to-one correspondence between two sets of signals, $\mathcal{R} \subseteq sig(b_1) \times sig(b_2)$ where $b_1, b_2 \in block(\mathcal{D})$ such that $\forall (s_1, s_2) \in \mathcal{R}$, type(s_1) $\neq$ type(s_2).*

SysML design supports the notion of pragma. Pragmas enable us to describe properties of the system in the initial state, and to query a property of the design that will be checked during verification. To simplify this description, we will consider only two types of pragmas which: - express that two attributes have the same value at the beginning of the execution ($\mathcal{P}_{init}$); - query the confidentiality of an attribute ($\mathcal{P}_{secret}$).

**Definition 4 Pragma.** *Let $\mathcal{D}$ be a design. We define a pragma as a pair: $\mathcal{P} = (\mathcal{P}_{init}, \mathcal{P}_{secret})$ where*

$$\mathcal{P}_{init} \subseteq \left(\bigcup_{b \in block(\mathcal{D})} att(b)\right)^2 \text{ and } \mathcal{P}_{secret} \subseteq \bigcup_{b \in block(\mathcal{D})} att(b)$$

A state machine diagram is a labelled transition system with variables named attributes; a state machine diagram can have guards and assignments of attributes on transitions. Attributes can be manipulated, defined, or accessed. Let $f$ range over function names, $x_i$ range over variable names, and $c$ are channel names. The set $\mathcal{A}ctions$ of action terms in state machine diagrams is defined as follows:

$$
\begin{array}{lll}
a \in \mathcal{A}ctions ::= & f(x_1, \ldots, x_n) & \text{function call} \\
& | \ x := exp & \text{assignment expression} \\
& | \ c\langle x \rangle & \text{input action} \\
& | \ \bar{c}\langle x \rangle & \text{output action} \\
& | \ \nu.x & \text{random action} \\
& | \ \varepsilon & \text{empty action}
\end{array}
$$

Expressions ($exp$) in SysML-Sec can be variables and function calls ($x$ and $f(x_1, \ldots, x_n)$). The set $\mathcal{G}uards$ is the set of boolean expressions.

**Definition 5 State Machine Diagram.** *A state machine diagram is a rooted directed graph:* $\mathsf{behav} = \langle \mathcal{Q}, q_0, q_\perp, \mathcal{E} \rangle$ *where*

- $\mathcal{Q}$ *is a set of nodes.*
- $q_0 \in \mathcal{Q}$ *is an initial state node.*
- $q_\perp \in \mathcal{Q}$ *is a (possibly empty) final state node.*
- $\mathcal{E} \subseteq \mathcal{Q} \times \mathcal{G}uards \times \mathcal{A}ctions \times \mathcal{Q}$.

A name is given by the designer to each state. We define a labelling function $\mathbb{L}$ that returns the name of a given state. Given an edge $e = (q, g, a, q')$, we define functions $source(e) = q$, $guard(e) = g$, $action(e) = a$, and $target(e) = q'$. A trace $\sigma \in \mathcal{A}ctions^*$ is a sequence of actions $a_0 \ a_1, \ldots a_n$ such that there is a sequence of states $q_0 \ q_1, \ldots q_n$ and $(q_{i-1}, g, a_i, q_i) \in \mathcal{E}$ for all $i = 1, \ldots, n$.

*Syntactic Constraints on Activity Diagram.* TTool enforces some basic properties on the state machine diagrams, namely:

1. The initial state node may only occur in the source of an edge.
2. The final state node may only occur in the target of an edge.
3. For any state node, there is a path from the initial state node to this node.

4. Any state node different from the final state node has at least one outgoing transition.

We introduce the notion of *basic block* that we will use in our translation. A basic block can be seen as a sub-design that offers a single point of entry and that can be triggered by several points. Precisely, it is a connected sub-graph for which all the states have exactly one incoming edge, except for one state that we name *root*. We will use $Out$ function that returns the set of transitions outgoing from a given state. We also define a predicate *UniqueOut* and *UniqueIn* that take a state $q$ and return true only if no two different transitions have $q$ as a source and target state respectively.

$$UniqueOut(q) \Leftrightarrow \left( \begin{array}{c} \forall (q_1, g_1, a_1, q_1'), (q_2, g_2, a_2, q_2') \in \mathcal{E}. \\ q_1 = q \wedge q_2 = q \Rightarrow g_1 = g_2 \wedge a_1 = a_2 \wedge q_1' = q_2' \end{array} \right)$$

$$UniqueIn(q) \Leftrightarrow \left( \begin{array}{c} \forall (q_1, g_1, a_1, q_1'), (q_2, g_2, a_2, q_2') \in \mathcal{E}. \\ q_1' = q \wedge q_2' = q \Rightarrow q_1 = q_2 \wedge g_1 = g_2 \wedge a_1 = a_2 \end{array} \right)$$

Figures 2a and b show the graphical representation of the two state machine diagrams of *Alice* and *Bob* respectively. Note that empty actions and "true" guards are not shown in the diagrams. States are depicted by colored boxes (except for the initial state which is a circle), transitions by arrows, and actions are either represented by textual expressions next to arrows (for function calls and assignment expression) or by white boxes with various forms (for the other types of actions). For instance, the state machine of Alice is composed of an initial state linked to a state named *generateNewKey* by an empty transition. This state is linked to another state *sendSecret* by a transition bearing 4 actions: a random action and 3 assignment expressions. Another transition links *sendSecret* to *generateNewKey* and bears an output action. Note that in the diagrams, multiple actions appear on each transition. This is semantically equivalent to multiple chained transitions, each of which bearing a single action and a `true` guard.

# 3   From SysML-Sec to Proverif

Our goal is to provide an environment to design safe and secure systems with the SysML language. Our plan is to give a formal definition of the behavioural semantics of SysML, and get a standard code to do the security analysis. This section describes the behavioural semantics of SysML design allowing security analysis.

## 3.1   ProVerif Language

ProVerif [7] is a cryptographic protocol verification tool operating on a symbolic model. ProVerif specifications are described in a custom language following a well-defined structure [8]. It consists of a sequence of declarations and a process. Our translation use a core of ProVerif language, excluding only some declarations. In detail, it covers the following features, which form a complete language for generating well-formed code for security analysis:

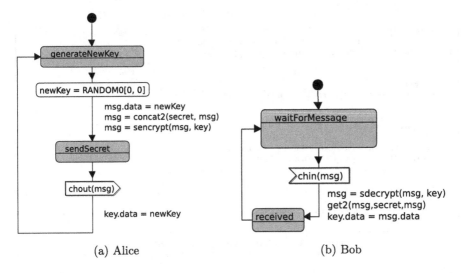

(a) Alice                              (b) Bob

**Fig. 2.** State machine diagrams in the SysML-Sec methodology

- **Function** declaration (referred to by *fun* and *reduc* keywords). They are typically used to describe cryptographic primitives such as *hash, symmetric encryption*, etc. and they don't depend on the particular design we are translating.
- **Variable** declaration (denoted by *channel* and *free* keywords). They declare channels and other variables that are shared by every participant and can be either public or private.
- **Queries** (referred to by *query* keyword) express the security properties that a user wishes to prove on the design
- **Sub-processes** declaration (referred to by *let* keyword). Each sub-process declaration contains a behavioral description of part of the state machine diagrams of the design. They may be referenced by other sub-processes or by the main process. If they are not referenced by anyone, they are simply ignored.
- The **main process** (referred to by *process* keyword), which is the entry point of the design. It can reference any sub-process.

Global structure of an example of ProVerif code is presented in Listing 1.1.

In particular, we see a constructor declaration (`sencrypt`), a destructor declaration (`sdecrypt`), two shared variables declarations (`token___Bob___0` and `token___Alice___0`), a confidentiality query, the declaration of a sub-process (`Bob___0`) and the main process which creates a new private name (`Alice___key___data`).

```
(* Functions *)
fun sencrypt (bitstring , bitstring ): bitstring .
reduc forall x: bitstring , k: bitstring;
        sdecrypt (sencrypt (x, k), k) = x.
...
```

```
(* Variables *)
free token___Bob___0: bitstring [private].
free token___Alice___0: bitstring [private].
...

(* Queries *)
query attacker(new Alice___secret__data).
...

(* Sub-processes *)
let Bob___0 =
    new strong___Bob___02: bitstring;
    out (chControl, strong___Bob___02);
    ...

(* Main process *)
process
    new Alice___key__data: bitstring;
    ...
```

**Listing 1.1.** Global structure of a ProVerif file

### 3.2 Translation of SysML-Sec Design to ProVerif

We now give the semantics of a SysML-Sec design, expressed as a translation from SysML-Sec designs into ProVerif specifications. For each SysML-Sec design $\mathcal{D}$, the interpretation function is expressed under the form:

$$\llbracket \mathcal{D} \rrbracket_{\mathcal{E}} = F_{\mathcal{E}}(\mathcal{D}) \oplus V_{\mathcal{E}}(\mathcal{D}) \oplus Q_{\mathcal{E}}(\mathcal{D}) \oplus P_{\mathcal{E}}(\mathcal{D}) \oplus \text{"process"} \oplus Main_{\mathcal{E}}(\mathcal{D})$$

It relies on several auxiliary functions for expressing the semantics of specific parts of the designs. The core entities of this semantics include five functions: $F_{\mathcal{E}}(\mathcal{D})$ for generating the set of functions, $V_{\mathcal{E}}(\mathcal{D})$ for generating the set of variables, $Q_{\mathcal{E}}(\mathcal{D})$ for generating the set of queries from pragmas, $P_{\mathcal{E}}(\mathcal{D})$ for generating the set of processes, and $Main_{\mathcal{E}}(\mathcal{D})$ that generates the main process that manages global instantiation of other processes. The construction of these functions relies on the notion of *environment* denoted $\mathcal{E} = (\mathcal{E}_q, \mathcal{E}_v)$ that keeps track of the states that have to be visited ($\mathcal{E}_q$) and those that have already been visited ($\mathcal{E}_v$) during state machine traversal.

Before defining the interpretation function, it is helpful to introduce some notations. We use the quote (") character to indicate the beginning and ending of a string (corresponding to ProVerif instruction). Quoted strings placed next to each other are concatenated (by $\oplus$ operator) to produce a whole string (complete source code). $\overrightarrow{a}^{a \in \mathcal{S}}$ denotes a list of parameters over the set $\mathcal{S}$.

**(1) Declarations part**
**Functions.** They include a list of common cryptographic primitives that can be used in all SysML-Sec designs. They also include additional functions tok and untok (used to protect variables), and a pair of encryption and decryption functions that are added to each private channel.
**Variables.** They consist of three types channels used for public communication, channels controlling messages (referred to by chctrl) and variable for each basic

block (referred to by token_...). Note that the token_... variables can only be generated once the sub-processes are generated.

**Queries.** In this paper, we focus on the confidentiality property. For each variable v for which the designer would like to check the confidentiality, we generate a query of the form "query attacker(new v)".

## (2) Processes generation

**Sub-processes.** They are generated by walking through the state machine diagram of every basic block of the SysML-Sec design. To do this, the interpretation function relies on a queue of states to be visited $\mathcal{E}_q$ that is initialized to contain the *root* state of each basic block, and a list $\mathcal{E}_v$ that contains all the states that have already been visited (which is empty at the beginning). While there are unexplored states, one state $s$ is picked from the $\mathcal{E}_q$ set, it is added to the explored set $\mathcal{E}_v$ set, a sub-process is created by using the first function $[\![s]\!]_{\mathcal{E}}^p$ (see Table 1). The idea is that the translation function goes through the whole *basic block* starting from the root and generates a Proverif instruction for each constructor encountered by calling the appropriate interpretation function. All interpretation functions are defined in Table 1. They use the terminology *fresh* variable which means that the variable is a new one and it has no occurrence anywhere in the code except in the instruction that creates it. Informally, the interpretation functions, as described in Table 1, translate states to a corresponding ProVerif event used for reachability queries; and transitions by translating their guards into if conditions $([\![.,.]\!]_{\mathcal{E}}^t)$ and their actions into ProVerif instructions $([\![.,.]\!]_{\mathcal{E}}^a)$. The continuation of the translation of following states is completed by $[\![.]\!]_{\mathcal{E}}^c$ function. Two interpretation functions require special attention: multiple outgoing transitions and transitions linking states of two different basic blocks. For the former, the resulting ProVerif process generates a token for each possible transitions and makes them available to the attacker $([\![.]\!]_{\mathcal{E}}^m)$. Then, it triggers the path by asking the attacker to accept one token. For the latter, the process also generates a token $([\![.]\!]_{\mathcal{E}}^b)$. This token must contain the current state of the block (as described by its attributes) and the identifier of the basic block to be called (the token_ variables). In order to prevent the attacker from replaying previous tokens, the token includes a nonce that is issued by the callee. This token is protected from modification and spying by the attacker by encapsulating it into a private function tok.

**Main Process.** The main process is then appended to the end of the ProVerif specification. Its purpose is first to create one unique tok(...) message for each state machine so that the attacker can *call*[2] the process corresponding to each basic block whose root is the initial state of a state machine. To create each token for a block, the main process needs to instantiate the attributes of the block, wait for a nonce and send the token. Then, it runs all the created processes in parallel (as denoted by the | operator) infinitely (as denoted by the ! operator).

---

[2] The term *call* here is abusive. Indeed, the attacker has no control over the execution flow of each process. It is however able to pass a token to a particular process which is blocked waiting for it.

**Table 1.** Interpretation function of state machine diagrams

$$[\![q]\!]_{\mathcal{E}}^{p} = \begin{cases} \text{"let proclabel\_L}(q) = \\ \text{new nonce;} \\ \text{out (chctrl, nonce);} \\ \text{in(chctrl, token);let (=token\_L}(q), \text{=nonce, } args) = \text{untok(token)"} \oplus [\![q]\!]_{\mathcal{E}}^{s} \\ \text{with } args = \overrightarrow{a}^{a \in att(b)} \end{cases}$$

$$[\![q]\!]_{\mathcal{E}}^{s} = \begin{cases} \text{"."} & \text{if } q = q_{\perp} \\ \text{"event enteringState\_L}(q)();\text{"} \oplus [\![q, e]\!]_{\mathcal{E}}^{t} & \text{if } UniqueOut(q) \\ \text{"event enteringState\_L}(q)();\text{"} \oplus [\![q]\!]_{\mathcal{E}}^{m} & \text{otherwise} \end{cases}$$

$$[\![q, e]\!]_{\mathcal{E}}^{t} = \begin{cases} \text{"if } guard(e) \text{ then"} \oplus [\![q, e]\!]_{\mathcal{E}}^{a} & \text{if } guard(e) \neq \text{true} \\ [\![q, e]\!]_{\mathcal{E}}^{a} & \text{otherwise} \end{cases}$$

$$[\![q]\!]_{\mathcal{E}}^{m} = \begin{cases} \bigoplus_{e \in Out(q)} \text{"new } x_e \text{;out (chctrl, } x_e); \text{"} \oplus \text{"in (chctrl, } c); \text{"} \bigoplus_{e \in Out(q)} \left( \text{"if } c = x_e \text{ then"} \oplus [\![q, e]\!]_{\mathcal{E}}^{t} \right) \\ \text{where } c \text{ and } x_e \text{ are fresh variables} \end{cases}$$

$$[\![q, e]\!]_{\mathcal{E}}^{a} = \begin{cases} \text{"let } x = exp \text{ in"} \oplus [\![target(e)]\!]_{\mathcal{E}}^{c} & \text{if } action(e) = x := exp \\ \text{"new } x; \text{"} \oplus [\![target(e)]\!]_{\mathcal{E}}^{c} & \text{if } action(e) = \nu.x \\ \text{"out } (c, x); \text{"} \oplus [\![target(e)]\!]_{\mathcal{E}}^{c} & \text{if } action(e) = \bar{c}\langle x \rangle \\ \text{"in } (c, x); \text{"} \oplus [\![target(e)]\!]_{\mathcal{E}}^{c} & \text{if } action(e) = c\langle x \rangle \\ [\![target(e)]\!]_{\mathcal{E}}^{c} & \text{if } action(e) = f(x_1, \ldots, x_2) \mid \varepsilon \end{cases}$$

$$[\![q]\!]_{\mathcal{E}}^{c} = \begin{cases} [\![q]\!]_{\mathcal{E}}^{s} & \text{if } UniqueIn(q) \\ [\![q]\!]_{\mathcal{E}}^{b} & \text{otherwise} \end{cases}$$

$$[\![q]\!]_{\mathcal{E}}^{b} = \begin{cases} \text{"in(chctrl, nonce);out(chctrl, tok(token\_L}(q)), \text{nonce, } args)).\text{"} & \text{if } q \in \mathcal{E}_v \text{ or } q \in \mathcal{E}_q \\ \text{"in(chctrl, nonce);out(chctrl, tok(token\_L}(q)), \text{nonce, } args)).\text{"} & \text{otherwise} \\ \mathcal{E}_q = \mathcal{E}_q \cup \{q\} \\ \text{with } args = \overrightarrow{a}^{a \in att(b)} \end{cases}$$

$$Main_{\mathcal{E}}(\mathcal{D}) = \left( \bigoplus_{b \in block(\mathcal{D})} \left( \bigoplus_{a \in att(b)} \text{"new } a; \text{"} \oplus \text{"in(chctrl, nonce);} \right. \right.$$
$$\left. \left. \text{out(chctrl, tok(token\_L}(q_0), \text{nonce, } args))\text{"} \right) \right)$$
$$\text{"} \mid \text{"}_{q \in \mathcal{E}_v} \left( \text{"! proclabel\_L}(q)\text{"} \right)$$

with $args = \overrightarrow{a}^{a \in att(b)}$

## 4   Validation

The purpose of this section is to provide arguments validating the semantics given in this paper. The first part shows formally that we didn't introduce any new information in our translation process; the second part focuses on an example to show how our translation works in practice.

### 4.1 Correctness Theorem

We first proved that our translation algorithm is sound: if there is a possible disclosure of a secret in the software design, then there is a disclosure in the ProVerif specification. Soundness of translation algorithm states that each ProVerif code generated by $Main_{\mathcal{E}}(\mathcal{D})$, is compliant with the software design $\mathcal{D}$, according to the property of confidentiality.

**Proposition 1.** *If a term M is a secret in the SysML-Sec model, then M is a secret in the generated Pro Verif specification.*

The proof is done by induction on the length of all possible execution traces of SysML-Sec model (proof detailed in [15]).

For checking properties like confidentiality, ProVerif tries to prove it by finding all possible *execution traces* that would lead to a violation of this property in an *approximated model*. This approximated model—which is needed since proving secrecy properties in the Dolev-Yao model has been proved to be undecidable in the general case [4, 10]—is constructed so that each possible trace on the *real* model produces a possible trace in the approximated model. As such, ProVerif can issue three types of results (given for secrecy here):

- Property is **true**. ProVerif did not find any trace leading to a violation of the property in the approximated model. Since the approximation is sound, this means that the property is true also on the real model.
- Property is **false**. ProVerif has found a trace on the approximated design and has managed to construct a corresponding trace on the real model. The trace found is provided with the result by ProVerif.
- Property **cannot be proved**. ProVerif has found a trace on the approximated design but this trace did not match a valid trace on the real model. In this case, ProVerif is not able to conclude but the trace on the approximated model is returned so that the designer can decide whether this matches a valid trace or not.

We keep these three possible results and make them available to the designer through the TTool interface.

### 4.2 Verification Results in TTool

In order to enable the designer to simultaneously see the results of the previous verification and accordingly continue modeling, verification results are displayed on the diagrams that are built by the designer. Results for the reachability, confidentiality and authenticity properties are displayed on the block and state machine diagrams in the form of green (when property is true) or red (when property is false) locks. For instance, we can see in Fig. 3a that the *waitForMessage* and *received* states are reachable. Also, in order to ease debugging and when it is available, the designer is provided with a trace that shows why the property is true (for instance how a state is reachable) or false (how a secret can be disclosed). This trace is automatically constructed based on the trace issued by ProVerif and displayed as a sequence diagram. As such, the trace presents the messages exchanged by the participants (all blocks and the attacker) and the states that each block goes through. As shown in Fig. 3b, we see how the *received* state inside Bob's state machine can be reached by receiving the message sent by Alice to Bob containing the data: (sencrypt((Alice.secret, Alice.newKey), Alice.Key).

## 5   Related Work

Assessing security properties when designing software components mostly relies on formal approaches. For example, [20] proposes verifying cryptographic protocols with a probabilistic analysis approach. Protocols are represented as trees whose nodes capture knowledge while edges are assigned transition probabilities. Although these trees could include malicious agents in order to model attacks and threats, nevertheless security properties are not explicitly represented. Moreover, for threat analysis, attacks should be explicitly expressed and manually solved. [21] defines a formal basic set of security services for accomplishing security goals. In this approach, security property analysis strongly relies on the designer's experience. Moreover, threat assessment is not easily feasible. There are numerous approaches for formal verification of security properties. Most of them are not automated and cannot be used as an engineering tool e.g. [9,17] and [2]. Among the research dedicated to engineering-oriented security verification that we are aware of, the closest are [13,14] and [19]. UMLsec [13] is a modeling framework aimed at defining security properties of software components and their composition within a UML framework. It also features a rather complete framework addressing various stages of model-driven secure software engineering from the specification of security requirements to tests, including

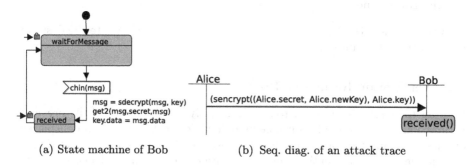

(a) State machine of Bob          (b) Seq. diag. of an attack trace

**Fig. 3.** Trace expressing ProVerif results (Color figure online)

logic-based formal verification regarding the composition of software components. In [14], Kordy et al. exposed a formal description of attack-defense trees. In these diagrams, interactions between the attacker and the system (defender) are modeled as attacks and countermeasures. In this sense, our approach is different as it relies on attacker capabilities and on a description of the system behaviour, meaning that the verification algorithm presented in this paper is able to prove that a design is secure against a certain class of attacker, without prior knowledge of the form of the attack. On the other hand, verification algorithms on attack-defense trees can solely prove that a countermeasure is efficient against a specific attack. More recently, [19] developed an expanded UML model extending the sequence diagrams of UML for security protocol verification. Their approach includes translating models into ProVerif for verification of confidentiality and correspondence. While sequence diagrams are particularly well suited to evaluating observational equivalence properties as they show the messages exchanged between participants, state machine diagrams –as used in this paper– allow modeling of precise behavioural properties more intuitively (such as conditional statements or loops). Furthermore, our process includes verification of weak and strong authenticity.

This paper expands on previous publications on SysML-Sec, proposing how to better model certain situations (e.g., loops) and their models-to-ProVerif transformation, taking into account the capabilities and limitations of ProVerif. We thus manage to limit cases where the proof of security properties would fail, without impacting the verification capabilities of SysML-Sec diagrams.

## 6 Conclusion

The paper describes a formal and novel Model-Driven Approach for (safety) and security modeling and verification of embedded systems. The paper itself focuses on the formal SysML-to-ProVerif transformation, and sketches a proof of the soundness of our approach. Last but not least, this new transformation is already available in TTool, and it includes backtracing capabilities. The overall approach is exemplified with a toy example. However, it has already been successfully applied to a large range of systems, including an authenticated and non-authenticated versions of the TLS protocol, an implementation of the X3DH protocol used by messaging applications such as Signal/Telegram or a key exchange protocol targeting Intel SGX architecture, and the design of the embedded architecture of an autonomous vehicle. Our formal description set the frameworks for a future proof of equivalence or soundness. Proof limitations of ProVerif could also be addressed using other proving techniques, e.g. relying on Prolog.

# References

1. Abadi, M., Blanchet, B.: Analyzing security protocols with secrecy types and logic programs. J. ACM **52**, 102–146 (2005)
2. Ali, Y., El-Kassas, S., Mahmoud, M.: A rigorous methodology for security architecture modeling and verification. In: Proceedings of the 42nd Hawaii International Conference on System Sciences (2009)
3. Allamigeon, X., Blanchet, B.: Reconstruction of attacks against cryptographic protocols. In: 18th IEEE Workshop on Computer Security Foundations, CSFW-18 2005 (2005)
4. Amadio, R.M., Lugiez, D., Vanackère, V.: On the symbolic reduction of processes with cryptographic functions. Theor. Comput. Sci. **290**, 695–740 (2003)
5. Apvrille, L., Roudier, Y.: Designing safe and secure embedded and cyber-physical systems with SysML-Sec. In: Desfray, P., et al. (eds.) Model-Driven Engineering and Software Development, vol. 580, pp. 293–308. Springer, Switzerland (2016). https://doi.org/10.1007/978-3-319-27869-8_17
6. Armando, A., et al.: The AVISPA tool for the automated validation of internet security protocols and applications. In: Etessami, K., Rajamani, S.K. (eds.) CAV 2005. LNCS, vol. 3576, pp. 281–285. Springer, Heidelberg (2005). https://doi.org/10.1007/11513988_27
7. Blanchet, B., et al.: An efficient cryptographic protocol verifier based on prolog rules. In: CSFW, vol. 1, pp. 82–96 (2001)
8. Blanchet, B., Smyth, B., Cheval, V.: Automatic cryptographic protocol verifier. User Manual and Tutorial, Technical report (2015)
9. Drouineaud, M., Bortin, M., Torrini, P., Sohr, K.: A first step towards formal verification of security policy properties for RBAC. In: QSIC 2004 (2004)
10. Durgin, N., Lincoln, P., Mitchell, J., Scedrov, A.: Undecidability of bounded security protocols. In: Workshop on Formal Methods and Security Protocols (1999)
11. Eames, D.P., Moffett, J.D.: The integration of safety and security requirements. In: Felici, M., Kanoun, K. (eds.) SAFECOMP 1999. LNCS, vol. 1698, pp. 468–480. Springer, Heidelberg (1999). https://doi.org/10.1007/3-540-48249-0_40
12. OM Group: System modeling language specification (SysML), version 1.5. Technical report
13. Jürjens, J.: Developing secure embedded systems: pitfalls and how to avoid them. In: 29th International Conference on Software Engineering (2007)
14. Kordy, B., Mauw, S., Radomirović, S., Schweitzer, P.: Foundations of attack–defense trees. In: Degano, P., Etalle, S., Guttman, J. (eds.) FAST 2010. LNCS, vol. 6561, pp. 80–95. Springer, Heidelberg (2011). https://doi.org/10.1007/978-3-642-19751-2_6
15. Lugou, F.: Environments for analyzing the security of smart objects. Ph.D. thesis, Télécom ParisTech, France (2018)
16. Lugou, F., Li, L.W., Apvrille, L., Ameur-Boulifa, R.: SysML models and model transformation for security. In: 4th International Conference on Model-Driven Engineering and Software Development (2016)
17. Maña, A., Pujol, G.: Towards formal specification of abstract security properties. In: The Third International Conference on Availability, Reliability and Security. IEEE (2008)
18. Pedroza, G., Knorreck, D., Apvrille, L.: AVATAR: a SysML environment for the formal verification of safety and security properties. In: The 11th IEEE Conference on Distributed Systems and New Technologies, NOTERE 2011 (2011)

19. Shen, G., Li, X., Feng, R., Xu, G., Hu, J., Feng, Z.: An extended UML method for the verification of security protocols. In: 19th International Conference on Engineering of Complex Computer Systems (ICECCS) (2014)

20. Toussaint, M.J.: A new method for analyzing the security of cryptographic protocols. IEEE J. Sel. Areas Commun. **11**, 702–714 (1993)

21. Trcek, D., Blazic, B.J.: Formal language for security services base modelling and analysis. Elsevier Sci. J. Comput. Commun. **18**, 921–928 (1995)

# The Challenge of Safety Tactics Synchronization for Cooperative Systems

Elena Lisova$^{(\boxtimes)}$ and Svetlana Girs

Malardalen University, Vasteras, Sweden
{elena.lisova,svetlana.girs}@mdh.se

**Abstract.** Given rapid progress in integrating operational and industrial technologies and recent increase in the level of automation in safety-related systems, cooperative cyber-physical systems are emerging in a self-contained area requiring new approaches for addressing their critical properties such as safety and security. The notion of tactics is used to describe a relation between a system input and its corresponding response. Cooperative functionalities often rely on wireless communication and incoherent behavior of different wireless channels makes it challenging to achieve harmonization in deployment of systems' tactics. In this work we focus on safety tactics for cooperative cyber-physical systems as a response to inputs related to both safety and security, i.e., we are interested in security informed safety, and formulate a challenge of synchronization of safety tactics between the cooperating systems. To motivate the requirement on such synchronization we consider a car platoon, i.e., a set of cooperative vehicles, as an example and illustrate possible hazards arising from unsynchronized tactics deployment.

**Keywords:** Cooperative CPSs · Safety tactics · Synchronization · Platooning

## 1 Introduction

Today we are witnessing a significant progress in industrial and operational technologies allowing to merge them in a system that combines physical processes and computational capabilities, can have external connections, communicate and cooperate with other systems and have different degrees of autonomy. Such cooperative cyber-physical systems (CO-CPSs) are more efficient and can have functionalities that are exceeding the onces coming from traditional systems. However, new challenges arise in these systems as well, as, e.g., wireless solutions, together with benefits in terms of reconfiguration, weight and complexity, also bring a challenge towards security due to openness of wireless channels possibly allowing an adversary to receive transmitted messages or interfere with the channel. Moreover, the majority of such systems are safety-critical as they have humans in the loop and thus, their safety has to be addressed. Safety of CO-CPSs cannot be guaranteed without incorporating security considerations,

© Springer Nature Switzerland AG 2019
B. Hamid et al. (Eds.): ISSA 2018/CSITS 2018, LNCS 11552, pp. 50–58, 2019.
https://doi.org/10.1007/978-3-030-16874-2_4

as a security breach can potentially contribute to hazards. Thus, CO-CPSs are required to have safety reactions to inputs coming from the sub-systems and surrounding environment, which might indicate on failures caused by both safety or security reasons. Moreover, given the complexity of CO-CPSs and frequent system updates due to security considerations, e.g., patches, safety reactions can be required to evolve with time. Emerging behavior is an immense challenge to address for such systems, and one of the aspects to solve in this domain is alignment of how CO-CPSs are seeing each other, e.g., common awareness of communication channels failures, and how their reactions are synchronized.

As system reactions are based on inputs from environment or other systems, communicational infrastructure and its state assessment play an important role. By assessment here we mean estimation of its current reliability level, as this level is directly connected to how much a CO-CPS can trust in correctness of inputs from other CO-CPSs and consequently to which extent the CO-CPS shall make decisions on its own. Moreover, grounds for further analyses and decision making need to be considered already during the system architecture design, once a particular architecture for collaborative systems is chosen [3].

On the system architectural level, safety can be discussed in terms of tactics. A tactic can be defined as "a design decision that influences the control of a quality attribute response" [2]. Initially this term was proposed for six quality attributes (availability, modifiability, security, performance, usability and testability), but later extended by Wu and Kelly [16] to be applied for safety. A safety tactic captures how to get a desired system safety response for various stimuli coming as inputs to the system. Each attribute can be associated with a set of attribute primitives, e.g., some of security primitives are encryption, integrity, firewalls [2]. Such primitives can be developed in architectural patterns that incorporate features necessary for such primitive being in place. The notion of tactics is defined on the system architecture level, however, system tactics influence the quality of the considered attribute, i.e., they influence the decision making process and system response. In this work we use the term tactic as it was initially proposed on the architectural level, but also to refer to its exact implementation. Thus, the discussed above challenge of safety responses synchronization and their implementations for CO-CPSs falls into safety tactics synchronization challenges. As was proposed by Wu and Kelly, safety tactics may include aim, description, rationale expressed with Goal-Structuring Notation (GSN), applicability, consequences, side effects, practical strategies and related patterns and other tactics. From what is important for our consideration, a tactic includes a logical input-processing-output chain along with deadlines for each step and can be refined further depending on the required level of details. We assume that safety tactics include possible input to the system that can be also provoked by an attack on it. Thus, we advocate security informed safety tactics instead of pure safety tactics as communication interfaces of a CO-CPS significantly increase its attack surface and make it impossible to claim a CO-CPS being safe if it is not secure.

This paper is our initial effort in tackling CO-CPS's wireless communication assessment and handling of failures originated in communication channels and related to both safety and security. These failures have to be addressed as CO-CPSs depend on communication. It is crucial to analyze how a communication channel failure can be perceived by different cooperating systems, e.g., whether the failure is detected by all communicating systems, whether detection can be done within a predefined time range and whether the cause of the failure can be assessed in a similar way by all the cooperative systems. In this paper we look at a car platoon as an example of a set of CO-CPSs that cooperate (drive and maneuverer together) to achieve a common goal, e.g., reduction of fuel consumption. Some of the questions that arise in this example are whether a failure of the leading vehicle will be perceived in the same manner by all participants and, e.g., disengaging maneuver will be performed in a safe manner, whether a failure of one of the platooning vehicles will be detected by others in time (this is important as a not detected failure of one vehicle can be hazardous to the whole platoon, e.g., if a vehicle that is compromised by an adversary ruins the string stability of the system [5]). As CO-CPSs form a relatively new domain, a gap can be observed in literature discussing their architecture principles, which include communication infrastructure, and knowledge about their practical realization [11]. Looking at platooning, there are papers describing particular aspects of in-platoon communication, e.g., a platoon leader trustworthiness [7] or communication topologies [10] for vehicles within the platoon, but it is not straightforward to find information in regard to overall communication infrastructure [1], i.e., where intelligence/decision making is placed, what the vehicles' tactics and platoon strategies are. For example, it is clear that platoon members should estimate reliability of communication channels in order to understand when to stop following the commands from the leading vehicle, however a realization of this monitoring and a logic behind making such decisions is not well presented in the literature. Even though platoon demonstrators from such manufacturers as Volvo and SCANIA exist, due to novelty of the area and its continuous development there is a lack of common agreement on how to analyze such systems. Hence, the contribution of this paper is, looking at a car platoon as an example of CO-CPSs, formulation of safety tactics synchronization challenge and a proposal on how to address it. Two scenarios of a communication failure are used to illustrate the hazards arising from safety tactics being unsynchronized. Moreover, possible ways to address the challenge are discussed and proposed as future work.

The remainder of the paper is structured as following: Sect. 2 introduces platooning, while the considered scenarios of failure perception are presented in Sect. 3. Next, Sect. 4 discusses the synchronization of safety tactics and Sect. 5 concludes the paper.

## 2    Example – A Platoon

The use case considered in this work is a platoon of vehicles which drive close together and in a collaborative manner, led by the front vehicle, Fig. 1. Each vehicle has a set of sensors, radars and other equipment to sense the road and any other cars or obstacles in the proximity. Moreover, every vehicle within the platoon is equipped with communication infrastructure to exchange information with other platoon members. It was shown before that, having all necessary sensors, vehicles are able to operate safely and detect acceleration or breaking performed by the vehicle in front even without communicating [12]. However, performance of a platoon where vehicles do not communicate with each other is significantly lower as communication provides additional source of information in the system [17]. Moreover, with communication not only the following vehicle, but also the other members of the platoon can be timely informed about a maneuver. Various communication strategies for organizing information exchange between the vehicles within a platoon exist [9,10] including options with neighboring cars communicating only with each other or with each other and also the platoon leader, scenarios with the platoon leader sending commands to all vehicles directly or intermediate members forwarding the information. Selection of a concrete communication scheme is outside of the scope of this paper, but to have a more specific scenario we consider a case where the leading vehicle coordinates the platoon by communicating to every member directly and informing the members about its position, speed and maneuver intentions. To make this possible, there exist a communication link between every platoon member and the leader vehicle. Additionally, platoon as a whole establishes connection with the surrounding environment such as other vehicles or road infrastructure nodes. This information exchange supports the work of various safety applications such as, e.g., cooperative forward collision warning, warning about an approaching emergency vehicle, pre-crash sensing warnings, and aims at providing drivers with information about critical situations in order to prevent accidents. One important feature of cooperative driving is the way the cooperating vehicles influence each other's behavior, e.g., by triggering auto brake in following vehicles if the lead one issues such command. Performance of such collaborative schemes depends of reliability of the communication between the members and timely reaction on the changes both in behavior of the vehicles and communication quality.

## 3   Failure Perception in a Platoon

As demonstrated in Fig. 1, we consider two scenarios of a failure occurrence and its propagation in a platoon. In *Scenario A*, one of the platooning vehicles experiences a failure of its communication channel to the leading vehicle, i.e., this vehicle cannot rely on timely and correct transmission of its messages and cannot trust in correctness of incoming packets (if any comes). We do not consider a particular cause of the failure, e.g., packet losses or delays, failure of receiving hardware [6], but assume that it can be triggered by causes associated with both safety and security domains. We assume that such failure is detected by the platooning vehicle and a decision about consequent actions, i.e., safety mechanisms, aligned with the corresponding safety tactic is made. In *Scenario A*, there are two aspects to consider. First, is whether the failure is detected in a similar way by both ends of this communication channel, i.e., if both the leading and the platooning vehicles recognize the failure and if they do it synchronously, i.e., the difference between moments of failure detection is below a certain threshold. Upon failure detection, both vehicles are supposed to activate safety mechanisms from their predefined safety strategies; obviously, these tactics have to be aligned with each other. If the failure is not recognized in the same way by the two vehicles, then, for example, the platooning vehicle can make a decision about leaving the platoon (one of possible safety mechanisms for the platooning vehicle upon a communication failure), while there is no command from the leading vehicle to the rest of the platoon to make space for the disengaging vehicle (for disengaging, the distances between the vehicle leaving the platoon and its neighbors have to be increased). We assume alike mechanisms for channel reliability estimation and failure detection being deployed within communicating nodes, however the same mechanism does not guarantee the same response as nodes communicating over the same wireless channel might not experience the same channel quality.

The second aspect to consider in *Scenario A* is the perception of such failure by other platooning vehicles. It is important both that other platoon members cooperate and allow the vehicle that detected the failure to disengage, but also that they have situation awareness in general (i.e., which failures have been detected and by whom), which may be of interest for all platooning vehicles as they all influence each-other's decision making process. Such awareness of the status of platooning vehicles can be seen as redundant and not needed during the normal operation of the platoon, given that control of the platoon is managed by the leading vehicle. However, it can be of use when failures occur, especially if they are caused by related attacks as then additional measures may be required to take back the control over vehicles.

*Scenario B* represents a situation where the platoon leader experiences a communication failure, e.g., its communication hardware has failed or its communication channels have been jammed. Obviously, such a failure needs to be recognized by the platooning vehicles and a corresponding action has to be taken, e.g., the whole platoon can disengage or it has to be reconfigured into a platoon with a new leader. Different vehicles can assess the same wireless communication channel differently and thus, timely detection of a failure in such communication channel is a challenge from a CO-CPS design point of view. Moreover, to disengage, vehicles need to increase the distances between each other, which requires cooperation and negotiation to complete the maneuver. And, as such maneuver is a part of safety tactics of platooning vehicles, we again see the need for synchronization of the safety tactics.

These examples of communication failures and how they are perceived by CO-CPSs are indicating that the challenge of synchronization of CO-CPSs' safety tactics (which include a particular failure and its cause, safety reaction to the failure and timing requirements for the reaction) needs to be addressed.

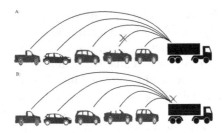

**Fig. 1.** Examples of failure scenarios in a platoon: A – communication failure of a single platooning vehicle; B – communication failure of the leading vehicle.

## 4 Safety Tactics Synchronization for CO-CPSs

In the previous section we showed how a failure in a wireless communication channel can be perceived differently within a set of CO-CPSs and how it can potentially contribute to a hazard. Based on the considered example we can distinguish three levels of required synchronization in CO-CPSs' safety tactics. Accordingly, we formulate three following sub-challenges:

1. Alignment of sets of the predefined safety tactics in different CO-CPSs (e.g., having in mind different manufactures).
2. Sufficient synchronization of communication reliability assessment done by different CO-CPSs.
3. Synchronized deployment of selected safety tactics by CO-CPSs.

The first sub-challenge belongs to the design phase of CO-CPSs and requires corresponding standardization grounds. Having platooning as an example, in a perspective it is expected that all platoon eligible vehicles would be able to join an existing platoon, regardless of their manufacturer. This can be addressed via a corresponding legislation, making manufacturers synchronize the set of safety tactics between each other, or at least have the same minimum set of required tactics. From a design point of view, to achieve such unification among vehicle components responsible for failure detection and deployment of corresponding safety mechanisms, one can look at the concept of Safety Element out of Context (SEooC) proposed by the automotive functional safety standard ISO 26262 [8]. The SEooC concept enables design of an element outside of the context of a specific system, but upon assumptions about safety relevant properties that need to be validated later during integration of the element. Given that such CO-CPS component needs to be reused in all communicating CO-CPSs, its development may be required to comply with high integrity demands. In this regard, SEooC development and assurance process have been already extended with semi-formal assumption/guarantee contract methodology [14]. Thus, the concept of SEooC can be a good candidate to be used for component design for CO-CPSs responsible for assessment of communication quality.

The second sub-challenge is provoked by the nature of wireless communication. Packets transmitted over wireless media are subjects to bit errors and packet delays and losses caused by pathloss, i.e., degradation of the signal strength with distance, multipath fading and shadowing. Moreover, wireless channels are not necessary symmetrical in both directions, change their characteristics with time and in space. Thus, communicating nodes might observe different levels of packet errors and losses, making channel estimation and common agreement on its reliability level a challenging task. If a communication channel is not reliable anymore, all CO-CPSs using this channel need to make the same estimation and decision about channel reliability. This is required as correct operation of the system needs cooperation. When channel quality estimation is done at the communication end-points, the "black channel" model proposed in IEC 61508 [4] can be used for handling the inherent unreliability of wireless links. This model implies that we cannot guarantee communication properties of the channel and a challenge of communication assessment and corresponding reactions should be handled by the CO-CPSs.

The last sub-challenge refers to a necessity for a CO-CPS "to understand" what other CO-CPSs are doing, what they are responding to and what may follow, i.e, which particular safety tactic is being currently deployed. It may be of high importance for a CO-CPS to be aware if one of other CO-CPSs has detected a communication failure and whether its cause comes from safety or security domain. This is important as it may, for example, indicate a general problem with communication that can affect other channels with time or a security breach that can lead to jeopardizing all involved CO-CPSs. Distinguishing between security and safety causes of a failure is a separate challenging task and may require additional techniques being deployed to determine the origin of the failure. Identification of the cause is crucial, as, e.g., in case of a security breach some of the usual fail-safe modes as shutting down and rebutting can make the situation worse, unless the adversary is located and isolated from communication network. Otherwise, the adversary can gain even more advantage if being present during the network reboot.

As the first step to address the challenge of safety tactics synchronization presented by a combination of sub-challenges above, we propose to design a CO-CPS channel state manager. Such manager can be developed as a part of a CO-CPS aiming to assess the reliability of the black channel in light of communication anomalies. This can be done by, e.g., extending the SEooC contract-based development process by detailing it further for a particular case of a CO-CPS channel state manager. To be able to assess the reliability level of communication, the channel state manager needs to have an incorporated monitor assessing parameters that are chosen based on related security and safety analyses. Even though traditionally safety and security analyses are conducted separately [13], for such monitor we need to consider them jointly as we want to catch possible interdependencies. Thus, first we need to develop a methodology of such monitor design as it will require corresponding joint analyses to determine relevant failure modes and attacks. The next step in regard to the CO-CPS channel state manager is its evaluation in terms of effectiveness and applicability. Further, the CO-CPS channel state manager needs to be integrated into a CO-CPS state manager [15], which is responsible for making a decision about the current system state and a particular safety mechanism being deployed, as information gained from the channel state manager can affect the decisions made by the CO-CPS state manager.

## 5   Conclusions

In this paper we formulated and motivated a challenge of safety tactics synchronization for cooperative systems. We considered two scenarios of possible failure occurrences in a system of platooning vehicles that illustrate the need of common perception of a wireless communication channel state among the collaborating systems. The challenge was refined into three sub-challenges reflecting the need for design of common safety tactics, coherent failure perception and synchronization of corresponding safety reactions. We also proposed a CO-CPS channel state manager as the fist step in addressing the formulated challenges.

Future work includes development of a design methodology for a CO-CPS channel state manager in which safety and security are threated jointly and its further evaluation. The latter includes simulations to evaluate applicability and effectiveness of the manager and later implementation. In parallel, we plan to consider how a system response is handled, i.e., to integrate the CO-CPS channel state manager into the system state manager.

**Acknowledgments.** The work is supported by the Swedish Foundation for Strategic Research (SSF) via the Future factories in the Cloud (FiC) and the Secure and Dependable Platforms for Autonomy (Serendipity) projects.

## References

1. Axelsson, J.: Safety in vehicle platooning: a systematic literature review. IEEE Trans. Intell. Transp. Syst. **18**(5), 1033–1045 (2017)
2. Bass, L., Clements, P., Kazman, R.: Software Architecture in Practice. Addison-Wesley, London (2003)
3. Bauer, B., Müller, J.P., Roser, S.: Decentralized business process modeling and enactment: ICT architecture topologies and decision methods. In: Dastani, M., El Fallah Seghrouchni, A., Ricci, A., Winikoff, M. (eds.) ProMAS 2007. LNCS (LNAI), vol. 4908, pp. 1–26. Springer, Heidelberg (2008). https://doi.org/10.1007/978-3-540-79043-3_1
4. CENELEC: IEC 61508: Functional Safety of E/E/PE Safety-Related Systems. Part 2: Requirements for E/E/PE Safety-Related Systems (2007)
5. Dadras, S., Gerdes, R.M., Sharma, R.: Vehicular platooning in an adversarial environment. In: Proceedings of the 10th ACM Symposium on Information, Computer and Communications Security, ASIA CCS 2015, pp. 167–178 (2015)
6. Girs, S., Sljivo, I., Jaradat, O.: Contract-based assurance for wireless cooperative functions of vehicular systems. In: IECON 2017–43rd Annual Conference of the IEEE Industrial Electronics Society, pp. 8391–8396 (2017)

7. Hu, H., Lu, R., Zhang, Z., Shao, J.: REPLACE: a reliable trust-based platoon service recommendation scheme in VANET. IEEE Trans. Veh. Technol. **66**(2), 1786–1797 (2017)
8. International Organization for Standardization (ISO): ISO 26262: Road Vehicles - Functional Safety (2011)
9. Jia, D., Lu, K., Wang, J., Zhang, X., Shen, X.: A survey on platoon-based vehicular cyber-physical systems. IEEE Comm. Surv. Tutor. **18**(1), 263–284 (2016)
10. Michaud, F., Lepage, P., Frenette, P., Letourneau, D., Gaubert, N.: Coordinated maneuvering of automated vehicles in platoons. IEEE Trans. Intell. Transp. Syst. **7**(4), 437–447 (2006)
11. Pop, P., Scholle, D., Šljivo, I., Hansson, H., Widforss, G., Rosqvist, M.: Safe cooperating cyber-physical systems using wireless communication: the SafeCOP approach. Microprocess. Microsyst. **53**, 42–50 (2017)
12. Sheikholeslam, S., Desoer, C.A.: Longitudinal control of a platoon of vehicles with no communication of lead vehicle information: a system level study. IEEE Trans. Veh. Technol. **42**(4), 546–554 (1993)
13. Čaušević, A.: A risk and threat assessment approaches overview in autonomous systems of systems. In: Proceedings of the XXVI International Conference on Information, Communication and Automation Technologies (ICAT), pp. 1–6 (2017)
14. Šljivo, I., Gallina, B., Carlson, J., Hansson, H.: Using safety contracts to guide the integration of reusable safety elements within ISO 26262. In: Proceedings of the IEEE 21st Pacific Rim International Symposium on Dependable Computing (PRDC), pp. 129–138 (2015)
15. Šljivo, I., Gallina, B., Kaiser, B.: Assuring degradation cascades of car platoons via contracts. In: Proceedings of the 6th International Workshop on Next Generation of System Assurance Approaches for Safety-Critical Systems, September, pp. 317–329 (2017)
16. Wu, W., Kelly, T.: Safety tactics for software architecture design. In: 2004 Proceedings of the 28th Annual International Computer Software and Applications Conference, COMPSAC 2004, vol. 1, pp. 368–375 (2004)
17. Xu, L., Wang, L.Y., Yin, G., Zhang, H.: Communication information structures and contents for enhanced safety of highway vehicle platoons. IEEE Trans. Veh. Technol. **63**(9), 4206–4220 (2014)

# SAM: A Security Abstraction Model for Automotive Software Systems

Markus Zoppelt[✉] and Ramin Tavakoli Kolagari[✉]

Nuremberg Institute of Technology, Nuremberg, Germany
{markus.zoppelt,ramin.tavakolikolagari}@th-nuernberg.de

**Abstract.** Due to the emergence of (semi-)autonomous vehicles and networked technologies in the automotive domain, the development of secure and reliable vehicles plays an increasingly important role in the protection of road users. Safe and secure road transport is a major societal and political objective, which is substantiated by the concrete goal of the European Commission to "move close to zero fatalities in road transport" (White Paper of the European Commission *Roadmap to a Single European Transport Area—Towards a competitive and resource efficient transport system*, 2011, page 10.) within the next three decades. One historically often neglected aspect of this objective in automotive system development is security, i.e., freedom from maliciously implemented threats. In the automotive software industry, model-based engineering is the current state of the practice. Instead of integrating security into the entire system development process, it currently tends to be an afterthought. Because of the tight interdependencies and integration of components, the consequences of gaping security flaws are grave. The contribution of this paper is a secure modeling approach enabling the automotive engineer to analyze the software system in the context of industrial model-based engineering in an early phase. The security modeling language specification is presented as a proposed annex to the relevant industry standard EAST-ADL, and therefore offers a common modeling approach for architectural and security aspects. All security extensions are in line with this standard and its meta level, which is shared with AUTOSAR. The security modeling language specification is demonstrated in a small modeling example, along with a formal evaluation which applies the Grounded Theory method to a set of expert interviews, showing that it is comprehensive and embraces even non-standardized pertinent research.

**Keywords:** Automotive security · Safety and security · Security requirements

## 1 Introduction

The growing complexity of electrical automotive systems forces original equipment manufacturers (OEMs) to have expertise in all software-relevant quality

Supported by the ZD.B and the BayWISS Consortium Digitization.

B. Hamid et al. (Eds.): ISSA 2018/CSITS 2018, LNCS 11552, pp. 59–74, 2019.
https://doi.org/10.1007/978-3-030-16874-2_5

objectives, in particular security, safety and dependability. Moreover, the context of the industry is changing and the controllability is shifting away from OEMs, i.e., they do not fully control the aftermarket of external components such as smartphones, tablets, infotainment systems etc. Nonetheless, they are responsible for providing a common platform with secure interfaces to the required exterior components. Customers of automobiles ask for reliability, privacy and safety along with common convenience features like keyless entry and internet connectivity. In most cases, these convenience features collide with basic security principles and ultimately lead to a less secure product. A lack of security can effectuate safety risks as well as endanger the driver, fellow passengers and other road users. Car hacking, route sponsoring and even lethal accidents may be the impending consequence. The manufacturer's reputation is at stake as well. Therefore, it is expedient to provide a platform-independent base for modeling secure software for automotive systems. The problem addressed in this paper is the lack of constructive security applied during systems engineering processes associated with automotive systems. Instead of integrating security into the entire system development process, it currently tends to be an afterthought. Neglecting security is always fatal, especially regarding the tight interdependencies and integration of components in modern automotive systems. System architects and software engineers need a common basis for collaboration and sharing concepts in the early phase of the system's development. An overview of the automotive core development process is described in Sect. 3.1.

In this paper we show:

- A combination of security principles and architectural system models, formalizing and transferring established security properties to the automotive software engineering context.
- A user story of a conventional security modeling method as a basis for extracting relevant requirements for automotive security modeling.
- An extension of the automotive-specific architecture description language EAST-ADL to compensate for the lack of methods and tools for security modeling in the automotive domain.
- A practical example based on the user story, applying the extension, proposed to illustrate the solution approach at hand.
- A short analysis of the practical relevance of our combined approach through Grounded Theory interviews with industry experts.

It is not in the scope of the paper, though, to provide an empirical feasibility study, because the used techniques are feasible themselves. We only propose a combined approach in form of a language specification, modeling the interplay of security and safety within architectural models.

## 2 Targeting "Driving Computers"

Developing secure automotive systems is a major challenge in particular for intelligent cars acting more as a computer than a traditional vehicle. Modern cars are interconnected networks, with potentially more than 150 Electronic Control Units (ECUs) in luxury models [18] communicating with each other and with the environment (Car-2-X communication). Attackers do not target cars in the same way like they would attack standard computer systems; cars use different networks, protocols and architectures [30, 33]. Countermeasures like firewalls do not exist for cars, yet. Even trivial Denial-of-Service (DoS) attacks are easy to perform [23]. Moreover, cars carry burdensome legacy mechanisms with insecure and unencrypted protocols (e.g., CAN, Controller Area Network) in their system design and were originally not designed in line with contemporary security principles [8, 13]. Secure automotive network architectures were not prioritized in the past due to the general preconception in the last three decades that cars are secure because of their technical complexity (security by obscurity). However, numerous attack vectors [20, 31] on cars and their network of ECUs, actuators and sensors exist. In contrast to desktop computers, human lives are at stake when these "driving computers" are the target of an attack. Cyber attacks should always be considered highly critical when passengers' lives are at risk. Today, everybody is fully aware of the necessity to increase the security standard of cars and we are constantly reminded of that fact by regular press releases about car attacks [20]. This paper tackles the automotive security problem by addressing security at the beginning of the automotive system development process, enabling the automotive engineers to document, analyze and control the security design, which is the crucial prerequisite for even implementing security in the automotive system.

## 3  Automotive Software Systems Engineering

This section gives an overview of automotive software systems engineering with a special focus on modeling automotive systems according to EAST-ADL and AUTOSAR, two major international automotive standards. It is necessary to understand the specifics of the automotive software development process in general and the (meta)modeling approach applied by EAST-ADL and AUTOSAR in particular to understand the remainder of the paper, especially Sect. 5 describing the innovative contribution. A reader knowledgeable in the automotive software development process can skip this section.

### 3.1  Automotive Core Development Process

The automotive core development process is basically organized according to the traditional software engineering V-Model [14]. The core development process reflects the fact that automotive systems are typically embedded—with specific demands on hardware and software—by a parallel illustration of the product development on hardware and software level, according to the respective structure in the ISO26262 standard [12], an international standard for functional safety of automotive systems, see Sect. 5.2. Each phase of the V-Model stands for a coherent set of process steps in which a set of artifacts are produced. The phases are logically organized, not temporally. In the System Analysis phase, requirements are elicited and documented, in the System Design phase, a logical, function-oriented architectural structure is developed that is the basis for both the hardware and software development phases, which finally results in the implementation of the automotive system. The descending branches of the "Vs" cover constructive phases of the system development process: an artifact produced in a lower phase (concrete artifact) must be compliant to all artifacts produced in the immediate upper phase (abstract artifacts), i.e., concrete artifacts are validated by abstract artifacts. Ascending branches of the "Vs" cover verification and integration phases. The core development process is accompanied by a set of supporting processes like functional safety, configuration, change, requirements management etc., but these processes are not in the scope of this paper.

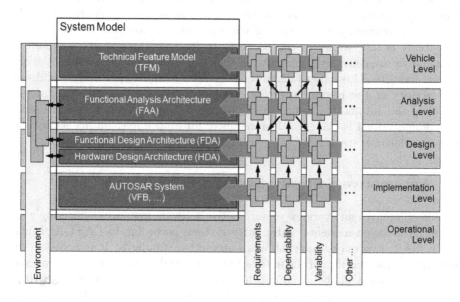

**Fig. 1.** EAST-ADL abstraction layers and extensions [4]

### 3.2    Modeling Automotive Systems with **EAST-ADL** and **AUTOSAR**

EAST-ADL [4] is a language to describe system architectures of automotive software-intensive systems by an information model that represents technical information in a standardized way. Aspects covered include vehicle functions and features as well as functional and hardware architecture. The EAST-ADL model is structured in abstraction levels, with each sub-model representing the complete embedded system in relevant details of the respective abstraction level.

The architecture models can be translated to various software architectures, including AUTOSAR [1], JasPar [26] and in-house frameworks, see Fig. 1.

The Technical Feature Model describes the system at the topmost level of abstraction and does not constitute an architecture. It is developed in the analysis phases (System Analysis, Hardware Analysis, Software Analysis) together with the corresponding requirements. The FunctionalAnalysisArchitecture is developed in the System Design phase. The HardwareDesignArchitecture is developed in the Hardware Design phase and the FunctionalDesign Architecture is developed in the Software Design phase. The AUTOSAR specification (see Sect. 3.3) of the automotive system is produced in the Software Implementation phase. The semi-formal modeling language EAST-ADL is described and explained by a language specification. This specification presents all language features, i.e., all notions, their essential meanings, interrelationships, applicable uses and constraints. Essentially, this specification could be described in a natural language (only fully formal languages require a logical/mathematical specification) but it is common practice to describe the language specification model-based as well. The model that is used to specify a language resides on the so-called metalevel (abbreviated M2); therefore, the concrete language specification model is called the metamodel. This metamodel comprises the aforementioned precise definition of the language. A concrete model of a system that makes use of the entities set forth in the metamodel resides on the type-level (abbreviated M1, sometimes also called User Models). Selected metamodel entities are instantiated and populated with concrete values, if necessary.

## 3.3 Adaptive AUTOSAR

AUTOSAR [1] is an international consortium formed by all major OEMs, suppliers, and tool vendors with the aim to develop a standard for automotive software architectures, i.e., a language specification (M2) for implementation modules. These implementation modules are called Software-Components and are used to encapsulate runnables, which are elementary C functions. The approach of AUTOSAR is to abstract away from all (irrelevant) details, hiding them in a Runtime Environment; in doing so, the system engineer is able to develop an application on the system level, and the complete car—with its complex underlying hardware topology—acts seemingly as a single computer. The AUTOSAR Adaptive Platform [2] goes one step further than the traditional approach (AUTOSAR Classic) and implements the Runtime Environment (RTE) for adaptive applications, which will become increasingly relevant with the perspective of (fully) autonomous automotive systems in near future. This platform uses virtual machines instead of embedded systems and its RTE dynamically links services and clients during runtime. The Adaptive Platform also features a dedicated component "Security Management", which is responsible for the crypto stack, identity and access management, secure communication, and a protected runtime environment [2, p. 7]. Furthermore, it offers protection against memory corruption attacks, horizontal isolation through virtual memory and OS-level visualization, and vertical isolation (i.e., "sandboxing").

# 4   User Story

In order to motivate the need for a dedicated security modeling support, this section gives a brief overview of the current state of practice when an automotive software system development team identifies security threats. Our main contribution is described in Sect. 5.

## 4.1   Automotive Security Management—State of the Practice

Our assumption: A car company assembles a task force to increase the security of their engine ECU. The task force consists of a system architect, security experts and software engineers. The security experts try to identify threats and vulnerabilities of a system, while the software engineers try to fix bugs and implement security functionality, e.g., cryptographic functions. The system architect defines the architecture of the system (i.e., the software and hardware topology), taking—among other things—security requirements into consideration. The team's job is to identify threats, attacks and vulnerabilities to address them in the current development. They start by creating a threat-risk analysis of different attacks against their main product line. Their company uses EAST-ADL to design a functional architecture. The team's security experts need to report threats and circumstances for real-world scenarios to the team. The security experts have already constructed attack trees [27] and estimated the attack potential [10] of possible attacks. The team's findings are documented in a textual requirements specification. The security experts attach a textual note to the modeled design function (`DesignFunction`) explaining an identified threat and possible countermeasures. The software engineers now need to check for the textual notes manually and implement them. The system architect, though, is usually not responsible for checking the notes or validating the content of the note. During subsequent testing of the system, the security experts wonder why no countermeasures have been implemented for this design function. They figure out that the software engineers did not take the note into account in the first place because the engineers have not interpreted the relevance of the threat correctly or could not decide for what purpose or security goal the note was intended.

The team's work will be interrupted as they discuss the use-case again to find out what the originally intended security goal was in the first place. Because the only documentation of the attack and adversary's motivation was only captured as a single textual note, the security experts also need to re-imagine the attack vector completely. Security has an inner complexity, though, which a textual note cannot fully explain, especially considering the requirements entailed. In addition, requirements alone are not sufficient enough. The system architect and the security experts need some sort of reciprocity and mutual possibilities for annotating the same model. Only then they can make the necessary adjustments to the system's architecture. To this date, there is no defined interaction through an iterative process between the system architect and the security experts. Moreover, information about safety precautions may pile up and show cross-references to other quality characteristics, like safety, security and timing. This might indicate that a certain component might be badly engineered in the first place.

### 4.2 Identifying Requirements for Automotive System Modeling

Classic AUTOSAR is the de-facto standard to this date. However, it allows the use for embedded ECUs only in the car and its model representation. This fact alone limits the focus on security. Some domain-specific architecture description languages (ADLs) exist, like EAST-ADL and AADL[1], but the modeling environment is scattered and not platform-agnostic.

The most relevant requirements for our combined approach of established security techniques and automotive security modeling are:

- Classifying attacks and security threats.
- Defining security goals.
- Extending the metamodel with entities to represent actors and link them to consequences and affected modeling entities.
- Representing the attack vector and all its stages—from attacker to breach—to affected vehicle features.
- A core solution idea for the attack vector handling.

## 5  SAM—Security Abstraction Model

In this section we describe our innovative contribution; a Security Abstraction Model (SAM) language specification for the automotive modeling environment as an extension for the EAST-ADL. SAM is a solution approach for the challenges and implications from the user story pictured in Sect. 4. We clarify the differences between security modeling and functional safety modeling and describe our metamodel entities of SAM. SAM is available as an open source project[2]. The complete metamodel of SAM (including entity descriptions) is also available as an online HTML version[3].

### 5.1  SAM Metamodel

SAM contains a concrete set of security modeling entities that are fully compliant to the EAST-ADL and AUTOSAR specifications. As such, SAM is a proposition for an annex extending EAST-ADL with security modeling facilities, which are currently not covered by the existing language specification. To provide a sufficient modeling environment for automotive security modeling we introduce new entities for the EAST-ADL metamodel. These entities can be used on the type-level (M1) to create functional architectures for safe and secure automotive systems.

---

[1] www.aadl.info.
[2] https://github.com/MarkusZoppelt/SAM.
[3] http://www.in.th-nuernberg.de/SAM.

The entities are:

- **Attack**: Represents a cyber-physical attack on the system described by an attack vector. An attack vector is a path or means by which an adversary can gain unauthorized access to a target system [29] or hurts one or more **SecurityGoals**. Attack vectors can be identified and extracted via attack trees.
- **Adversary**: Attacks are performed by either an individual or the system's environment. Either way, adversaries are derivates of the system environment because they are not part of the main systems model and interact from the outside. An adversary can, however, come from within the system, e.g., from an unauthorized part or device.
- **AttackMotivation**: An abstract representation of the adversary's motivations. There is at least one **AttackMotivation** in an attack tree (its root). **AttackMotivations** collide with **SecurityGoals**.
- **Harm**: A threat by an attack meant to actively or passively harm passengers and other road users.
- **InformationRetrieval**: A threat by an attack meant to, e.g., invade the privacy of passengers, other road users and other situational or political stakeholders, e.g., the OEM. Furthermore, getting access to other types of info, e.g., software/firmware by performing reverse engineering.
- **FinancialGain**: A threat by an attack meant to steal or cause financial or material gain for the adversary, service workshops or insurance companies. This usually leads to a financial loss for the owner or the OEM.
- **ProductModification**: A threat by tampering with the product's specification, e.g., getting more functionality out the car or tampering with the software in general, e.g., down-/upgrading.
- **AbstractFailure**: An abstract failure of a set of items, i.e., an inability to fulfill one or several of its requirements.
- **AttackableProperty**: Characteristics or certain properties of items an adversary searches / needs for his attack to succeed, e.g., wireless communication capabilities.
- **Vulnerability**: In order to represent the weak spots in the system architecture, **Vulnerability** describes the weakness and affiliation to one or more **Items**.
- **SecurityGoal**: This entity offers enumerations for common security goals [6] across any communication or data flow. These goals are: **Confidentiality, Integrity, Availability, Authenticity, Reliability** and **Accountability**.
- **Requirement**: To define **Requirements** to fix **Vulnerabilities**, a so-called **Requirement** is the packed result of lesson's learned and is derived from **Attack**.
- **FunctionalSecurityConcept**: Represents the set of functional security requirements that together fulfill a **SecurityGoal**, e.g., according to Common Criteria (CC) ISO/IEC 15408.

- `TechnicalSecurityConcept`: Represents the set of technical security requirements that together fulfill a `FunctionalSecurityConcept` and `SecurityGoal`, e.g., according to Common Criteria (CC) ISO/IEC 15408.
- `SecL`: SecL is an enumeration metaclass with enumeration literals indicating the level of security in accordance with the SAHARA method [17].
- `Environment`: The `Environment` is not a newly introduced entity as it already exists in its own package, though it is extended due to the adversary's ability to use the environment for his attacks and himself being conceptually part of the environment.
- `SecurityExpert`: An abstract class that is used to provide an attribute *knowledgeLevel* to be inherited by the `Adversary`. It can be useful to know where the `Adversary` has gotten his knowledge or skill-set from, even if the security expert may not be the direct cause of an attack.
- `VehicleFeature`: Provided by the Dependability package, a `VehicleFeature` represents a special kind of feature intended for use on Vehicle Level. `Items` enable a feature.

### 5.2   Methodical Context for SAM

In order to protect and defend a system from attacks and threats it is necessary to identify and classify these threats first. The categorization of AttackMotivations already creates methodological benefits with regard to the identification of attacks. Systematic security analyses can be used to quantify the required effort for a potential attack. There is a constant battle between the attacker with his efforts and the layers of security devised by system engineers. Because no system can be completely secured against any sort of attack, system engineers compromise on varying levels of security abstractions to reach an acceptable degree of security. Hence, any security system ultimately results in a trade-off.

Although SAM does not instill security in the system design, it enforces reflection about attacks and their consequences for the system, ideally as a collaboration between system engineers and security experts. While SAM's metalevel is rather abstract, its application becomes concrete on metalevel M1. Notice that the multiplicity from `AttackMotivation` to `Item` is 1..* to 1..*, requiring the system engineer to describe at least one attack motivation for every item of the automotive system. This is an important methodical support for the discovery of threats. If a single item has no associated motivation for an attack, increased caution is required, e.g., because no attack against the item is known yet. In this case, system engineers might simply desist to scrutinize an item for possible attack motivations.

SAM has structural and methodical similarities to safety modeling (dependability). The main difference between safety modeling and security modeling for automotive software systems is the classification of hazards (safety) versus attacks (security). For functional safety, hazards are classified according to the ISO 26262 [12] ASIL levels. An equivalent standard for security threats does not yet exist. There is an ISO standard, called ISO/SAE AWI 21434

"Road Vehicles—Cybersecurity engineering", which is currently under development at the time of writing this paper. SAM has no explicit specifications for a FunctionalSecurityConcept or a TechnicalSecurityConcept. However, SAM proposes Common Criteria (CC) ISO/IEC 15408 protection profiles [32] as a possible solution. Common Criteria is an established standard in the security domain to provide guidance during the development of dependable systems.

The main difference between safety risks and security threats is that security threats do not happen at random (i.e., they are not bound by probability) but always occur in worst-case scenarios. For safety hazards, a statistical probability can be assumed. Cyber attacks are performed by an intelligent attacker at the most suitable time for the adversary and at the lowest defense barrier. Applicable measurements to classify attacks in levels are used in the SAHARA method [17]. The SAHARA approach combines the automotive HARA (hazard analysis and risk assessment) with the security domain STRIDE [5] to further strengthen the compatibility between functional safety and security. This is why SAM uses SecL from the SAHARA method as a classifier. Furthermore, it can be misleading to confuse safety goals with security goals. Security threats, however, *can* cause safety hazards and vice-versa. Though it is not recommended to treat them in the same way during the system design phase for reasons mentioned above. Additionally, text annotations are bad practice. Usually, the transfer from annotations in natural language is imprecise and the original intent of the security experts, which is needed to represent the system model and its security mechanisms accordingly, might be lost during the transfer. An extensive reuse of security solutions can be established by embedding SAM in the "Dependability" package of EAST-ADL and the subsequent integration into AUTOSAR. This makes it possible to keep the development effort at a minimum and to implement comprehensive safety and security solutions in a wide range of applications in the vehicle.

SAM offers the possibility to model socio-technical systems by providing the modeling entity Adversary. Security goals need to be fulfilled in a *socio-technical context* or a *socio-technical system*. The definition of a socio-technical system is an organized group of humans and connected technologies, which are constructed in a certain manner to produce a specific result [6]. Nevertheless, trying to improve security simply by adding cryptography to the system is a fallacy. At best, cryptography can ensure confidentiality but cannot cover security goals like availability, reliability or accountability. With our approach, we offer co-engineering processes of security and safety for automotive software engineering (security and safety by design).

## 6   Evaluation

To prove that SAM is feasible, we have evaluated our solution approach via conducting a modeling example and through "Grounded Theory" [7] interviews with experts from the automotive industry. The modeling example takes up the scenario from the user story and illustrates the methods introduced in Sect. 5

as an instantiation of the metamodel. The interviews give convincing evidence that the entities added in the SAM metamodel are correct or sufficient enough to address the problem of automotive systems modeling.

## 6.1    Modeling Example

SAM enables the system architect from the user story described in Sect. 4 to model a security architecture for automotive software systems. By using the model entities provided, the system architect is able to represent attacks and model threats accordingly. His team plans to do an analysis on a hijacking attack vector via wireless keyfobs. The adversary performing the attack is a **Thief**. He is the only person attacking the vehicle and wants to steal another person's vehicle by opening the car wirelessly and driving away undetected. His knowledgeLevel is equal to the defined minimalKnowledgeLevel of a **KeyfobAttack**. To perform the attack, he is searching for the AttackableProperty **RollingCode** and the target vehicle needs to be parking, i.e., its condition is "standing and locked" (Mode). The SecL of a possible **KeyfobAttack** is classified as 2. The attack motivation is FinancialGain, which is associated with **CarTheft**. If the adversary successfully performs the attack this would mean a **WirelessVulnerability** affecting Items used for the VehicleFeature KeylessEntry. To counter a possible attack the team needs to define **WirelessEncryption** as a resulting requirement. This modeling example is illustrated as a M1 model in Fig. 2.

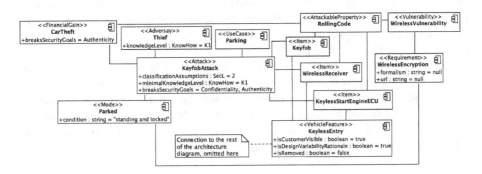

**Fig. 2.** Exemplary architecture model for hijacking attack on M1.

## 6.2    Interviews with Experts from the Automotive Industry

We conducted an empirical analysis through 'Grounded Theory' [7] by interviewing two experts (security and software engineering) from the automotive industry. The interviews were aimed at finding out whether the entities added in the SAM metamodel are correct or sufficient enough to address the problem of secure automotive systems' modeling. Both interview partners have a professional background in automotive systems engineering and/or embedded security. Although the number of interview partners seems rather small, they were very qualified and fitting for this evaluation due to their strong overlappings with automotive, security and software engineering. The results of our evaluation are also available publicly online[4], including the Grounded Theory code networks, selected quotes and code tables. The interview was structured into multiple parts: At first, we asked some general questions about automotive security to find out how pertinent our proposed solution is. Afterwards, we explained our approach and showed SAM and its metamodel to the experts. We continued to interview them about details, such as the concept and the introduced entities. Finally, we asked them about their estimation for the acceptance in the industry.

The following is a corresponding summary of the interview transcript: We asked the experts how they would define requirements for a secure automotive system and how they would visually describe attacks. The requirements they mentioned (e.g., tamper protection in a way that does not jeopardize lives and economic values, not being able to get unauthorized information out of the vehicle, etc.) were compliant to our defined security goals. They also all agreed on using diagrams and graphs to describe attack scenarios rather than text. The use of attack trees was also proposed.

We asked if our attack motivations are sufficient or if the experts were missing some additional category. Beside some minor wording differences (e.g., `FinancialGain` was previously named `FinancialLoss`) the interviewees completely agreed with our categorization. The experts even put emphasis on the importance of the unique attack motivations for their own fields of work and helped clarifying the benefit of different attack motivations for different scenarios. They also accepted the introduction of the `Adversary` entity to represent the attacker in the EAST-ADL model.

According to the experts, the SAM extension tends to be more useful for the security experts than the system engineers. "Though, to some extent, it's the system engineer who has derived some software requirements that can be diffused from a model like this", one expert said, "its main value is early in the development chain. Consequently, as soon as the developers are looking at the software architecture and software implementation as well, the developers will make sure to have this information".

One of the experts underlined the aspect of attack motivations and the SecL classification level. He said that combining attack motivations with SecL would be a good way to "present to managers" how important some security scenario can or will be. We also presented SAM to a member of the EAST-ADL Association and he confirmed our approach as valuable and valid, especially because the symmetry to the dependability package is clearly noticeable. The described medium would also be in line with the EAST-ADL paradigm. Since the interviews have been conducted, we have made all necessary changes to SAM to meet the expectations and suggestions of the experts.

---

[4] https://www.in.th-nuernberg.de/Professors/AS2E/SAM/GT-Eval.pdf.

# 7    Related Work

With SAM we are trying to fill the gap between other approaches and solutions achieved in related work and transfer the knowledge to an automotive context to actually be used in the industry by integrating it in the EAST-ADL. This section discusses related work from security modeling, security requirements analysis and automotive software systems engineering. SAM utilizes common concepts of the listed projects and related work. A non-trivial foundation includes the work of Holm [11], featuring a Cyber Security Modeling Language (CySeMoL) for enterprise architectures, Mouratidis [21] (Secure Tropos), papers such as "Model-based security engineering for cyber-physical systems: A systematic mapping study" [22], Juerjens [15], featuring UMLSec which allows to express security-relevant information within the diagrams in a system specification, INCOSE work on integrating system engineering with system security engineering [9], NIST SP 800-160 [25] and other NIST work on cyber-physical systems [16]. SAM's unique characteristic and advantage over those existing approaches is that it is already integrated into an existing system model (i.e. EAST-ADL). SAM uses existing entities of the EAST-ADL system model (e.g., `Environment`, `Hazard`, `Item`, etc.) and is therefore tightly coupled with the system model. This enables a seamless integration of a security model into a system model that is extensively used in the automotive industry.

A well-explained taxonomy of attacks and defenses in the automotive context was given by Thing and Wu [29] to describe common terms from the point of view of attacker and defender. Smith [28] describes many different penetration testing techniques for monitoring and manipulating car functionalities are shown and illustrated. He also gives an introductory explanation of threat rating systems [28, pp. 11–14] like DREAD [24] and CVSS [19] in comparison to the ISO 26262 ASIL levels. Cars use the CAN bus to transmit and receive information between their ECUs. Smith lists the basic and essential hardware and software tools to get started with monitoring the CAN bus and reverse engineering car functions.

Beside Adaptive AUTOSAR (see Sect. 3.3), there are other projects dedicated to security for automotive systems and cyber-physical systems: PRESERVE was an "EU-funded project running from 2011 to 2015 and contributed to the security and privacy of future vehicle-to-vehicle and vehicle-to-infrastructure communication systems. It provides security requirements of vehicle security architectures" [3]. The EVITA project tries to "design, verify and prototype an architecture for automotive on-board networks where security-relevant components are protected against tampering and sensitive data are protected against compromise. It focuses on V2X (vehicle to anything) communications and provides a base for secure deployment of electronic safety applications" [10].

# 8    Conclusion and Future Work

In this paper we have presented a solution for modeling secure automotive systems in the early system development phase in order to reduce risks connected to late identification of security threats and vulnerabilities in the automotive system life cycle. The approach tightly couples security management and model-based systems engineering by an abstract description of automotive security modeling principles. The resulting SAM language specification is based on security requirements elicited from common industrial scenarios. It is a suitable solution for representing attack vectors on vehicles and provides a thorough security modeling for the automotive industry. By conducting a qualitative analysis in accordance with the methodology of Grounded Theory we gathered evidence that our solution is relevant to the industry and is conform to the general paradigms of automotive software engineering. By improving the identification and probing of security attack vectors, we provide a robust foundation for automotive security testing.

Future work will concentrate on implementing the results of our current work in form of a novel application for OEMs to apply and implement security principles as shown in this paper. For example, the concepts and benefits from SAM and our work could serve as a motivation for further development of the Adaptive AUTOSAR Platform (see Sect. 3.3). Moreover, the SecL levels lack certain dynamics. Once an attack is published, the scenario immediately changes to level 3 and this particular attack is suddenly notoriously undervalued. There is a need for a more dynamic security level system which covers this aspect as well. A major challenge that goes beyond the language-centric scope of this paper is support for security experts to systematically derive a systematic `TechnicalSecurityConcept` from a `FunctionalSecurityConcept`. Even CC does not provide a systematic derivation process. As soon as this process is available anyone can define the hardware and software at the implementation level. Further work may also focus on developing an integrated development environment (IDE) for SAM that performs checks for consistency, completeness and integrity on each SAM-based software project, e.g., in MetaEdit+. Ideally, this would validate the scalability of SAM with respect to the size and real-world complexity of automotive software and the wide range of cyber and physical attacks against it. Furthermore, our top-down approach for a functional architecture description provides the groundwork for one of the main applications of networked vehicle technology: ECU architectures for highly automated and autonomous driving.

# References

1. AUTOSAR: Enabling Continuous Innovations (2018). https://www.autosar.org/
2. AUTOSAR AP Release 17–10: Requirements on Security Management for Adaptive Platform. https://www.autosar.org/fileadmin/user_upload/standards/adaptive/17-10/AUTOSAR_RS_SecurityManagement.pdf
3. Bißmeyer, N., et al.: PREparing SEcuRe VEhicle-to-X Communication Systems - Deliverable 1.3 - V2X Security Architecture v2 (2014)
4. Blom, H., et al.: EAST-ADL-an architecture description language for automotive software-intensive systems-white paper version 2.1.12. http://www.maenad.eu/public/conceptpresentations/EAST-ADL_WhitePaper_M2. Accessed Jan 2013

5. Chen, M., Qian, Y., Mao, S., Tang, W., Yang, X.: Software-defined mobile networks security. Mob. Netw. Appl. **21**(5), 729–743 (2016)
6. Dalpiaz, F., Paja, E., Giorgini, P.: Security requirements engineering via commitments. In: Socio-technical Aspects in Security and Trust (STAST), pp. 1–8. IEEE (2011). https://doi.org/10.1109/STAST.2011.6059249
7. Glaser, B.G., Strauss, A.L., Strutzel, E.: The discovery of grounded theory; strategies for qualitative research. Nurs. Res. **17**(4), 364 (1968)
8. Happel, A., Ebert, C.: Security in vehicle networks of connected cars. In: Bargende, M., Reuss, H.C., Wiedemann, J. (eds.) 15. Internationales Stuttgarter Symposium: Automobil- und Motorentechnik (March), pp. 233–246. Springer, Wiesbaden (2015). https://doi.org/10.1007/978-3-658-08844-6_16
9. Haskins, C., Forsberg, K., Krueger, M., Walden, D., Hamelin, D.: Systems engineering handbook. In: INCOSE (2006)
10. Henniger, O., Apvrille, L., Fuchs, A., Roudier, Y., Ruddle, A., Weyl, B.: Security requirements for automotive on-board networks. In: 2009 9th International Conference on Intelligent Transport Systems Telecommunications, ITST 2009, pp. 641–646. IEEE (2009). https://doi.org/10.1109/ITST.2009.5399279
11. Holm, H., Ekstedt, M., Sommestad, T., Korman, M.: A Manual for the Cyber Security Modeling Language (2014)
12. International Organization for Standardization: Road vehicles - functional safety - Part 2: Management of functional safety. International Organization for Standardization **066**(20), 26 (2009)
13. ISO/IEC: ISO/IEC 15408–1:2009 - Evaluation Criteria for IT Security **2009**, 64 (2009)
14. Johansson, C., Bucanac, C.: The V-Model. IDE, University Of Karlskrona, Ronneby (1999)
15. Jürjens, J.: UMLsec: extending UML for secure systems development. In: Jézéquel, J.-M., Hussmann, H., Cook, S. (eds.) UML 2002. LNCS, vol. 2460, pp. 412–425. Springer, Heidelberg (2002). https://doi.org/10.1007/3-540-45800-X_32
16. Lee, J., Bagheri, B., Kao, H.A.: A cyber-physical systems architecture for industry 4.0-based manufacturing systems. Manuf. Lett. **3**, 18–23 (2015)
17. Macher, G., Höller, A., Sporer, H., Armengaud, E., Kreiner, C.: A combined safety-hazards and security-threat analysis method for automotive systems. In: Koornneef, F., van Gulijk, C. (eds.) SAFECOMP 2015. LNCS, vol. 9338, pp. 237–250. Springer, Cham (2015). https://doi.org/10.1007/978-3-319-24249-1_21
18. Mash, C.: Ethernet set to bring about radical shift in how automotive networks are implemented, January 2018. http://www.digitimes.com/news/a20180115PR203.html
19. Mell, P., Scarfone, K., Romanosky, S.: A complete guide to the common vulnerability scoring system version 2.0. In: Published by FIRST-Forum of Incident Response and Security Teams, vol. 1, p. 23 (2007)
20. Miller, C., Valasek, C.: A survey of remote automotive attack surfaces. Defcon **22**, 1–90 (2014)
21. Mouratidis, H., Giorgini, P.: Secure tropos: a security-oriented extension of the tropos methodology. Int. J. Softw. Eng. Knowl. Eng. **17**(02), 285–309 (2007). https://doi.org/10.1142/S0218194007003240
22. Nguyen, P.H., Ali, S., Yue, T.: Model-based security engineering for cyber-physical systems: a systematic mapping study (2017). https://doi.org/10.1016/j.infsof.2016.11.004

23. Palanca, A., Evenchick, E., Maggi, F., Zanero, S.: A stealth, selective, link-layer denial-of-service attack against automotive networks. In: Polychronakis, M., Meier, M. (eds.) DIMVA 2017. LNCS, vol. 10327, pp. 185–206. Springer, Cham (2017). https://doi.org/10.1007/978-3-319-60876-1_9

24. Rao, K.R.M., Pant, D.: A threat risk modeling framework for Geospatial Weather Information System (GWIS): a DREAD based study. Int. J. Adv. Comput. Sci. Appl. 1(3) (2010)

25. Ross, R., McEvilley, M., Carrier Oren, J.: Systems security engineering: considerations for a multidisciplinary approach in the engineering of trustworthy secure systems, vol. 160, November 2016. https://doi.org/10.6028/NIST.SP.800-160. http://nvlpubs.nist.gov/nistpubs/SpecialPublications/NIST.SP.800-160.pdf

26. Sandelin, A., Alkema, W., Engström, P., Wasserman, W.W., Lenhard, B.: JASPAR: an open-access database for eukaryotic transcription factor binding profiles. Nucleic Acids Res. 32(Suppl. 1), D91–D94 (2004)

27. Schneier, B.: Attack trees. Dr. Dobb's J. 24(12), 21–29 (1999)

28. Smith, C., Francisco, S.: The Car Hacker's Handbook a Guide for the Penetration Tester About the Contributing Author About the Technical Reviewer (2016)

29. Thing, V.L., Wu, J.: Autonomous vehicle security: a taxonomy of attacks and defences. In: Proceedings - 2016 IEEE International Conference on Internet of Things; IEEE Green Computing and Communications; IEEE Cyber, Physical, and Social Computing; IEEE Smart Data, iThings-GreenCom-CPSCom-Smart Data 2016, pp. 164–170 (2017). https://doi.org/10.1109/iThings-GreenCom-CPSCom-SmartData.2016.52

30. Tuohy, S., Glavin, M., Hughes, C., Jones, E., Trivedi, M., Kilmartin, L.: Intra-vehicle networks: a review (2015). https://doi.org/10.1109/TITS.2014.2320605

31. Valasek, C., Miller, C.: Adventures in automotive networks and control units. Technical White Paper, vol. 21, p. 99 (2013)

32. Van Tilborg, H.C.A., Jajodia, S.: Encyclopedia of Cryptography and Security. Springer, New York (2014)

33. Zeng, W., Khalid, M.A., Chowdhury, S.: In-vehicle networks outlook: achievements and challenges. IEEE Commun. Surv. Tutor. 18(3), 1552–1571 (2016). https://doi.org/10.1109/COMST.2016.2521642

# Car Security

# CAN-FD-Sec: Improving Security of CAN-FD Protocol

Megha Agrawal[1]([✉]), Tianxiang Huang[2], Jianying Zhou[3],
and Donghoon Chang[1]

[1] Indraprastha Institute of Information Technology, Delhi, India
meghaa@iiitd.ac.in
[2] Chongqing University of Posts and Telecommunications, Chongqing, China
[3] Singapore University of Technology and Design, Singapore, Singapore

**Abstract.** A modern vehicle consists of more than 70 Electronic Control Unit (ECUs) which are responsible for controlling one or more subsystems in the vehicle. These ECUs are interconnected through a Controller Area Network (CAN) bus, which suffers from some limitations of data payload size, bandwidth, and the security issues. Therefore, to overcome the CAN bus limitations, CAN-FD (CAN with Flexible Data) has been introduced. CAN-FD has advantages over the CAN in terms of data payload size and the bandwidth. Still, security issues have not been considered in the design of CAN-FD. All those attacks that are possible to CAN bus are also applicable on CAN-FD. In 2016, Woo et. al proposed a security architecture for in-vehicle CAN-FD. They used an ISO 26262 standard that defines the safety level to determine the security requirements for each ECU, based on that they provided encryption, authentication, both or no security to each ECU. In this paper, we propose a new security architecture for the communication between ECUs on different channels through gateway ECU (GECU). Our experimental results also demonstrate that using an authenticated encryption scheme has better performance than applying individual primitives for encryption and authentication.

**Keywords:** Controller Area Network (CAN) ·
CAN-FD (CAN with flexible data rate) · Security of in-vehicle network

## 1 Introduction

Over the past 30 years, with the emergence of vehicle information and communication technology (ICT), several electronic communication devices have been installed in the vehicles. These electronic communication devices, known as Electronic Control Units (ECU) are responsible for controlling the one or various subsystems of the vehicle including the break, doors, tyre pressure and so on. Nowadays, a typical vehicle consists of more than 70 ECUs [8]. These ECUs are generally on a single chip, using an 8-bit microcontroller with around 100 bytes of RAM, 32 kB of ROM and a few I/O pins to connect to sensors, actuators,

© Springer Nature Switzerland AG 2019
B. Hamid et al. (Eds.): ISSA 2018/CSITS 2018, LNCS 11552, pp. 77–93, 2019.
https://doi.org/10.1007/978-3-030-16874-2_6

and a network interface [16]. Data exchange among these ECUs is facilitated through various communication networks such as Local Interconnect network (LIN), Controller Area Network (CAN), Byteflight [6], and FlexRay [9]. Among all these communication networks, CAN [7] has been standardized for all the communications among various ECUs.

Controller Area Network (CAN) is a serial bus based communication protocol. It was introduced by Robert Bosch GmBH in 1983 and standardized in 1994 under the ISO 11898-1 [1]. All the ECUs in the vehicle are interconnected through CAN bus. There is no security consideration in the design of CAN bus except the standard CRC-15. All the messages between ECUs are transmitted in plaintext without any security feature. An adversary can eavesdrop all communications between ECUs and later can launch a replay attack [12] or he can modify the existing message and inject into the system to alter the usual vehicle behaviour. These kind of attacks can result in some catastrophic consequences. Various attacks on the CAN bus security are shown in [12–15,17,21]. All these attacks become possible because of no implementation of the essential security features: confidentiality, authentication, and integrity. Confidentiality of the data can be achieved using encryption whereas authentication and integrity can be incorporated by using MAC algorithm (Message Authentication Code). One of the other disadvantages of the CAN is the small data packet size. CAN can support data payload of up to 8 bytes only. Due to the low payload size, it is impossible to use MAC algorithm as it adds a tag to the data, which increases the data payload size at least twice.

To match the modern vehicle requirements and to overcome the current limitation of CAN, Bosch developed a new protocol in 2011 known as CAN-FD (CAN with flexible data) [11]. CAN-FD has an almost similar structure as CAN with some additional advantages. Following are the advantages of CAN-FD over CAN [2]:

- CAN-FD supports data payload of up to 64 bytes.
- It can support bandwidth up to 8 Mbps whereas CAN can support up to 1 Mbps only.
- It has lower latency and better real-time performance.
- CAN-FD is compatible with CAN and can support existing software and applications with the minimum changes.

CAN-FD is supposed to replace CAN gradually by 2020 [4]. However CAN-FD also suffers from the same security issues as CAN. Here data is transmitted in the plaintext without any security. Hence all the existing attacks on CAN are also applicable to CAN-FD. In [21], authors have shown a practical wireless attack using a real vehicle in a connected car environment where driver's smartphone is connected to the in-vehicle CAN. This attack assumes that a driver downloads the malicious self-diagnostic application that has been uploaded by an adversary. Once it has been downloaded to the driver's smartphone, the adversary can control the driver's smartphone and can inject malicious CAN data frame that may cause an abnormal behaviour leading an accident or any devastating scenario. The same attack is also applicable on CAN-FD as it does not have any security features as well. Later in [20], authors proposed a security architecture for CAN-FD to resist against these kind of attacks. In that paper, it considered a characteristics of ISO 26262 Automotive Safety Integrity Level and defined the security requirements for ECUs. More details of their work is explained in the next section. We will demonstrate that the security architecture for CAN-FD proposed in [20] is not practical and has high overhead.

In this paper, we proposed an improvement over the existing security architecture for the CAN-FD bus. The main contributions of this paper are:

- Proposed a group-based approach to the communication among different ECUs. Groups are divided based on the existing channels.
- Modified the existing key management protocol to satisfy the group communication.
- Provided an experimental analysis by replacing the individual encryption and authentication scheme with a single primitive called authenticated encryption to provide confidentiality and authenticity.

## 2   Background and Related Work

A typical in-vehicle network consists of several ECUs responsible for controlling various subsystems. Controller Area Network (CAN) uses a serial bus communication to interconnect those ECUs in an in-vehicle network. It is a multicast message-oriented transport protocol which facilitates all in-vehicle data communication where each node (ECU) can act as a transmitter or receiver. An ECU that initiates a message is called a transmitter, which broadcasts the message to all other ECUs on the bus. All receiving ECUs read the message and decide if it is relevant to them. All these ECUs communicate with each other using a fixed length data packet over a CAN bus. It supports data payload of at most 8 bytes and data rate up to 1 Mbps. CAN-FD is built upon CAN protocol and retains most of its characteristics. It provides better real-time performance and supports higher bandwidth up to 8 Mbps. CAN-FD supports data payload of up to 64 bytes. CAN and CAN-FD data frames are shown in Fig. 1. As shown in the figure, some additional bits have been added to CAN-FD in control field.

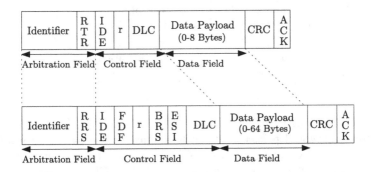

**Fig. 1.** CAN and CAN-FD data frame

*Communication.* In an in-vehicle network, ECUs are categorized into several subsystems or channels. All these channels are connected through a gateway ECU which is supposed to be more powerful than the usual ECUs. All ECUs on one channel form the internal subnetwork. The communication between these channels is facilitated through gateway ECU. If an ECU on one channel wants to send messages to another ECU on a different channel, it first sends to GECU. Then GECU broadcasts the messages to another channel.

*Related Work.* The area of securing CAN-based communication has drawn lots of attentions. As a result, various solutions for providing secure communication in CAN networks have been proposed. Vecure [19] and LeiA [18] are two authentication protocols designed for CAN which rely on symmetrically shared keys and MACs for data authentication. LiBrA-CAN [10] provides authentication based on key sharing in groups of nodes. With the introduction of CAN-FD, more efficient transmission of bigger payloads is possible, resulting in development of new security mechanisms. In [20], authors have proposed a security architecture for in-vehicle CAN-FD. The idea is to use an ISO 26262 standard to define security requirements for each ECUs. Based on this they define the four automotive security level (from 0–3) and categorize each ECU under these four levels. The higher the level number, more security it requires. Details are given in Table 1. If the ECU having ASL scale 0 wants to broadcasts a message, it just sends it to GECU without any security feature which further broadcast it. Others ECU belonging to ASL scale 1, 2 and 3 uses authentication, encryption and both respectively. If these ECUs want to send messages, they encrypt or compute MAC or do both and send it to GECU. GECU then decrypt and verify the MAC. Based on the verification it further encrypts and computes MAC using keys shared between different ECUs and GECU and sends it to respective ECU.

**Table 1.** Defining automotive security level

| ASL | Security requirement | Security provided |
|-----|----------------------|-------------------|
| 0 | No security | Inbuilt CRC |
| 1 | Data authentication | Authentication |
| 2 | Data confidentiality, data authentication | Encryption, athentication |
| 3 | Data confidentiality, data authentication, external access | Encryption, authentication, access control |

The main issue with this approach is the excess overload on GECU while broadcasting encrypted packet as it needs to encrypt the packet with an individual key for each ECU. For instance, if GECU wants to transmit it to 10 ECU's, then it needs to perform ten encryptions as all the ECU's shared their secret key with GECU only. If the message requires authentication also, then GECU again have to compute individual tags for each ECU as it uses the separate key for encryption and authentication.

## 3 Security Requirements

In the previous sections, we mentioned the existing vulnerabilities in CAN-FD bus that attacker can exploit to launch an attack to cause damage to the vehicle or the driver. Following are the security requirements that must be followed by CAN-FD bus to work without any vulnerabilities.

– **Confidentiality:** As all the messages over CAN-FD bus are communicated in plaintext, an adversary can eavesdrop the valid communication and analyze the messages to plan an attack. To overcome this, all communication should happen in encrypted form so that only legitimate parties can access the original data. This can be achieved by using an existing block cipher like AES in a valid encryption mode.
– **Authenticity:** Receiving node on a CAN-FD bus identify the data frame based on the sender information. An adversary can eavesdrop the communication and later can replay a data frame by masquerading a valid sender. CAN-FD uses CRC sequence only to check for the error, which fails to detect this kind of attacks. Hence, authentication must be used to verify the identity of the sender and to prevent this kind of attacks. A cryptographic Message Authentication Code(MAC) algorithm can be used to achieve authentication.

A cryptographic primitive that achieves Confidentiality and Authenticity simultaneously in a single step is called an Authenticated Encryption(AE). Introduce by Bellare and Rogaway in [5], an AE scheme $\Pi$ can be defined as set of 3 algorithms $\Pi = (\mathcal{K}, \mathcal{E}, \mathcal{D})$ where $\mathcal{K}$ is a non-empty set of strings, $\mathcal{E}$ is a randomized encryption algorithm and $\mathcal{D}$ represents a deterministic decryption algorithm. Encryption algorithm $\mathcal{E}$ takes a key $K$, message $M$ and associated data $A$ (optional) as an input and generate a ciphertext tag pair $(C, T)$. Decryption algorithm $\mathcal{D}$ takes a key $K$, $A$ and $(C, T)$ as an input and returns either $M$ or *Invalid* based on the verification of the tag. There is an advantage of using AE over an individual cryptographic primitive for confidentiality and authenticity. Individual primitive requires a separate key for encryption and authentication and two passes over the message while authenticated encryption uses only one key and require only one pass which results in better performance.

In this paper, we use the AEGIS [23] authenticated encryption from the ongoing CAESAR [3] competition for the implementation and compare its performance against using individual primitives for encryption(AES) and authentication(CCM).

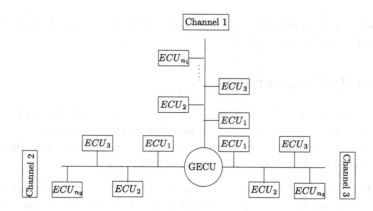

**Fig. 2.** CAN-FD architecture

**Table 2.** Notations

| Notations | Meaning |
|---|---|
| GECU | Gateway ECU |
| $i$ | $i^{th}$ channel |
| $j$ | $j^{th}$ ECU |
| $ECU_{ij}$ | Refers to $j^{th}$ ECU on $i^{th}$ channel |
| $K_{ij}^1, K_{ij}^2$ | Preshared long term keys between $ECUij$ and GECU |
| $seed_{ij}^k$ | Seed for $k^{th session}$ |
| $sk_{ij}^k$ | Individual key for $ECU_{ij}$ of $k^{th}$ session |
| $gk_i^k$ | Group key for $i^{th}$ channel of $k^{th}$ session |
| $AE_K$ | Authenticated encryption using key $K$ |
| $KDF_K$ | Key derivation function using key $K$ |
| $M$ | Plaintext |
| $(C, T)$ | Ciphertext tag pair |

## 4   A Secure CAN-FD Protocol

In this work, we present a new security architecture for the CAN-FD (Fig. 2).
Our proposed solution works on the following assumptions:

- All the communication between different ECUs is done through Gateway
  ECU (GECU), which is supposed to have more computing power than other
  ECUs.
- All ECUs are preloaded with the two keys that they share with GECU. Out
  of which, one is used to authenticate each other and other is used for further
  session key generation.
- All ECUs have been divided into the fixed no of channels and the communi-
  cation happens among these channels through gateway ECU (GECU).
  The notations we used in this paper are shown in Table 2.

## 4.1   Message Structure

Deployment of the proposed security approach will affect the structure of the message packets. Therefore, the data fields of different types of CAN-FD packets are processed in segments. The following rules need to be followed when adding a new feature to the protocol:

- The impact on non-encrypted data packets is as small as possible. If the protocol structure occupies more effective data segment length, the original communication architecture will be greatly affected, which will make it inconvenient for the deployment of the program, and will also have an impact on the real-time communication performance.
- Easy maintenance. For the later program improvement, we must reserve a certain amount of space.
- Consistency. Applicable to multiple nodes in the network, both parties can effectively identify the communication.

The details of the message structure formulated in this paper is shown in Fig. 3.

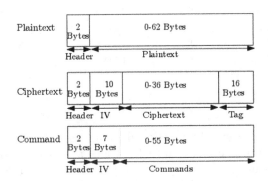

**Fig. 3.** Modified data field for CAN-FD packet

The CAN-FD network message is divided into three categories: plaintext, ciphertext, and command messages. The first two bytes of the data field out of 64 bytes are used as the header segment to distinguish among these 3 type of messages. At present, an only first byte is used where 0x55 represents the plaintext and 0xFF represents the ciphertext, and the second byte is reserved for the future use. For the plaintext message, an effective data payload can be up to 62 bytes. However, we restrict it up to 36 bytes as rest of the bytes we require for the tag and IV usage in the ciphertext. We used an authenticated encryption scheme to generate the ciphertext. Hence its valid data segment can be up to 36 bytes, followed by a 16-byte authentication tag and 10 byte IV(Initialization Vector). Command messages are used for key management. They are divided into address segments (used to indicate the receiving node) and content segments (used to transmit random numbers or authentication codes, etc.).

## 4.2   Proposed Security Architecture

The overall security procedure is divided into several steps. We will explain these steps in detail below (Fig. 4).

**Step 1: Initialization.** During the initialization phase, each ECU is loaded on their respective channel. A typical modern vehicle consists of following channels: powertrain, chassis, body, safety, and Infotainment serving different purposes. Details about the channels and ECUs under these channels are given in Table 3.

**Table 3.** Characteristics of various channels on an in-vehicle network

| Subsystems/ channels | Powertrain | Chassis | Body | Telematic | safety |
|---|---|---|---|---|---|
| Functions | Engine control, automatic transmission, hybrid control | Steering, brake, suspension | Instrumental panel, door, key, window | Audio, navigation, traffic information | Pre crash safety |
| No of ECUs | 3–6 | 6–10 | 14–30 | 4–12 | 11–12 |
| Safety | High | High | Low | Low | Very high |
| ECUs example | ECM TCM | BCM SUM | DDM PDM | TBOX | ABS |

**Step 2: Key Loading.** As mentioned above each ECU in the vehicle is preloaded with the two keys $K_{ij}$ and $LK_{ij}$ which are shared with GECU. So, if there are $n$ ECUs in the vehicle, GECU is loaded with total 2n keys ($n$ no. of $K'_{ij}s$ and $n$ $LK'_{ij}s$). These loading of the keys are done during the manufacturing of a vehicle or when some ECU need to be changed.

**Step 3: Session-Key Generation.** After a vehicle starts, each ECU performs a session key generation with GECU in a fixed order. This process is divided into 2 steps. In the first step, every ECU on different channels perform an individual session key generation with GECU. During the second step, when every ECU on the different channel have their session key, GECU generate a group key for each channel by hashing the individual session key for each ECU on that channel and then distribute this group key on that channel by encrypting it with the ECU's session key. Algorithms for individual session key generation and group key generation are shown in Algorithms 1 and 2 respectively.

**Step 4: Authenticated Encryption.** Once the individual session key and the group key has generated, confidentiality and authenticity is provided to the data frames using Authenticated Encryption (AE) scheme. For example, if $ECU_1$ on channel 1 wants to send a message to the ECU's on channel 2, then $ECU_1$ will use the AE using their session key and send it to GECU. GECU will then verify the message, if it gets verified, then GECU will encrypt the message with channel 2 group key and forward it on that channel otherwise it will discard the message. Details are given in Algorithm 3.

**Step 5: Key Update.** Individual and the group session key between ECUs and GECU are updated in the following scenarios:

– After a fixed predefined period say $T$.
– If any ECU leaves or joins the network.
– if any external device tries to connect.

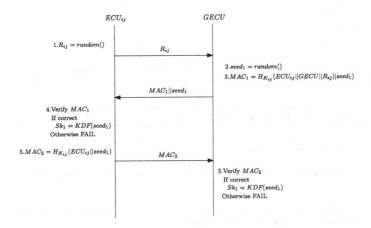

**Fig. 4.** Data flow diagram showing session key generation

## 5 Discussion on Security

Security of the proposed protocol depends on the underlying key management and authenticated encryption scheme.

### 5.1 Key Management

We assumed that each ECU is preloaded with two long-term symmetric keys during the manufacturing phase. Each ECU share these keys with GECU only. Further, these keys are used to generate individual session keys using existing

---

**Algorithm 1.** Individual session key generation

---

**for** $1 \rightarrow i$ **do**
    **for** $1 \rightarrow j$ **do**
        $ECU_{ij}$ generates random no $R_{ij}$ and send it to GECU.
        GECU generates random $seed_1$ and compute
        $MAC_1 = H_{K_{ij}}(ECU_{ij}||GECU||R_{ij}||seed_1)$
        GECU sends $seed_1||MAC_1$ to $ECU_{ij}$.
        $ECU_{ij}$ verifies $MAC_1$,
        **if** *correct* **then**
            |  $sk_{ij} = KDF_{LK_{ij}}(seed_1)$
        **else**
            |  FAIL
        **end**
        $ECU_{ij}$ generates $MAC_2 = H_{K_{ij}(ECU_{ij}||seed_1)}$ and send it to GECU.
        GECU verifies $MAC_2$,
        **if** *correct* **then**
            |  $sk_{ij} = KDF_{LK_{ij}}(seed_1)$
        **else**
            |  FAIL
        **end**
    **end**
**end**

---

---

**Algorithm 2.** Group key generation

---

**for** $1 \rightarrow i$ **do**
    |  $gk_i = H(sk_{i1}||sk_{i2}\ldots||sk_{ij})$
**end**

---

---

**Algorithm 3.** Authenticated Encryption

---

1. Sender $ECU_{ij}$ applies a AE scheme on message $M$ using his own session key and compute $(C, T) = AE_{sk_{ij}}(M)$ and send it to GECU.
2. GECU receives $(C, T)$ pair and verifies it.
3. **if** *correct* **then**
    GECU further applies AE algorithm using group key $gk_i$ of the receiving channel and compute $(C', T')$ and forward it on that channel.
**else**
    |  Discard the message.
**end**
4. All ECUs on the receiving channel will receive $(C, T)$ and do the verification.
5. **if** *correct* **then**
    |  Keep the message
**else**
    |  Discard
**end**

---

AKEP2 protocol. It is a three pass protocol and provides perfect forward secrecy which means compromise of long-term keys does not compromise the past session keys. A protocol is considered to be secure if compromise of these keys doesn't have any adverse effect like

– It should not subvert subsequent authentication.
– it should not reveal any information about other session keys.

Group session key is generated by taking a hash of all individual keys on the same channel whose security depends on the hash function used in the computation.

## 5.2    Authenticated Encryption

The proposed protocol is considered to be secure if the underlying AE scheme is secure. In this work, we used AEGIS, an existing authenticated encryption scheme from CAESAR competition. Hence, we can directly adapt their security analysis from [22].

## 6    Implementation Results

In this section, we will discuss the implementation results of our proposed security architecture. To make the implementation scenario more realistic, we design a small-size CAN-FD network and schedule communication of each ECU. Figure 5 shows the HIL (Hardware-In-the-Loop) network topology.

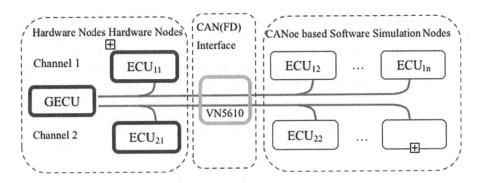

**Fig. 5.** CAN-FD network topology

To simulate nodes on the hardware, we use LPC54618 microcontroller which supports two CAN-FD channels and baud-rate up to 180 Mhz. On the software, we use CANoe testing tool to build virtual ECUs which are programmed in CAPL (Communication Access Programming Language). VN5610 is a CAN(FD) interface connecting those two parts. Figure 6 shows our setup for the hardware and software environments. We divide real-time performance test into 2 phases:

1. First phase known as initialization includes session key generation and distribution, group key generation and distribution.
2. Second phase includes authenticated encryption and decryption for a one message forwarding event by the ECU.

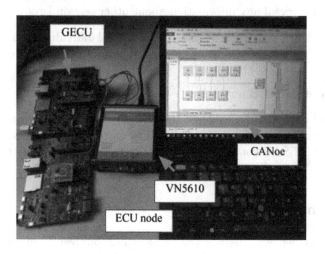

**Fig. 6.** Evaluation environment

**Initialization Phase.** During this phase initial key distribution time is recorded. The usual startup time of vehicle is around 200 ms after ignition turned on. All ECUs need to execute key distribution during these 200 ms only. Our mechanism, to some extent, is limited by the hardware performance of ECU nodes. We compute the initialization time by considering key distribution between GECU and $n$ no. of ECU's which includes individual and group key distribution. To compute the timing results more accurately, we use the Trace function of CANoe to capture the timestamp of first and last frame of this program. Results are shown in Fig. 7 considering different number of channels and ECU's.

We can see in the Fig. 8, with the increase in the number of ECU's over a channel, the delay also increase. But most of the points are within allowable limits.

**Message Forwarding Phase.** This test is about the real-time performance of secure data transmission. We consider a test scenario where GECU facilitates a transfer of message between two channels, Fig. 9 shows a data flow diagram.

| Test name | Channel N | Node N | ECU speed (Mhz) | Session key generation time(ms) | Group key distribution time (ms) | Total run time (ms) |
|-----------|-----------|--------|-----------------|--------------------------------|----------------------------------|---------------------|
| Case1 | 2 | 10 | 48 | 48 | 2 | 50 |
|       |   |    | 96 | 32 | 2 | 34 |
|       |   |    | 120 | 30 | 2 | 32 |
|       |   |    | 180 | 27 | 2 | 29 |
| Case2 | 2 | 20 | 48 | 98 | 2 | 100 |
|       |   |    | 96 | 66 | 2 | 68 |
|       |   |    | 120 | 61 | 2 | 63 |
|       |   |    | 180 | 55 | 2 | 57 |
| Case3 | 4 | 20 | 48 | 98 | 4 | 102 |
|       |   |    | 96 | 66 | 3 | 69 |
|       |   |    | 120 | 61 | 2 | 63 |
|       |   |    | 180 | 55 | 2 | 57 |
| Case4 | 4 | 48 | 48 | 236 | 5 | 241 |
|       |   |    | 96 | 160 | 4 | 166 |
|       |   |    | 120 | 151 | 3 | 154 |
|       |   |    | 18 | 133 | 3 | 136 |

**Fig. 7.** Key distribution results

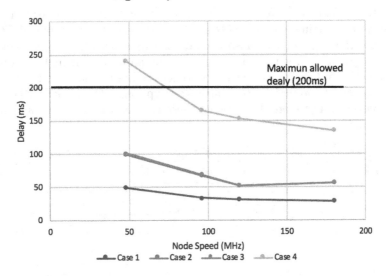

**Fig. 8.** Graph representation of key distribution results

As shown in Fig. 9 $ECU_{11}$ encrypt the original message $OMsg_p$ with the key $GK_1$ to get the ciphertext $OMsg_c$ and then sends it to GECU. On receiving $OMsg_c$, GECU decrypts and verifies it. If the verification fails, GECU discards the message otherwise it encrypts the decrypted message $OMsg_p$ with key $GK_2$ (group key for channel 2) to get ciphertext $FMsg_c$ and sends it over channel 2.

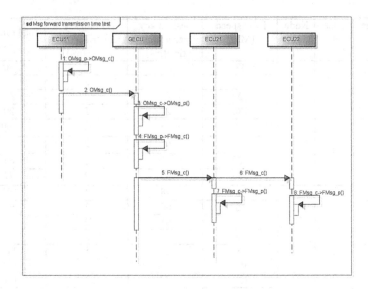

**Fig. 9.** Data flow diagram showing communication between ECU's over different channels through GECU.

All EC U's on channel 2 receive $FMsg_c$, and they decrypt and verify it with $GK_2$ to get the original message $OMsg_p$. By capturing the start time of $ECU_{11}$ to generate the $OMsg_p$ and finish time of $ECU_{21}$ and $ECU_{22}$ to decrypt and verify $FMsg_c$, we can get the total time of computation. Figure 10 shows the Trace interface of CANoe as we can see to get the start time, we add an initial message. After $ECU_{21}$ and $ECU_{22}$ finishes decryption and verification, they send an end message. Therefore, by noticing these two-time stamps, we can get the accurate time.

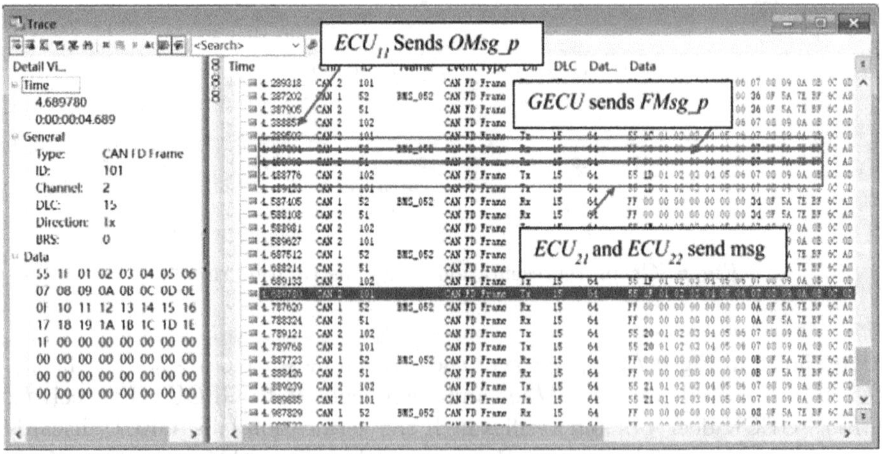

![Trace interface of CANoe]

**Fig. 10.** Trace interface of CANoe

As the GECU is always fixed, we set it's clock speed at 180 Mhz and varies the clock speed for rest of the ECU's. Figure 11 shows the time on the same microcontroller with different clock speed and different baud rate for CAN-FD. Here we use AEGIS [23] authenticated encryption scheme for the secure communication and compare its results against AES with CCM mode for authentication. In the graph shown in Fig. 11, solid lines shows the secure communication with AEGIS and the dotted line denotes no security at all. Obviously, in this result, the time depends on the microcontroller performance, and the time is controlled below 2 ms, which is allowed in-vehicle communication. The graph in Fig. 12 shows the results using AES (no hardware acceleration) with CCM. As we can see the time taken by AES-CCM is more than AEGIS, especially at lower frequency. Hence, we can conclude that use of fast authenticated encryption scheme can optimize the secure communication and meet the real-time requirements.

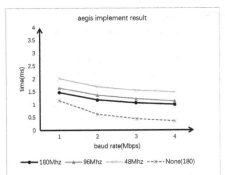
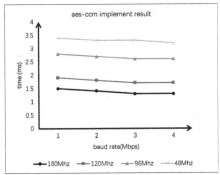

**Fig. 11.** AEGIS implementation results    **Fig. 12.** AES-CCM implementation results

## 7 Conclusion

In this paper, we provided an improved security architecture for the CAN-FD network. We proposed a new group-based approach for the secure communication between ECUs connected on the CAN-FD network. In addition, we also used the authenticated encryption scheme instead of applying individual primitives for encryption and authentication. We tested our results using AEGIS which is a fast authenticated encryption scheme satisfying real-time requirements. We compared the AEGIS implementation results against individual primitives (AES for encryption and CCM for authentication), and found that AEGIS performs better than AES-CCM. Hence, we can conclude authenticated encryption is a good choice for providing secure communication over CAN-FD network.

**Acknowledgement.** This work was supported by SUTD start-up research grant SRG-ISTD-2017-124. The first author's work was done during her internship in SUTD.

# References

1. Can standardization. http://elearning.vector.com/index.php?&wbt_ls_seite_id=48 9557&root=378422&seite=vl_can_introduction_en
2. Comparing can FD with classical can. https://www.kvaser.com/wp-content/ uploads/2016/10/comparing-can-fd-with-classical-can.pdf
3. Caesar: Competition for authenticated encryption: security, applicability, and robustness (2014). http://competitions.cr.yp.to/caesar.html
4. Can 2020: The future of can technology (2016). https://www.can-cia.org/news/ cia-in-action/view/can-2020-the-future-of-can-technology/2016/3/21/
5. Bellare, M., Namprempre, C.: Authenticated encryption: relations among notions and analysis of the generic composition paradigm. J. Cryptol. **21**(4), 469–491 (2008)
6. Berwanger, J., Peller, M., Griessbach, R.: Byteflight - a new protocol for safety critical applications (2000)
7. Can specification (1991). http://esd.cs.ucr.edu/webres/can20.pdf
8. Charette, R.N.: This car runs on code. IEEE Spectr. **46**, 3 (2009)
9. Next generation car network- flexray (2006). http://www.fujitsu.com/downloads/ CN/fmc/lsi/FlexRay-EN.pdf
10. Groza, B., Murvay, S., van Herrewege, A., Verbauwhede, I.: LiBrA-CAN: a lightweight broadcast authentication protocol for controller area networks. In: Pieprzyk, J., Sadeghi, A.-R., Manulis, M. (eds.) CANS 2012. LNCS, vol. 7712, pp. 185–200. Springer, Heidelberg (2012). https://doi.org/10.1007/978-3-642-35404-5_15
11. Florian Hartwich and Robert Bosch Gmbh. icc 2012 can in automation can with flexible data-rate, 2012
12. Hoppe, T., Dittman, J.: Sniffing/replay attacks on can buses: a simulated attack on the electric window lift classified using an adapted cert taxonomy. In: Proceedings of the 2nd Workshop on Embedded Systems Security (WESS) (2007)
13. Hoppe, T., Kiltz, S., Dittmann, J.: Security threats to automotive can networks – practical examples and selected short-term countermeasures. In: Harrison, M.D., Sujan, M.-A. (eds.) SAFECOMP 2008. LNCS, vol. 5219, pp. 235–248. Springer, Heidelberg (2008). https://doi.org/10.1007/978-3-540-87698-4_21
14. Huang, T., Zhou, J., Bytes, A.: ATG: an attack traffic generation tool for security testing of in-vehicle CAN bus. In: ARES (2018)
15. Huang, T., Zhou, J., Wang, Y., Cheng, A.: On the security of in-vehicle hybrid network: status and challenges. In: Liu, J.K., Samarati, P. (eds.) ISPEC 2017. LNCS, vol. 10701, pp. 621–637. Springer, Cham (2017). https://doi.org/10.1007/ 978-3-319-72359-4_38
16. Kopetz, H.: Automotive electronics: present state and future prospects. In: Proceedings of the Twenty-Fifth International Conference on Fault-tolerant Computing, FTCS 1995, pp. 66–75. IEEE Computer Society, Washington, DC (1995)
17. Koscher, K., et al.: Experimental security analysis of a modern automobile. In: Proceedings of the 2010 IEEE Symposium on Security and Privacy, SP 2010, pp. 447–462. IEEE Computer Society, Washington, DC (2010)
18. Radu, A.-I., Garcia, F.D.: LeiA: a lightweight authentication protocol for can. In: ESORICS (2016)
19. Wang, Q., Sawhney, S.: VeCure: a practical security framework to protect the can bus of vehicles. In: 2014 International Conference on the Internet of Things (IOT), pp. 13–18, October 2014

20. Woo, S., Jo, H.J., Kim, I.S., Lee, D.H.: A practical security architecture for in-vehicle CAN-FD. IEEE Trans. Intell. Transp. Syst. **17**(8), 2248–2261 (2016)

21. Woo, S., Jo, H.J., Lee, D.H.: A practical wireless attack on the connected car and security protocol for in-vehicle can. IEEE Trans. Intell. Transp. Syst. **16**(2), 993–1006 (2015)

22. Wu, H., Preneel, B.: AEGIS: a fast authenticated encryption algorithm. In: Lange, T., Lauter, K., Lisoněk, P. (eds.) SAC 2013. LNCS, vol. 8282, pp. 185–201. Springer, Heidelberg (2014). https://doi.org/10.1007/978-3-662-43414-7_10

23. Wu, H., Preneel, B.: AEGIS: A Fast Authenticated Encryption Algorithm (v1) (2015). http://competitions.cr.yp.to/round1/aegisv1.pdf

# INCANTA - INtrusion Detection in Controller Area Networks with Time-Covert Authentication

Bogdan Groza[✉], Lucian Popa, and Pal-Stefan Murvay

Faculty of Automatics and Computers,
Politehnica University of Timisoara, Timişoara, Romania
bogdan.groza@aut.upt.ro, lucian.popa.lp@gmail.com,
stefan.murvay@gmail.com

**Abstract.** We explore the use of delays to create a time-covert cryptographic authentication channel on the CAN bus. The use of clock skews has been recently proposed for detecting intrusions on CAN, using similar mechanisms that were previously exploited in computer or mobile networks in the past decade. However, the fine-grained control of timers easily allows controllers to adjust their clock potentially making such mechanisms ineffective as we argue here and was also proved by a recent research work. We exploit this potential shortcoming in a constructive sense, i.e., the accuracy of arrival times on in-vehicle buses and the fine-grained control of timer/counter circuits on automotive controllers allows us to use time as a covert channel to carry cryptographic authentication. Based on this procedure we propose an effective authentication and intrusion detection mechanism that is fully back-ward compatible with legacy implementations on CAN. Our proposal directly applies to any modern in-vehicle bus, e.g., CAN-FD, FlexRay, etc.

## 1 Introduction and Motivation

We are at a decade of research on attacks and countermeasures for in-vehicle networks. From proof-of-concept attacks on laboratory setups [11] to attacks on real-world vehicles [3,16,21,22] we are witnessing each year more and more threats to the future of automobiles. Without proper countermeasures, such attacks may jeopardize the development of future technologies such as self-driving cars, autonomous intersection management systems, etc. Many security proposals were brought to attention by research works. Various cryptographic authentication techniques are explored from regular message authentication codes [10,30] to well established protocols in sensors networks such as the TESLA protocol [9] or group key-sharing between nodes [8]. Attention is also payed to efficient allocation of signals in each frame [19]. Other works account for the physical layer in order to discard forged frames by error flags [17], hide authentication bits within regular CAN bits [37] or distinguish between nodes based on signal characteristics [26]. Particularities of the physical signalling on the bus have also been exploited to securely share a cryptographic key [12,25].

© Springer Nature Switzerland AG 2019
B. Hamid et al. (Eds.): ISSA 2018/CSITS 2018, LNCS 11552, pp. 94–110, 2019.
https://doi.org/10.1007/978-3-030-16874-2_7

Recently, the design of intrusion detection for the CAN bus has been explored by several research works. Solutions include the use of entropy [20,27], inclusion of anomaly detection sensors [28], the analysis of voltage levels on the bus [5] or the use of cryptographic authentication [2]. Hardware implementations based on the error-confinement mechanism of CAN are discussed in [7]. Artificial intelligence techniques have been also recently employed by the use neural networks in [13,14,34], machine learning [36] and regression learning [18]. Other techniques include hidden Markov models [29], multivariate time series [35] and finite-state automatons [33].

Still, the most basic feature of the communication on the CAN bus which can be used to build intrusion detection mechanisms is the periodicity of messages on the bus. As industry implementations usually demand simplicity, such mechanisms cannot be neglected. Using frame periodicity to detect intrusions was discussed in several research works, e.g., [24] and [32]. Further, the periodicity of messages can be exploited to extract clock skews (which is a unique fingerprint due to physical imperfections in oscillators) and identify the sender of the message as discussed in [4]. The use of clock skews has been previously explored in computer networks [15] and was also applied to smart-phones [6]. However, as we point out in the analysis from the forthcoming section, the fine grained control of time-triggered interrupts and the low-level access to the system clock, may easily allow an embedded device to mimic the clock-skew of another. This was already proved by recent research in [31] which proposes cloaking attacks and may render mechanisms such as the work in [4] ineffective in detecting intrusions. In contrast, in this work we exploit this fine-grain control of timer-counter circuits in a constructive manner and envision the design of a time-covert cryptographic authentication and intrusion detection system for the CAN bus, i.e., INCANTA (INtrusion detection in Controller Area Networks with Time-covert cryptographic Authentication).

Our work is organized as follows. For clarity we begin by presenting the experimental setup in Sect. 2, this comprises high-end automotive-grade controllers as well as industry standard tools, e.g., CANoe, that are used both for simulating real-world in-vehicle traffic and measuring delays. In Sect. 3 we discuss some theoretical notions on measuring clock offsets and present our first experimental results on measuring delays in our setup. Then, in Sect. 4 we embed authentication information in delays, i.e., we create a time-covert authentication channel, and present experimental results. Section 5 holds the conclusions of our work.

## 2   Experimental Setup

For gathering frame arrival timestamps we employed off-the-shelf devices and applications to build an experimental setup. Our setup, as suggested in Fig. 1, consists on three nodes linked over a 500 kbit/s CAN bus. Two of the nodes were implemented on AURIX development boards, while the third was a Vector VN1610 PC to CAN adapter. The Vector VN device was connected to a PC running CANoe 8.0.35 used to record all frames sent over the bus along with their

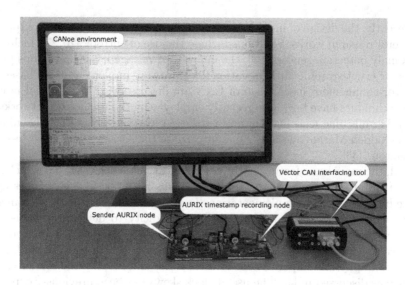

**Fig. 1.** Experimental setup used for gathering frame arrival timestamp data

arrival timestamps. A second set of frame arrival timestamps was recorded on one of the AURIX development boards which acted as a receiver node. To assure consistency of the results, the receiver node was generally either the VN1610 or a TC277 board which used the System Timer module to generate a 10ns base tick for recording the local time.

The target bus traffic was generated by the second of the AURIX-based nodes. Table 1 presents specifications for the 6 different AURIX boards featuring three different Infineon AURIX microcontrollers used as sender nodes in our data recording setup. The sender node was set to send a cyclic message once every 100 ms. The timing functionality is implemented on the AURIX nodes using the on-chip System Timer module configured in the Compare Match Interrupt Control mode to generate interrupts at 100 ms.

**Table 1.** Features of AURIX development boards employed in our experiments

| Microcontroller characteristics | Development board model | | |
|---|---|---|---|
| | AURIX TC224_TFT | AURIX TC277_TFT | AURIX TC299_TFT |
| RAM | 96 KB | 472 KB | 728 KB |
| FLASH | 1 MB | 4 MB | 8 MB |
| EEPROM | 128 KB | 384 KB | 384 KB |
| Top frequency | 133 MHz | 200 MHz | 300 MHz |
| CAN nodes | 3 | 4 | 6 |
| Employed board count | 2 | 2 | 2 |

To provide more realistic results under normal bus operating conditions, a separate set of message arrival timestamps was recorded while generating additional bus traffic in the previously described setup. The additional traffic consisted of traffic recorded on a real-world high-end vehicle and replayed on our CAN bus setup by CANoe through the VN CAN adapter. The additional traffic consists of ≈100 different CAN message types sent on event or periodically with various cycle times. By introducing the recorded traffic the busload increased from 0.49% to around 50%.

# 3 Analysis of Clock Accuracy in Automotive-Grade Controllers

We begin with some theoretical foundations then proceed to a practical analysis of delays on the automotive-grade platforms of our setup.

## 3.1 Theoretical Background

Existing definitions from [23] provide sufficient theoretical background on clock offsets, skews and drifts that characterize differences between clock measurements. These were used in the works from [4] for in-vehicle networks, [15] for computer networks and [6] for smart-phones over wireless-networks. In all these scenarios, delays are used to identify a particular sender. We stay to the same notions but make small modifications according to our needs.

Distinct to the case of a general clock-adjustment scenario in computer networks, e.g., [15] or [6], we are missing the time-stamps of each participant and rely only on local clocks. Subsequently, we want to infer on the clock offset based on local timestamps and also from the a-priori knowledge of the precise time intervals at which frames are broadcast. We note that delays are generally fixed in automotive applications and thus we can infer on the intended delay since this is usually a hardcoded constant $10, 50, 100, 500, 1000$ ms, etc.

Figures 2 and 3 shows how the local timestamps are formed and how they account for delays that are expressed as random variables. Whenever principal $\mu C_1$ sends a cyclic frame, the frame is sent at delay $\delta_{\mu C_1}$ which is a random variable that accounts for imperfections in the local clock of $\mu C_1$. Subsequently, the frame travels on the bus and propagation delays are accounted which are again represented by a random variable $\delta_{\mu C_1, \mu C_2}$ (the propagation delay includes delays due to arbitration loss or mere propagation of the packet on the bus, etc.). Finally, the time-stamp of the frame is quantized on $\mu C_2$ this time accounting for new clock imperfections due to the local clock of $\mu C_2$ that are represented in the random variable $\delta_{\mu C_2}$. In principle, random variable $\delta_{\mu C_2}$ has a mean that is smaller than the mean of $\delta_{\mu C_1, \mu C_2}$ which can get significantly larger when the busload is high, while the mean of $\delta_{\mu C_1}$ is much larger than any of the two as it accounts for the delays at which the frame is sent.

We formally refine the timing metrics that we use in the following definition in attempt to set a theoretical background for our experimental measurements.

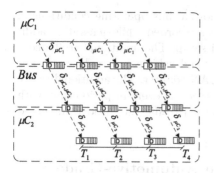

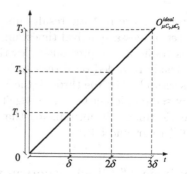

**Fig. 2.** The travelling time for a frame from $\mu C_1$ over the CAN bus to $\mu C_2$

**Fig. 3.** Offset of the recorded time-stamps in case of ideal clocks

*Definition 1.* Let $\Delta T$ be the random variable that accounts for the delay between consecutive occurrences on the bus of frame identified by its ID sent by principal $\mu C_1$ and let $\mathbb{T}_{\mu C} = \{\Delta T_1, \Delta T_2, \ldots, \Delta T_n\}$ be a recording by principal $\mu C_2$ of $n$ consecutive values of variable $\Delta T$, i.e., $\Delta T_i = T_i - T_{i-1}, i = 1 \ldots n$, $T_0 = 0$. We define the following non-random variables that correspond to reference clocks:

   i. $C^{\star}_{\text{ideal}}(t) = t\delta$ where $\delta$ is the intended constant delay between frames,
  ii. $C^{\star}_{\text{min}}(t) = tv_{\text{min}}$ where $v_{\text{min}}$ is the minimum value in $\mathbb{T}_{\mu C}$,
 iii. $C^{\star}_{\text{med}}(t) = tv_{\text{med}}$ where $v_{\text{med}}$ is the median of the values in $\mathbb{T}_{\mu C}$,
 vi. $C^{\star}_{\text{mean}}(t) = tv_{\mu}$ where $v_{\mu}$ is the mean of the values in $\mathbb{T}_{\mu C}$.

Subsequently, we define the cumulative clock offset of principals $\mu C_1$ and $\mu C_2$ with respect to reference clock $C^{\star}_{\blacklozenge}$ where placeholder $\blacklozenge \in \{\text{min}, \text{mean}, \text{med}\}$ as $C_{\mu C_1, \mu C_2}(t) - C^{\star}_{\blacklozenge}(t)$ where $C_{\mu C_1, \mu C_2} = \sum_{i=1,t} \Delta T_i$. In the following subsection we analyze the variation of delays with respect to these four reference clocks. While in the protocol description we analyze variations only with respect to $C^{\star}_{\text{ideal}}$, evaluating the other three clocks should not appear meaningless since without proper evaluation it would have been improper to rule them out as possible indicators.

## 3.2   Experimental Measurements of Delays

We first perform experiments in order to choose which of the four metrics $C^{\star}_{\text{ideal}}$, $C^{\star}_{\text{min}}, C^{\star}_{\text{med}}, C^{\star}_{\text{mean}}$ is best suited for our approach. We also analyze the case when forced constant delays are added to each packet. For illustration purposes, these delays are fixed to $\pm 100$, $\pm 250$ and $\pm 500$ clock ticks. In case of the TC277 boards (the main actor of our experiments) 1 tick of the System Timer is the equivalent of 10ns. Then we focus on the impact on changing delays by very small variations (in the order of hundreds of clock ticks) on the measurements from the receiver side. Nonetheless we discuss the behavior of lower priority IDs which may lose arbitration and thus add more to the propagation delay.

Our experimental measurements clearly point toward $\mathcal{C}^\star_{ideal}$ as the best reference value for the clock drift. Indeed, $\mathcal{C}^\star_{ideal}$ is a constant fixed at design time, but it is also easy to determine by empirical evidence on an existing network since manufacturers always choose fixed delays, e.g., 50 ms, 100 ms.

We now comment why the other indicators, i.e., $\mathcal{C}^\star_{min}, \mathcal{C}^\star_{med}, \mathcal{C}^\star_{mean}$ do not seem to offer a better approximation. The main problem consists in the gap between measurements on a free bus and measurements on a bus that features regular network traffic. We do rely on the minimum, median and mean of the first 100 received packets (by increasing this value the results do improve but not enough to justify the use of these three reference clocks) the subsequent plots are done over the next 1400 frames. When the bus is free of additional traffic the variations between the mean and median values are very small and results computed over a limited number of packets prove to be a bad indicator. The plots appear to be mixed between distinct delays with no obvious separation. This is plotted on the upper side of Figs. 4 and 5. When the bus becomes loaded, variations increase by two orders of magnitude and become stable, this is plotted on the lower side of Figs. 4 and 5. For $\mathcal{C}^\star_{min}$ apparently there is good separation both in the case of a free bus and a bus that is loaded with regular network traffic, this is depicted in Fig. 6. However, the variations are not correctly aligned with the value of the delay, which suggests that the difference toward the minimum value is again a poor separator. For the same measurements $\mathcal{C}^\star_{ideal}$ proves to be a very good classifier with or without network traffic, measurements are presented in Fig. 7.

In Figs. 4, 5, 6 and 7 we have contrasted between independent measurements on the Infineon board and CANoe since the similarities between the independent measurements prove the correctness of the results. The plots suggest that using the clock drift from a single packet may lead to wrong classifications but the cumulative clock drift computed over a few dozen packets is a very good separator to identify a specific delay.

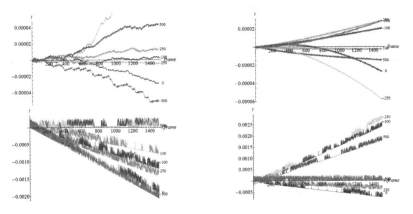

**Fig. 4.** $\mathcal{C}^\star_{mean}$ for a frame sent from an Infinenon TC277 as measured on another Infineon board (left) and on CANoe (right) - results over a free bus (up) or with network traffic (down)

### 3.3  Forcing Delays on the Bus

We now discuss the impact on manipulating delays at fine grain clock modifications. This discussion is essential for embedding the authentication values in delays which is the objective of the INCANTA protocol.

Figure 8 shows these delays (±100, ±250 and ±500 clock ticks) when they are measured from another TC277 board without (left) and with additional traffic (right). In Fig. 9 we show the same delays when measured from a CANoe/VN device at the same time. Here we choose to present the plot at finer grain by taking only 500 packets, otherwise these plots are consistent with the plots already shown in Fig. 7. The slope of the lines are distinct since the clock of the reference

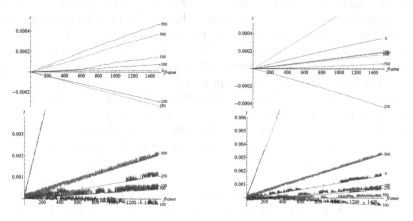

**Fig. 5.** $\mathcal{C}^\star_{\text{med}}$ for a frame sent from an Infinenon TC277 as measured on another Infineon board (left) and on CANoe (right) - results over a free bus (up) or with network traffic (down)

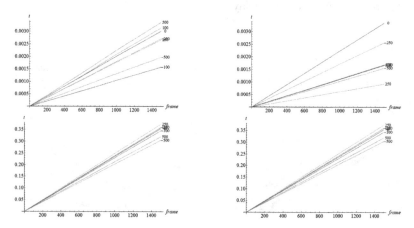

**Fig. 6.** $\mathcal{C}^\star_{\text{min}}$ for a frame sent from an Infinenon TC277 as measured on another Infineon board (left) and on CANoe (right) - results over a free bus (up) or with network traffic (down)

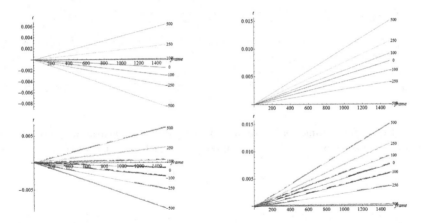

**Fig. 7.** $C^*_{ideal}$ for a frame sent from an Infinenon TC277 as measured on another Infineon board (left) and on CANoe (right) - results over a free bus (up) or with network traffic (down)

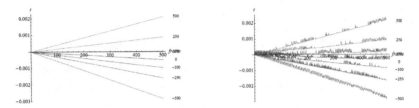

**Fig. 8.** Delays for a frame sent from an Infinenon TC277 as measured on another Infineon board without (left) and with network traffic (right)

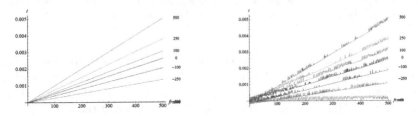

**Fig. 9.** Delays for a frame sent from an Infinenon TC277 as measured from CANoe/VN CAN adapter without (left) and with network traffic (right)

clock from the VN CAN adapter device is distinct. Overlapping the plots in the two cases (with and without traffic) for each reference clock in Fig. 10 shows that traffic does not cause significant changes in the clock skew over multiple packets. While small variations can be encountered, the slopes are close for the two cases.

*Low Priority IDs.* Switching to low priority IDs leads to significant changes in the delay at which packets arrive. Computed over multiple packets, the clock

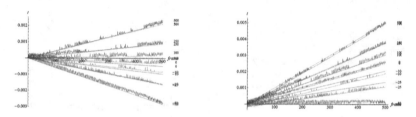

**Fig. 10.** Delays for a frame sent from an Infinenon TC277 as measured by an Infineon board (left) or from CANoe/VN CAN adapter (right) with and without traffic (overlap)

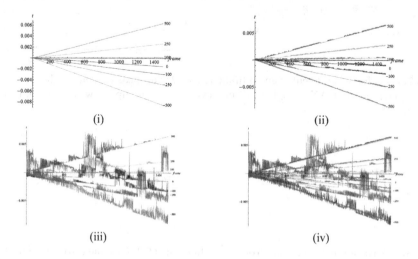

**Fig. 11.** Delays for TC277 on several testbeds: a bus with no traffic (i), with regular traffic and high priority ID (ii) and regular traffic with lowest priority extended ID (iii) and overlap of the three cases (iv) (the slope is similar in all cases)

skew remains the same, but individual packets may come at significant delays. In Fig. 11 we illustrate delays for one of the TC277 boards in the case with no additional traffic on the bus (i), a bus loaded at 50% with delays computed on a packet with the highest priority ID (ii) and delays in case of the lowest priority extended ID (iii). In the later case, it is easy to note that inter-packet delays may have large variations. In part (iv) we overlap these 3 plots and the result confirms that the clock skew is the same for the node. Small variations appear in the case when the delay is set to $0, \pm100$ and $\pm250$ between the three cases but the slope of the line that mediates these values is still close, making identification possible.

*Repeated Randomized Trials.* To get a convincing image on the correctness of the results we proceed to a set of randomized trials that consist in taking small portions of the trace at random positions and compute the variation of clock on the smaller data set. We consider both the case of a free bus and that of a bus loaded with regular network traffic. We performed these tests with 4 Infineon controllers: TC277, TC297, TC224 and a second TC224. Moreover, these tests are again performed for all the induced delays on packet arrival: ±100, ±250 and ±500, Fig. 12 graphically depicts the results. For each board the first set of data which is encircled in the figure represent the packet arrival time without any forced delay, the subsequent tests are for plus 100, 250 and 500 ticks and it can be clearly seen that the arrival time increases and is correctly determined by the receiver. Then the delay decreases by 100, 250 and 500 ticks and so does the arrival time measured by the receiver. In the case when regular traffic is present, variations exists due to the obvious fact that the bus may not be free when data is sent and the time-stamp of these packets alone does not offer sufficient information to identify a sender node (or the intended delay). Fortunately, even with a loaded bus for the majority of packets the delay is correctly estimated as can be seen in Fig. 12. In the next section we do discuss how to exploit this delay in order to hide authentication information and how additional traffic influences the accuracy of our estimation (some packets do deviate significantly from the expected delay and unavoidably they will contribute to the false positive rate).

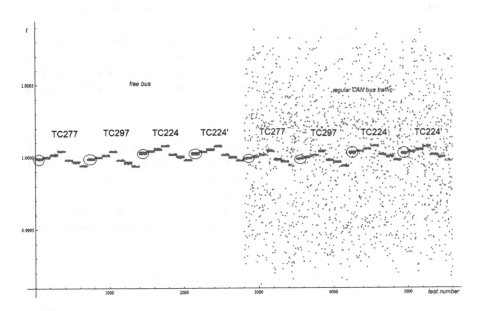

**Fig. 12.** Results after 100 tests at randomized locations in the trace for all 4 Infineon controllers: TC277, TC297, TC224 and a second TC224 and the six added delays ±100, ±250 and ±500 with (right) and without (left) regular network traffic

## 4    The Proposed Protocol and Results

In this section we give a brief overview of the proposed protocol which uses a covert timing channel to embed authentication tags. Then we present experimental results.

## 4.1    Protocol Overview

The protocol description is written for frames which are cyclic in nature. Fortunately the large majority of CAN bus traffic fits into this category. Frames that are on-event can be treated distinctly provided that there is a reference frame for computing the delay. For example one can use the delay toward the previous cyclic frame as a covert channel. It is out of scope for the current work to address on-event frames.

We consider that a shared secret key $k$ exists on each ECUs from the CAN bus. We do not discuss how this key is shared since procedures for this are well known. The INCANTA (INtrusion detection in Controller Area Networks with Time-covert cryptographic Authentication) protocol consists in the following set of actions that are to be followed by each node:

1. SendCyclic($id$, m) is the procedure triggered at some fixed delay $\delta$ for a frame with identifier field $id$ at which the sender computes the tag $tag = MAC_k(i, id, m)$ where $i$ is a counter that is incremented for each ID. The sender then sets $T = \lfloor tag \rfloor_\ell$ and performs a wait operation $wait(T)$ then broadcasts message $(id, m)$,
2. RecCyclic($id$, m) at which a message having identifier $id$ and data-field m is received at time $t$, the receiver computes $tag = MAC_k(id, m)$ and $T = \lfloor tag \rfloor_\ell$ then checks if $|t - i\delta + T| \leq \epsilon$ and if this fails it drops the frame and reports an intrusion by returning Intrusion (here $i$ is the counter for the corresponding frame).

In the description above, we assume that the CAN message having the identifier $id$ is sent at delay $\delta$ while the expected arrival time differs by a small constant $\epsilon$ which compensates for both synchronization error and propagation/computation delays. The desired security level is denoted by $\ell$. For practical purposes this must be set to a value that introduces a reasonable delay. For example, by using $\ell = 16$ and assuming signed values the maximum delay would be $\pm 2^{15}$ ticks, i.e., $327680\,\mathrm{ns}$, and the $327\,\mathrm{\mu s}$ should be negligible considering a frame that regularly arrives at $100\,\mathrm{ms}$.

## 4.2    Results on Embedding Authentication in Delays

The analysis in this section deals with deviations of the arrival time from the expected value and with the analysis of the adversarial success rate in injecting forged frames. The broader image in Fig. 12 makes it clear that in case when regular bus traffic is present, frame arrival time may deviate by large amounts. We do discuss how this affects the detection rate and the improvements that can be done.

*Deviations from the Expected Value.* Due to existing traffic (and also due to measurement imprecisions but by a much smaller amount) some of the genuine frames may be marked as potential intrusions, i.e., the false positives rate FPR. To begin with, in Fig. 13 we show the deviations as recorded in our experiments in case when there is no additional traffic on the bus (i)–(ii) and in case when the bus is loaded with additional traffic (iii)–(iv). Clearly, the distribution of delays is Gaussian in both cases but it is greatly influenced by existing traffic. Figure 14 proves that these deviations are mostly independent on the receiver's clock by illustrating the distribution of delays as recorded both on CANoe vs. the Infineon board. Indeed, the distributions are similar which suggests as expected that the busload is the only cause for the delays.

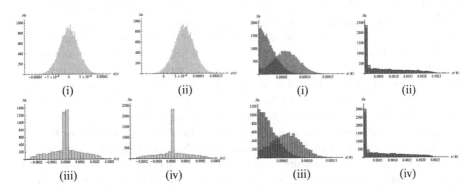

**Fig. 13.** Delay deviations on a free bus recorded by Infineon receiver (i) vs. CANoe trace (ii) and on a bus with regular traffic recorded by Infineon receiver (iii) or CANoe trace (iv)

**Fig. 14.** Comparative deviations between delays on Infineon and CANoe traces with MD5 (i–ii) and SHA2 (iii–iv) on a free bus (left) and a bus with regular traffic (right)

*Detection Rate, True Negatives and False Positives.* The experiments are performed both with MD5 and SHA256 as the underlying hash functions (messages are hashed along with a secret key as required by regular Message Authentication Codes) and the delay is fixed to the last 16, 20 or 22 bits of the resulting authentication tag. MD5 is known to be insecure but this is irrelevant to our experiments since our security level is even lower than that of MD5. Experimental data is used to compute the acceptance rate for legitimate frames, i.e., the true negatives rate TNR, while we estimate the success rate of an adversary, i.e., false negatives rate FNR, synthetically as:

$$\epsilon_{adv} = \frac{\epsilon}{\theta 2^\ell}$$

Here $\epsilon$ is the delay tolerance for accepting a frame, $\theta$ is the value of a tick (in seconds) and $\ell$ is the security level. This comes from the assumption that an adversary can at best insert a frame at some random point and hope that it will match the expected delay. Figure 15 shows the contrast for the advantage of legitimate frames when compared to frames injected by an adversary. Plots (i) and (ii) address the case without additional bus-load. Since there are no delays, the probability of accepting a legitimate frame quickly increases to 1 by using a tolerance of several hundreds ticks. The bus-load however greatly affects the acceptance rate and in case when additional traffic is present the tolerance needs to be increased to more than ten thousands ticks. While the advantage of an adversary is much higher, the acceptance rate for legitimate frames is still superior. The results are also summarized in Table 2 for the case of a free bus and Table 3 for the case of a bus loaded with regular traffic. As expected on the free bus, by considering a tolerance of around one thousand ticks, legitimate frames are accepted at a 99.9% rate while a false negative can occur between 1.40% and 0.02% according to the security level. This is a very good detection/acceptance rate. For the case of a bus loaded with regular network traffic only by a tolerance close to 20,000 ticks we get an acceptance rate of 90% for legitimate frames and from 1.80% to 0.47% false negative rate at 20–22 bit security for the embedded authentication delay. This is satisfactory but not perfect and may be improved by better allocation of bus traffic which out reach for our current work. For 16-bit authentication tags hidden in delays the false negative rate is somewhat high at 27% which suggest that 20–22 bits should be preferred.

Nonetheless we find it relevant to note that the chance of legitimate frames to be accepted increases rapidly after only several hundred ticks in tolerance and then reaches a first 0-growth point (a point where the acceptance probability does not increase at the next tick that is added in tolerance). At the 0-growth point the advantage of the adversary is extremely small, e.g., 0.0002% to 0.4%, while the acceptance rate (TNR) of legitimate frames is much higher, e.g., 4.89% to 25%. While such an acceptance rate is too low to be useful for practical scenarios, the discrepancy between the TNR and FNR can be positively exploited by deciding the intrusion over several consecutive frames. This happens because in case of legitimate frames there is a high chance that at least one frame fits the expected arrival time while it is less likely for any of the adversarial frames to match the expected arrival time. For example, if each authentication tag is computed over the content of the previous $k$ frames, then each frame may eventually benefit from

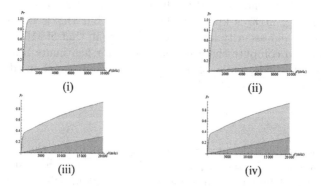

**Fig. 15.** Advantage of genuine frames in front of adversarial frames at a security level of 16 bits with no bus-load as recorded by the Infineon receiver (i) or CANoe trace (ii) and with bus-load by the Infineon receiver (iii) or CANoe trace (iv)

**Table 2.** Detection rate in case of a bus with no traffic

|                 | Tolerance at 90% TNR | FNR at 90% TNR | Tolerance at 99.9% TNR | FNR at 99.9% TNR |
|-----------------|----------------------|----------------|------------------------|------------------|
| 16 bit (MD5)    | 469                  | 0.70%          | 941                    | 1.40%            |
| 16 bit (SHA256) | 505                  | 0.77%          | 1033                   | 1.57%            |
| 20 bit (SHA256) | 510                  | 0.04%          | 981                    | 0.09%            |
| 22 bit (SHA256) | 504                  | 0.01%          | 998                    | 0.02%            |

**Table 3.** Detection rate in case of a bus with regular traffic

|                 | 0-growth point tolerance | TNR at 0-growth | FNR at 0-growth | Tolerance at 90% TNR | FNR at 90% TNR |
|-----------------|--------------------------|-----------------|-----------------|----------------------|----------------|
| 16 bit (MD5)    | 312                      | 25.00%          | 0.4%            | 18289                | 27.00%         |
| 16 bit (SHA256) | 291                      | 26.00%          | 0.44%           | 17976                | 27.00%         |
| 20 bit (SHA256) | 65                       | 4.89%           | 0.006%          | 19596                | 1.80%          |
| 22 bit (SHA256) | 121                      | 9.16%           | 0.002%          | 19814                | 0.47%          |

a tag embedded in $k$ distinct delays. The probability for at least a single frame out of the $k$ frames to yield the correct delay which matches the authentication tag is $1 - \text{FPR}^k = 1 - (1 - \text{TNR})^k$ while the probability that an adversary injects one frame with a correct delay remains $1 - \text{TPR}^k = 1 - (1 - \text{FPR})^k$. Substituting with data from the second row of Table 3 we get for $k = 8$ a correct classification rate of $1 - (1 - 0.26)^8 = 91\%$ while the false negative rate is $1 - (1 - 0.0044)^8 = 3\%$. This is only a quick estimation and further experiments in this direction will be subject of future work for us.

## 5  Discussion and Conclusion

Our work proves that the cyclic nature of in-vehicle communication and the accuracy of timers on automotive-grade controllers can facilitate the creation of an efficient time-covert authentication channel on the CAN bus.

INCANTA stays at the borderline between a conventional intrusion detection mechanism and regular cryptographic authentication. By relying on cryptography our detection system should be superior to conventional intrusion detection systems which can be easily fooled by messages build to satisfy intrusion classification rules (e.g., simulating the delay of another device/frame). Since false-negatives are still present, we do not eliminate the need for a conventional IDS which may easily coexist with the current solution. Since the security level that can be embedded in delays, i.e., 16–20 bits, is obviously lower than the size of a regular cryptographic MAC, e.g., 128 bits, we cannot claim to achieve perfect security in a cryptographic sense. However, recently introduced standards in automotive security require only 24 bits of security [1] for authentication values used on in-vehicle modules (this may be enough for real-time communication). Depending on the network traffic, by cumulating authentication data over consecutive frames we may get closer to this limit.

Besides relying on cryptography which makes it more solid than regular intrusion detection systems, INCANTA has at least two merits: first it is fully backward compatible and second it does not increase the bus-load which is already at its limit on the CAN bus. Nonetheless, the solution is bus independent and can be ported on modern buses such as CAN-FD, FlexRay or BroadRReach without much modifications. Limitations do exist as in the case of a loaded bus a small rate of false positives and true negatives does occur. But we hope that this limitation can be overcome by better allocation of the rest of the traffic from the bus. For the moment this was out-of-reach for our work and we used a real-world trace from a vehicle bus that was not specifically designed for our experiments. As future work we do believe that better allocation of the traffic on the bus can lead to excellent results and we hope that our work opens road in this direction where clever engineering can merge with cryptographic techniques to build efficient intrusion detection by using covert timing channels on CAN or other in-vehicle buses.

**Acknowledgement.** We thank the reviewers for their comments which have helped us to improve our work. This work was supported by a grant of the Romanian National Authority for Scientific Research and Innovation, CNCS-UEFISCDI, project number PN-II-RU-TE-2014-4-1501 (2015–2017) http://www.aut.upt.ro/~bgroza/projects/cseaman/.

# References

1. AUTOSAR: Specification of Secure Onboard Communication, 4.3.1 edn (2017)
2. Boudguiga, A., Klaudel, W., Boulanger, A., Chiron, P.: A simple intrusion detection method for controller area network. In: 2016 IEEE International Conference on Communications (ICC), pp. 1–7. IEEE (2016)
3. Checkoway, S., et al.: Comprehensive experimental analyses of automotive attack surfaces. In: USENIX Security Symposium, San Francisco (2011)
4. Cho, K.-T., Shin, K. G.: Fingerprinting electronic control units for vehicle intrusion detection. In: 25th USENIX Security Symposium (2016)
5. Choi, W., Joo, K., Jo, H.J., Park, M.C., Lee, D.H.: VoltageIDS: low-level communication characteristics for automotive intrusion detection system. IEEE Trans. Inf. Forensics Secur. **13**(8), 2114–2129 (2018)
6. Cristea, M., Groza, B.: Fingerprinting smartphones remotely via ICMP timestamps. IEEE Commun. Lett. **17**(6), 1081–1083 (2013)
7. Giannopoulos, H., Wyglinski, A.M., Chapman, J.: Securing vehicular controller area networks: an approach to active bus-level countermeasures. IEEE Veh. Technol. Mag. **12**(4), 60–68 (2017)

8. Groza, B., Murvay, S., van Herrewege, A., Verbauwhede, I.: LiBrA-CAN: a lightweight broadcast authentication protocol for controller area networks. In: Pieprzyk, J., Sadeghi, A.-R., Manulis, M. (eds.) CANS 2012. LNCS, vol. 7712, pp. 185–200. Springer, Heidelberg (2012). https://doi.org/10.1007/978-3-642-35404-5_15

9. Groza, B., Murvay, S.: Efficient protocols for secure broadcast in controller area networks. IEEE Trans. Industr. Inf. **9**(4), 2034–2042 (2013)

10. Hartkopp, O., Reuber, C., Schilling, R.: MaCAN-message authenticated CAN. In: 10th International Conference on Embedded Security in Cars (ESCAR 2012) (2012)

11. Hoppe, T., Dittman, J.: Sniffing/replay attacks on can buses: a simulated attack on the electric window lift classified using an adapted cert taxonomy. In: Proceedings of the 2nd Workshop on Embedded Systems Security (WESS), pp. 1–6 (2007)

12. Jain, S., Guajardo, J.: Physical layer group key agreement for automotive controller area networks. In: Gierlichs, B., Poschmann, A.Y. (eds.) CHES 2016. LNCS, vol. 9813, pp. 85–105. Springer, Heidelberg (2016). https://doi.org/10.1007/978-3-662-53140-2_5

13. Kang, M.-J., Kang, J.-W.: Intrusion detection system using deep neural network for in-vehicle network security. PLoS One **11**(6), e0155781 (2016)

14. Kang, M.-J., Kang, J.-W.: A novel intrusion detection method using deep neural network for in-vehicle network security. In: 2016 IEEE 83rd Vehicular Technology Conference (VTC Spring), pp. 1–5. IEEE (2016)

15. Kohno, T., Broido, A., Claffy, K.C.: Remote physical device fingerprinting. IEEE Trans. Dependable Secure Comput. **2**(2), 93–108 (2005)

16. Koscher, K., et al.: Experimental security analysis of a modern automobile. In: 2010 IEEE Symposium on Security and Privacy (SP), pp. 447–462. IEEE (2010)

17. Kurachi, R., Matsubara, Y., Takada, H., Adachi, N., Miyashita, Y., Horihata, S.: CaCAN - centralized authentication system in CAN (controller area network). In: 14th International Conference on Embedded Security in Cars (ESCAR 2014) (2014)

18. Li, H., Zhao, L., Juliato, M., Ahmed, S., Sastry, M.R., Yang, L.L.: POSTER: intrusion detection system for in-vehicle networks using sensor correlation and integration. In: Proceedings of the 2017 ACM SIGSAC Conference on Computer and Communications Security, pp. 2531–2533. ACM (2017)

19. Lin, C.-W., Zhu, Q., Sangiovanni-Vincentelli, A.: Security-aware modeling and efficient mapping for CAN-based real-time distributed automotive systems. IEEE Embed. Syst. Lett. **7**(1), 11–14 (2015)

20. Marchetti, M., Stabili, D., Guido, A., Colajanni, M.: Evaluation of anomaly detection for in-vehicle networks through information-theoretic algorithms. In: Research and Technologies for Society and Industry Leveraging a better Tomorrow (RTSI), pp. 1–6. IEEE (2016)

21. Miller, C., Valasek, C.: Adventures in automotive networks and control units. DEF CON **21**, 260–264 (2013)

22. Miller, C., Valasek, C.: Remote exploitation of an unaltered passenger vehicle. Black Hat USA (2015)

23. Moon, S.B., Skelly, P., Towsley, D.: Estimation and removal of clock skew from network delay measurements. In: INFOCOM 1999, Eighteenth Annual Joint Conference of the IEEE Computer and Communications Societies, Proceedings, vol. 1, pp. 227–234. IEEE (1999)

24. Moore, M.R., Bridges, R.A., Combs, F.L., Starr, M.S., Prowell, S.J.: Modeling inter-signal arrival times for accurate detection of can bus signal injection attacks: a data-driven approach to in-vehicle intrusion detection. In: Proceedings of the 12th Annual Conference on Cyber and Information Security Research, pp. 11. ACM (2017)

25. Mueller, A., Lothspeich, T.: Plug-and-secure communication for CAN. CAN Newsl. **4**, 10–14 (2015)

26. Murvay, P.-S., Groza, B.: Source identification using signal characteristics in controller area networks. IEEE Signal Process. Lett. **21**(4), 395–399 (2014)

27. Müter, M., Asaj, N.: Entropy-based anomaly detection for in-vehicle networks. In: 2011 IEEE of the Intelligent Vehicles Symposium (IV), po. 1110–1115. IEEE (2011)

28. Müter, M., Groll, A., Freiling, F.C.: A structured approach to anomaly detection for in-vehicle networks. In: 2010 Sixth International Conference on Information Assurance and Security (IAS), pp. 92–98. IEEE (2010)

29. Narayanan, S.N., Mittal, S., Joshi, A.: OBD_SecureAlert: an anomaly detection system for vehicles. In: 2016 IEEE International Conference on Smart Computing (SMARTCOMP), pp. 1–6. IEEE (2016)

30. Radu, A.-I., Garcia, F.D.: LeiA: a Lightweight authentication protocol for CAN. In: Askoxylakis, I., Ioannidis, S., Katsikas, S., Meadows, C. (eds.) ESORICS 2016. LNCS, vol. 9879, pp. 283–300. Springer, Cham (2016). https://doi.org/10.1007/978-3-319-45741-3_15

31. Sagong, S.U., Ying, X., Clark, A., Bushnell, L., Poovendran, R.: Cloaking the clock: emulating clock skew in controller area networks. In: Proceedings of the 9th ACM/IEEE International Conference on Cyber-Physical Systems, pp. 32–42. IEEE Press (2018)

32. Song, H.M., Kim, H.R., Kim, H.K.: Intrusion detection system based on the analysis of time intervals of can messages for in-vehicle network. In: 2016 International Conference on Information Networking (ICOIN), pp. 63–68. IEEE (2016)

33. Studnia, I., Alata, E., Nicomette, V., Kaâniche, M., Laarouchi, Y.: A language-based intrusion detection approach for automotive embedded networks. Int. J. Embed. Syst. **10**(1), 1–12 (2018)

34. Taylor, A., Leblanc, S., Japkowicz, N.: Anomaly detection in automobile control network data with long short-term memory networks. In: 2016 IEEE International Conference on Data Science and Advanced Analytics (DSAA), pp. 130–139. IEEE (2016)

35. Theissler, A.: Detecting known and unknown faults in automotive systems using ensemble-based anomaly detection. Knowl.-Based Syst. **123**, 163–173 (2017)

36. Tian, D., et al.: An intrusion detection system based on machine learning for CAN-Bus. In: Chen, Y., Duong, T.Q. (eds.) INISCOM 2017. LNICST, vol. 221, pp. 285–294. Springer, Cham (2018). https://doi.org/10.1007/978-3-319-74176-5_25

37. Van Herrewege, A., Singelee, D., Verbauwhede, I.: CANAuth-a simple, backward compatible broadcast authentication protocol for CAN bus. In: ECRYPT Workshop on Lightweight Cryptography, vol. 2011 (2011)

# Detection of Injection Attacks in Compressed CAN Traffic Logs

András Gazdag[1(✉)], Dóra Neubrandt[1], Levente Buttyán[1], and Zsolt Szalay[2]

[1] Laboratory of Cryptography and System Security,
Department of Networked Systems and Services,
Budapest University of Technology and Economics, Budapest, Hungary
{agazdag,dneubrandt,buttyan}@crysys.hu
[2] Department of Automotive Technologies,
Faculty of Transportation Engineering and Vehicle Engineering,
Budapest University of Technology and Economics, Budapest, Hungary
zsolt.szalay@gjt.bme.hu

**Abstract.** Prior research has demonstrated that modern cars are vulnerable to cyber attacks. As such attacks may cause physical accidents, forensic investigations must be extended into the cyber domain. In order to support this, CAN traffic in vehicles must be logged continuously, stored efficiently, and analyzed later to detect signs of cyber attacks. Efficient storage of CAN logs requires compressing them. Usually, this compressed logs must be decompressed for analysis purposes, leading to waste of time due to the decompression operation itself and most importantly due to the fact that the analysis must be carried out on a much larger amount of decompressed data. In this paper, we propose an anomaly detection method that works on the compressed CAN log itself. For compression, we use a lossless semantic compression algorithm that we proposed earlier. This compression algorithm achieves a higher compression ratio than traditional syntactic compression methods do such as gzip. Besides this advantage, in this paper, we show that it also supports the detection of injection attacks without decompression. Moreover, with this approach we can detect attacks with low injection frequency that were not detected reliably in previous works.

**Keywords:** CAN · Anomaly detection · CAN traffic compression

## 1 Introduction

These days vehicles can be the target of various cyber attacks. In a modern automobile, there are numerous ECUs (Electronic Control Units) which are responsible for different functionalities. These ECUs are connected together with the Control Area Network (CAN) bus and they communicate with each other using the CAN protocol. There are several external interfaces which can be used to gain access to this inner network of the vehicle such as wireless interfaces (Bluetooth, WiFi, wireless TPMS) and the on-board diagnostic port (OBD). The design

© Springer Nature Switzerland AG 2019
B. Hamid et al. (Eds.): ISSA 2018/CSITS 2018, LNCS 11552, pp. 111–124, 2019.
https://doi.org/10.1007/978-3-030-16874-2_8

of the inner network and its protocol and interfaces makes the CAN vulnerable against several attacks. We will elaborate more on these attacks in Sect. 3. While in the past, such attacks were considered low risk and not a real concern, recently, researches have demonstrated [1–3] that they are not so difficult to carry out and, hence, the risk is indeed considerable.

Cyber attacks on vehicles can cause physical accidents. This means that when an accident happens, forensic analysis must be extended into the cyber domain, and investigators must analyze whether the accident was caused or made possible by a cyber attack. Imagine, for example, that a compromised ECU provides false data and as a consequence, misleading information is displayed to the driver on the dashboard, or the airbag is disabled silently before a crash, or some autonomous driving function is enabled and the driver loses control over the vehicle. All these can either lead to an accident or increase its fatality. As the cyber attack on the vehicle may occur well before the accident that it causes, forensic analysis can be successful only if detailed logs are recorded for an extended period of time, not just for a few seconds before the accident[1].

In our view, in the future, especially with the increased penetration of autonomous vehicles, it will be indispensable to continuously record CAN traffic in vehicles and efficiently store these logs for later forensic analysis. Efficient storage of CAN logs requires compressing them. Compression not only saves storage space, but it also makes it easier to off-load logs from the vehicle. Usually, the compressed log must be decompressed for analysis purposes, and the analysis is carried out on large amount of decompressed data. This increases the inefficiency of the analysis itself. In this paper, we study the problem of detecting anomalies that may indicate cyber attacks on the compressed CAN traffic log, hence making analysis faster by not requiring decompression and most importantly by reducing the amount of data on which the analysis must be performed.

Anomaly detection cannot be performed on any kind of compressed CAN log, but the compression method must support the analysis of the compressed data. Hence, for compression, we use a lossless semantic compression algorithm that we proposed earlier [4]. This compression algorithm achieves a higher compression ratio than traditional syntactic compression methods such as gzip. Besides this advantage, in this paper, we show that it also supports the detection of certain types of attacks in the CAN log without decompression. More specifically, we can easily detect flooding attacks, where the attacker (e.g., a compromised ECU) injects a given type of periodic CAN message with a smaller repetition time (higher frequency) than its normal repetition time. Most of the attacks demonstrated in prior work were of this kind [1–3]. The increased frequency of injected false messages usually results in "overriding" the information carried in the legitimate messages. We show that such an attack causes a well-identifiable anomaly pattern in the compressed log even when the frequency of the fake messages is just slightly larger than the normal frequency.

The remainder of the paper is organized as follows: In Sect. 2, we give an overview on the existing anomaly detection works on CAN traffic. In Sect. 3,

---

[1] https://www.nhtsa.gov/research-data/event-data-recorder.

we describe how the CAN protocol and the CAN compression algorithm we use work. In Sect. 4, we discuss the attack scenario and the possible attacks against the CAN protocol that we and recent works take into consideration. We present our anomaly detection approach and its evaluation in Sect. 5. Finally, we conclude in Sect. 6.

## 2    Related Work

Anomaly detection on the CAN bus has been an actively researched field recently. Multiple approaches have been proposed varying in the interpretation of the CAN traffic. If the interpretation of the CAN messages are accessible it is possible to collect the actual vehicle parameters. Approaches using this knowledge usually perform anomaly detection on this high level data. The researches not using a CAN matrix are mainly focused on the communications properties such as repetition times of the messages.

Taylor et al. proposed a method from the first approach in [8]. They interpreted the CAN massages to build a current state of the vehicle. Then with a Long Short-Term Memory Network (LSTM) predicted the next state of the car. If the actual state, based on the following messages, is diverging from the predicted state they detect it as an anomaly.

Narayanan et al. proposed a hidden Markov models based approach to anomaly detection [11]. They used the OBD port available in every modern car to access the CAN bus. Packets captured through this interface are interpreted then and used to build the Markov model. They also understand states of the vehicle and define the possible state transitions. If an unexpected state transition is detected that means an anomaly in their model.

In [10] Marchetti et al. showed that anomaly detection can be efficiently performed based on CAN ID sequences. From the CAN traffic they only use the ID field of the messages. They build a transition matrix to understand the connection between messages. If during normal traffic an ID follows another then this transition is marked as normal in the matrix. Their anomaly detection method analyzes whether a not allowed transition appears in the traffic.

In another paper Taylor et al. [5] presented an anomaly detection approach that is based on repetition times of the messages on the CAN bus. They first splitted the traffic into flows. For every flow various measures are calculated such as the number of packets in the flow, the average Hamming distance between successive packet data fields and the average time difference between successive packets. During their analysis they show that the only reliable parameter for anomaly detection is the average time difference between successive packets. They use a one-class support vector machine (OCSVM) to classify the benign traffic and to detect anomalies. They measure the efficiency of their work only on syntactically generated traffic.

Although anomaly detection on compressed traffic has several advantages, this idea was not researched so far. We aim to close this gap by analyzing normal and attacked compressed CAN traffic to determine what kind of anomalies could be detected with this approach.

# 3    Technical Background

## 3.1    CAN Protocol

In modern cars the ECUs are controlling several processes. They measure their surroundings and according to the available information they perform operations. They are connected together with the CAN bus and communicate by its protocol, the CAN protocol, which uses CAN messages. In the protocol there is no authentication, and broadcast is used, so every ECU gets every message and selects which interests it. That is, all traffic is visible to everyone and any controller can send any type of message. The above mentioned attributes make the CAN vulnerable against several attacks. For example an attacker can easily send arbitrary messages once he gained access to the inner network.

A CAN message has the following format. Every message has an ID which can be 11 or 29 bits long. The meaning and the range of the IDs are manufacturer specific. The lower the value of the identifier field the more prior is the message. After the ID comes the data length field then comes the data.

```
1481492674.734327 0x260 8 00 00 00 00 00 00 00 6a
1481492674.736055 0x2c4 8 05 c8 00 0f 00 00 92 3c
1481492674.738092 0x2c1 8 08 03 35 01 6a d9 00 4f
1481492674.754306 0x260 8 00 00 00 00 00 00 00 6a
1481492674.759605 0x2c4 8 05 c8 00 0f 00 00 92 3c
1481492674.769823 0x2c1 8 08 03 39 01 70 d9 00 59
1481492674.774302 0x260 8 00 00 00 00 00 00 00 6a
1481492674.783129 0x2c4 8 05 c2 00 0f 00 00 92 36
1481492674.794246 0x260 8 00 00 00 00 00 00 00 6a
1481492674.801541 0x2c1 8 08 03 3b 01 74 d9 00 5f
```

**Example 1.1.** Simplified CAN traffic log

In Example 1.1 a CAN traffic log is shown. Each row corresponds to a message. The first column is the arrival time of the message (Unix time), the second column is the message ID, in the third column there are specific flags (which in our captured data are not used), the fourth column shows the length of the data in the message, and the last column is the data.

## 3.2    CAN Compression Algorithm

We used a recently published semantic compression algorithm [4] made specifically for CAN traffic compression. It achieves a good compression ratio on CAN traffic, exceeding other state of the art syntactic compression algorithms, such as gzip. It is a lossless compression method which is a necessary requirement for being able to use it in forensic investigations after an incident.

```
0x260
start_time:1481492674.734327
period:19984
00 00 00 00 00 00 00 6a:  0#0,1#-5,1#12,1#-40,
                         1#-3,1#105,1#-87,
                         1#-16

0x2c4
start_time:1481492674736055
period:23540
05 c8 00 0f 00 00 92 3c:  0#0,1#10
05 c2 00 0f 00 00 92 36:  1#-16, 1#20
05 c5 00 0f 00 00 92 39:  1#111
05 c8 00 0f 00 00 92 3c:  1#-113, 1#-22

0x2c1
start_time:1481492674738092
period:31728
08 03 35 01 6a d9 00 4f:  0#0
08 03 39 01 70 d9 00 59:  1#3
08 03 3b 01 74 d9 00 5f:  1#440, 1#14
08 03 38 01 72 d9 00 5a:  1#-5
```

**Example 1.2.** Compressed CAN traffic log

The compression algorithm works as follows.

1. First, it separates the messages according to their message ID-s.
2. For each message ID, it records the time of the first message in the recorded traffic. (See 'start_time' in Example 1.2.)
3. It calculates the average time between messages with the same ID-s.
4. For a given ID, it sorts the messages into groups according to their data, so messages with the same data go into the same group.
5. Store the number of elapsed periods and the difference between the period based and the actual time stamp.

It is unnecessary to store the time for each message in every group, because the periodic nature of the bus arbitration can be exploited. Thus, it is enough to store how many periods elapsed since the previous message (in the group) and the difference from it in microseconds. For example 1#440 means that, after the previous message 1 period and 440 µs elapsed.

## 4   CAN Attacks

An attacker could try to interfere with the normal operation of the CAN bus in multiple ways depending on the malicious intent. It is possible to achieve an anomaly with just a few messages but in most cases to make an attack reliable a large number of messages are necessary. In the following paragraphs we describe the various possibilities of an attacker organized by the number of messages required. In the second part of this section we describe how we recorded infected CAN logs for this research.

### 4.1   Taxonomy of CAN Attacks

**DOS Against the CAN Bus:** In this scenario the goal of the attacker is to completely disable the communication on the CAN bus. This can be achieved at least with two extreme approaches.

An attacker could disturb the transmission of every CAN packet by starting its own dummy transmission in the middle of every other packet. This way an error will occur during the reception of every packet. This attack does not need a full packet to be sent by the attacker just a few bits with the correct timing.

Similar effect can be achieved with the transmission of packets with the ID 0. The ID field of the CAN packet is also determines the priority of the message. The value of the ID decides which packet can be transmitted in case of multiple colliding packets. The smaller the ID of a packet is the higher its priority is. If an attacker sends continuously packets with the ID 0 then there won't be any resource left for the normal traffic.

Both of these attacks are operation critical for a vehicle. A complete DOS against the CAN bus isolates the ECUs from each other disabling most of their operations. These scenarios are trivial to detect but very difficult to handle.

**Messages with New IDs:** It is common in car manufacturing that the same hardware parts are used in various car models. This practice makes it possible for an attacker to try to trigger functionality in a car that would not be used otherwise. On the CAN level this means that messages could appear with previously unseen IDs.

Some attacks are realized with the usage of debug packets [1]. These scenarios also introduce packets with new IDs on the bus.

If all benign IDs are known in advance, identifying these attacks is simple. Messages with IDs not seen before can effectively be found with basic white-listing or simple anomaly detection.

**Irregular Messages with Known IDs:** Some CAN messages are only transmitted as a response to certain events. These messages are encountered rarely because they are responses to environmental changes and are not part of the regular operation of a vehicle. An attacker could inject any of these messages at random times to force an inconsistency in the operation.

Without an external source of information the only way to detect these messages is to correlate information from other packets. This is a challenging task in most cases if even possible.

**Messages with Regular Repetition Times:** To interfere with the normal operation of a vehicle the regular communication of the ECUs should be altered. It is hard to remove a messages from the CAN bus (if en error occurs during transmission usually a re-transmission logic is triggered at the sender) thus the best possible option for an attacker is to send malicious packets additionally. A packet with fake content could force the vehicle into a compromised state until the next packet with correct content arrives. Most attacks require to keep the vehicle in a compromised state for the majority of the time. This means that the attacker is required to send a lot of malicious packets to minimize the effect of the original benign traffic.

Based on the goal of the attacker the frequency of the malicious packets could be anything between 1x and 10x of the original traffic. Our measurements and previous research [1] results also showed that a malicious traffic with ~10x the frequency of the original traffic forces the vehicle to stay in a compromised state almost constantly.

## 4.2   Realized Attacks

We used a test vehicle to demonstrate some of the attacks described previously. It allowed us to test our anomaly detection approach in a real life scenario as well.

**Speed Indicator Modification:** In this attack we were able to change the displayed speed of the vehicle. We achieved that even when the car was standing still without the engine running.

We performed this test with different attack frequencies. In the first attempt the frequency of the forged packets was the same as the original one effectively doubling the number of packets with the given ID. This caused the speed indicator to oscillate between the real speed (0 km/h) and the forged speed (30 km/h) (Fig. 1).

In our second attempt we increased the frequency of the malicious packets to 10x the frequency of the normal traffic. This created a stable attack where the indicator showed continuously the speed defined by our attack (Fig. 2).

**Transmission Dashboard Modification:** We also attacked the transmission signal for the dashboard (Fig. 3). The engine was still not running but we were able to force the display to show that the vehicle was in gear 1.

To achieve this goal we used a packet observed during previous test drives. The malicious packet injection frequency was also 10x of the original rate. As a side-effect we also modified the fuel level indicator and some control lights from the engine. In the original state the fuel level was low whereas during the attack it showed that the tank is half full (Fig. 4). This indicates that the fuel level and some of the control signals are transmitted in the same packet as the current gear.

**Fig. 1.** Speed indicator attack with 1x frequency caused oscillation of the indicator needle.

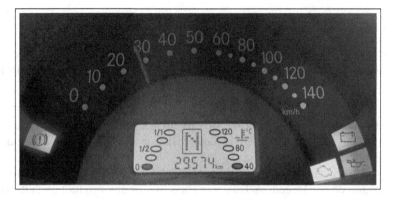

**Fig. 2.** Speed indicator attack with 10x frequency. The indicator shows 28 km/h while the real speed was 0 km/h.

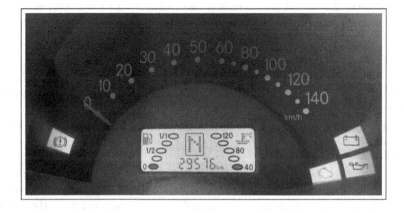

**Fig. 3.** Original state of the transmission display.

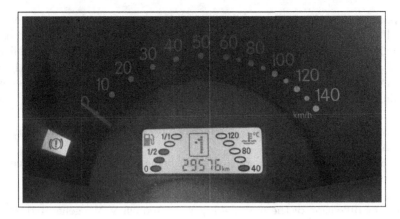

**Fig. 4.** Attack on the transmission display. The engine was not running but the indicator showed gear 1. The control lights were switched off and the fuel level was increased.

## 5   Anomaly Detection

### 5.1   Data Sets

During the research we created two data sets. First, we created a synthetic data set where the attacks were manually injected into a clean CAN traffic log. Then we also performed some attacks against a real vehicle that gave us real life infected traffic logs.

**Synthetic Data Set:** We have captured a few hours of benign traffic from a mid class vehicle. With reverse engineering we found the signal used to display the RPM of the engine on the dashboard. We used this signal during our attacks to simulate an attack where false information is displayed to the driver. The RPM value is sent by an ECU in a message with the ID 110. Normally this message is send in every 10 ms. This attack belongs to the "Messages with regular repetition times" category described in Sect. 4.

We created a packet with a malicious content to insert into the traffic. The packet contained a higher RPM value than found in normal traffic.

We generated the malicious traffic with multiple steps. First we splitted the normal traffic into smaller chunks. Each chunk contained approximately 1 min of traffic. As a base rule we decided that every attack should be at least 5 s long because a shorter attack on the dashboard would probably not disturb the driver thus it would not achieve any goal. We also generated longer attacks. For each attack scenario we increased the attack length with 5 s. This resulted in attacks with random length in these intervals: 5–10; 10–15; 15–20; 20–25 and 25–30 s.

For every attack scenario we generated 100 malicious samples. They were each tested in our algorithm together with 100 benign samples.

We generated the malicious traffic simulating the normal operation of the CAN bus (including the bus arbitration). First, we generated 10000 of the malicious packets. The time stamp of the first packet was randomly chosen from the first half of the benign sample, the rest of the time stamps were calculated based on the chosen attack frequency. Then, we merged the benign and the malicious packets according to the time stamps. If two messages overlapped than the one with the higher time stamp was shifted after the other. If there was enough time until the next message then the shifted message was simply inserted. Otherwise the same logic was repeated again to resolve further conflicts in the time stamps. Generally, the bus load was relatively low in our test vehicle resulting a low number of those conflicts.

Once we had the 100 malicious and 100 benign samples for every scenario we compressed all of the logs with the chosen compression algorithm.

Furthermore we examined how the detectability of such an attack changes with the modification of the message injection frequency. We generated attacks where the injection frequency was 10 times, 5 times and 2 times higher than the original frequency of the given ID. We considered the 10 times higher frequency the default frequency for a flooding attack as our real life tests and other researchers also demonstrated it is an adequate frequency for an attack to have a stable effect.

In our captured traffic there are 18 different IDs. There are IDs with regular (14) and irregular (4) repetition times. We only focused on the regular IDs.

**Real Life Data Set:** We implemented CAN attacks on a vehicle with real impact. We targeted both the speed and the transmission indicator. For the speed indicator we used 3 different attack frequencies: ~10 times higher, 2 times higher and the exact same frequency as the original messages have. For the transmission indicator we also used a frequency 10 times of the original. We also collected benign traffic from the vehicle to compare it to the malicious logs.

### 5.2    Our Anomaly Detection Algorithm

Our detection algorithm has the goal to decide whether a given message in the compressed CAN traffic log belongs to an attack or not. To address this, first we split the compressed log into separate ID files, where each file contains messages of a given ID. These files are analyzed separately.

We calculated different features of the malicious and benign logs to find the ones that distinguish them the most efficiently. Although, the changes of the repetition times had a significant impact on the structure of the compressed traffic log, the simplest and most powerful feature turned out to be the number of messages during a constant time window.

**Number of Messages per Minute:** In a time window of 1 min we count the number of messages for each ID. Thus we get a feature for each ID: the number of messages in a minute. This will be different in a normal and an attacked traffic log. This approach is also intuitive. If we inject additional messages of an

ID that has an approximately constant message rate per minute, the increase in the message rate per minute will indicate an attack.

This feature proved to be reliable for attacks both with higher and lower frequencies.

**Attack Detection:** Based on the previously suggested feature, attacks can be detected efficiently. As can be seen in Sect. 5.3, this approach separates malicious traffic logs from benign logs even visually making the decision easy.

## 5.3   Results

We evaluated our method on both synthetic and real life data with different attack frequencies.

On synthetic data we used the above mentioned 100-100 normal and attacked samples for attacks with different frequency. The histogram of the distribution of the attacks can be seen in Figs. 5 and 6. They demonstrate that the attacked traffic is efficiently distinguishable from the normal traffic even when the attack frequency is as low as 2 times of the original.

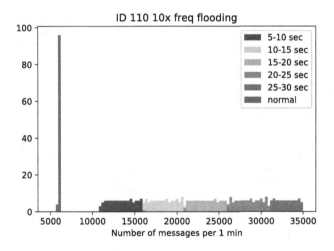

**Fig. 5.** The deviation of the number of messages per minute feature for 100 - 100 samples at 10x frequency (synthetic attack).

On the data from the real world attacks we performed the same calculations. Figs. 7 and 8 show that our algorithm achieves the same reliable results in the real life scenarios as well.

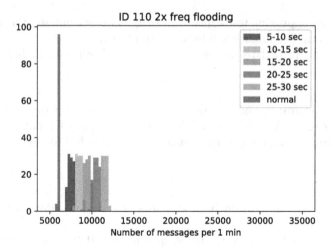

**Fig. 6.** The deviation of the number of messages per minute feature for 100 - 100 samples at 2x frequency (synthetic attack).

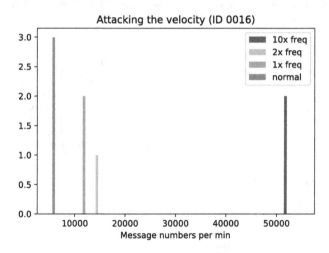

**Fig. 7.** Real attacks on the speed indicator. Comparison of the number of messages in normal and attacked scenarios.

These results show that with this approach it is possible to achieve correct classification in every case. For the stable attacks, where a high message frequency is used, the proposed method produces a reliable result with 0 false positive and false negative rates. As the message injection rate decreases the confidentiality is also reduced but even for attacks with 1x injection frequency it remains high enough for a correct decision.

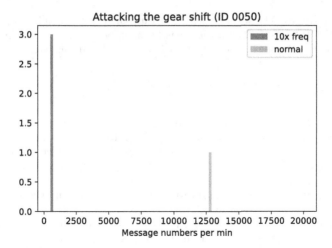

**Fig. 8.** Real attacks on the transmission indicator. Comparison of the number of messages in normal and attacked scenarios.

## 6    Conclusion

In this paper, we argued that cyber attacks on vehicles may cause physical accidents, therefore, forensic investigations must be extended into the cyber domain. In order to support this, CAN traffic in vehicles must be logged continuously and stored efficiently for later analysis. Our main contribution in this paper was a novel anomaly detection method that works on compressed CAN traffic logs. The advantage of running anomaly detection on the compressed logs is that less amount of data needs to be analyzed, hence, the efficiency of forensic investigations can be increased.

Our anomaly detection algorithm is based on analyzing the average frequencies of messages with given CAN IDs. The compression algorithm that we use preserves the number of messages per unit time in an easily extractable form in the compressed CAN log, which makes it possible to use our anomaly detection algorithm on the compressed logs. We demonstrated that this approach works reliably in a range of scenarios, including using data sets captured in real vehicles and modified with synthetically generated attacks as well as data sets captured in real vehicles under real attacks. Our algorithm was capable to identify attacks is both cases.

Observing the average frequencies of messages with given CAN IDs may appear to be a simplistic approach for anomaly detection; nevertheless, it works reliably for detecting injection attacks. In addition, many prior works suggested that injection attacks are easy to carry out and they have noticeable effects, hence, this type of attack is one of the most important attacks to consider. Whether our method of analyzing the compressed logs can be adapted to other types of attacks, where message frequencies are not changed, is an open question and subject of our future work.

**Acknowledgement.** The work presented in this paper was partially supported from the grant GINOP-2.1.1-15. The project has been supported by the European Union, co-financed by the European Social Fund. EFOP-3.6.2-16-2017-00002.

# References

1. Miller, C., Valasek, C.: Adventures in automotive networks and control units. Technical report, IOActive Labs Research, August 2013
2. Koscher, K., et al.: Experimental security analysis of a modern automobile, pp. 447–462 (2010)
3. Checkoway, S., et al.: Comprehensive experimental analyses of automotive attack surfaces. In: Proceedings of the 20th USENIX Conference on Security, SEC 2011. USENIX Association, Berkeley (2011)
4. Gazdag, A., Buttyan, L., Szalay, Z.: Efficient lossless compression of CAN traffic logs. In: 2017 25th International Conference on Software, Telecommunications and Computer Networks (SoftCOM), Split (2017)
5. Taylor, A., Japkowicz, N., Leblanc, S.: Frequency-based anomaly detection for the automotive CAN bus. In: World Congress on Industrial Control Systems Security (WCICSS), London, pp. 45–49 (2015)
6. Song, H.M., Kim, H.R., Kim, H.K.: Intrusion detection system based on the analysis of time intervals of CAN messages for in-vehicle network. In: 2016 International Conference on Information Networking (ICOIN), Kota Kinabalu, pp. 63–68 (2016)
7. Miller, C., Valasek, C.: Remote exploitation of an unaltered passenger vehicle. Black Hat USA (2015)
8. Taylor, A., Leblanc, S., Japkowicz, N.: Anomaly detection in automobile control network data with long short-term memory networks. In: 2016 IEEE International Conference on Data Science and Advanced Analytics (DSAA), Montreal, QC, pp. 130–139 (2016)
9. Evenchick, E.: Hopping On the CAN Bus. Black Hat Asia (2015)
10. Marchetti, M., Stabili, D.: Anomaly detection of CAN bus messages through analysis of ID sequences. In: IEEE Intelligent Vehicles Symposium (IV), Los Angeles, CA, pp. 1577–1583 (2017)
11. Narayanan, S.N., Mittal, S., Joshi, A.: OBD_SecureAlert: an anomaly detection system for vehicles. In: 2016 IEEE International Conference on Smart Computing (SMARTCOMP), St. Louis, MO (2016)

# Key is in the Air: Hacking Remote Keyless Entry Systems

Omar Adel Ibrahim[1(✉)], Ahmed Mohamed Hussain[2(✉)],
Gabriele Oligeri[1(✉)], and Roberto Di Pietro[1(✉)]

[1] Division of Information and Computing Technology,
College of Science and Engineering,
Hamad Bin Khalifa University, Doha, Qatar
oaibrahim@mail.hbku.edu.qa, {goligeri,rdipietro}@hbku.edu.qa
[2] Electrical Engineering Department, College of Engineering,
Qatar University, Doha, Qatar
ahmed.hussain@qu.edu.qa

**Abstract.** A Remote Keyless Systems (RKS) is an electronic lock that controls access to a building or vehicle without using a traditional mechanical key. Although RKS have become more and more robust over time, in this paper we show that specifically designed attack strategies are still effective against them. In particular, we show how RKS can be exploited to efficiently hijack cars' locks.

Our new attack strategy—inspired to a previously introduced strategy named *jam-listen-replay*—only requires a jammer and a signal logger. We prove the effectiveness of our attack against six different car models. The attack is successful in all of the tested cases, and for a wide range of system parameters. We further compare our solution against state of the art attacks, showing that the discovered vulnerabilities enhance over past attacks, and conclude that RKS solutions cannot be considered secure, calling for further research on the topic.

## 1 Introduction

Remote Keyless Systems (RKS) are a critical component of modern car security. Such systems allow the user to lock/unlock the car without resorting to any mechanical key but only by clicking a button on the car's fob or even by getting close to the car itself. RKS mainly implements a request-response protocol between the fob and the car's radio transceiver with minimal security protection [3]. During the years, several security flaws have been identified and RKS evolved mitigating such attacks. An interesting example is the so-called *rolling codes* that prevent an eavesdropper to reuse a code sequence from the past. At each transmission, a new code is generated invalidating the old one by resorting to hash function computations. Unfortunately, rolling codes do not protect against either *proxy attacks* or *jam-listen-replay* attacks [11]. The first class of attacks involve to proxy the code sequence from a further distance to the car without the user consent. This is a classical attack that is played as follows: a

© Springer Nature Switzerland AG 2019
B. Hamid et al. (Eds.): ISSA 2018/CSITS 2018, LNCS 11552, pp. 125–132, 2019.
https://doi.org/10.1007/978-3-030-16874-2_9

user, leaving the fob unattended, allows an adversary to activate the fob (without stealing it, just pressing the button) and to proxy the fob emitted code sequence to the car leveraging another radio technology such as WiFi, Bluetooth or either GSM. Proxy attacks can be mitigated using distance bounding and proximity solutions [12]. Nevertheless, jam-listen-replay attacks are still an open issue due to the difficulty of mitigating jamming attacks. Indeed, the adversary prevents the reception of the code sequence by jamming the car radio transceiver, and at the same time, he logs it for the future hijacking of the car.

**Contribution.** This paper pushes further the analysis of the jam-listen-replay attack proposed in [11]. We propose an improved attack scenario by exploiting cheap hardware and commonly available Linux tools. We show the results of a real measurement campaign highlighting the effectiveness of the proposed attacks and comparing it against the ones introduced by [11]. We observe how, given the current state of the art, these types of attacks cannot be solved without resorting to novel authentication mechanisms, hence justifying further research efforts by both industry an academia on this topic.

**Roadmap.** Next section reviews the current state of the art as for RKS security. Section 3 details the attack scenario; Sect. 4 introduces the adopted equipment and its configuration, while Sect. 5 reports on our measurement campaign and discuss the differences of our attack with respect to the state-of-the-art. Finally, some concluding remarks are presented in Sect. 6.

## 2 Related Work

A major family of attacks exploits jamming and two subsequent phases: preventing the delivery of the message to the car (by jamming) and recording the transmitted message for the subsequent re-transmission. An early contribution has been provided by [11]. Authors firstly propose an efficient brute-force technique for hacking garage doors remote controllers. Secondly, they introduce RollJam, a combined jamming and radio-recording technique enabling the adversary to hack the communications between the car and its associated fob. RollJam involves very cheap devices such as Teensy 3.1 and two CC1101 transceivers. RollJam works by preventing one or more messages to be delivered to the car from the fob while recording them. Eventually, RollJam allows the user to get in the car but a sequence of valid messages have been stolen and they can be reused later on for opening the car.

Van de Beek et al. in [5] and subsequently in [4], revised the jamming-based attack considering pulse electromagnetic interference despite of continuous interference. They analyzed the effects of pulsed interference on envelope detectors through both simulations and measurements. They also suggested an improved receiver design based on synchronous transmitter-receiver communications, which turn out to be more robust against pulsed interference.

Francillon et al. in [10] demonstrated the relay attack on Passive Key-less Entry Systems (PKES) used in modern cars. They set up two low-cost and powerful attack scenarios, using wireless and wired physical layer relays enabling the adversary to open the car and start the engine by relaying the messages between the key and the car.

A general overview describing several techniques of potential attacks against passive entry systems is introduced in [3]. Authors proposed a solution to protect the vehicle from such attacks by exploiting the difference in power levels of the received bits.

## 3   Scenario

Our attack scenario involves three entities: the *car*, the car's owner (*user*) and the *adversary* who wants to steal the user's car. The adversary implements his strategy in 3 subsequent steps as depicted in Fig. 1: (i) *set-up*, (ii) *jamming and recording*, and (iii) *hijacking*.

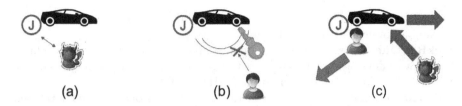

(a)                         (b)                         (c)

**Fig. 1.** The attack is performed in a sequence of 3 steps: (a) Set-up the jammer and activation, (b) Jamming the communication between the user and the car and forcing the user to use the mechanical key, and finally (c) when the user leaves the car unattended, the adversary hijacks the car.

**Set-Up.** This is a preliminary phase that is performed by the adversary when the car is left unattended by the user. Indeed, the adversary has to install a jammer on the car. As it will be clear in the following, the jammer is a very portable device mainly constituted by a Raspberry Pi v3 (RPiv3) connected to a HackRF One, a very cheap and ready to be deployed Software Defined Radio (SDR). The overall equipment can be hidden in several places outside of the car, e.g., by using a magnet under the car platform.

**Jamming and Recording.** The equipment should be activated after its installation and it will prevent the communication between the fob and the car by jamming a specific frequency. Since the user will not be able to open the car by using the fob, after several attempts, he will resort to the mechanical key. Conversely, the adversary will record one or more code sequences transmitted by the fob (and never received by the car) by eavesdropping the fob-car communication channel.

**Hijacking.** The car's owner will eventually drive the car away and close it still using the mechanical key. We recall that a jammer is installed on the car preventing the fob to control the lock mechanism of the car. Subsequently, the adversary will perform his attack by replaying one of the previously recorded code sequences, and allow him to hijack the car.

The only unknown parameter to the previous procedure is the communication frequency adopted by the car brand. The adversary can easily discriminate it by running a discovering session sensing fractions of the radio spectrum. Our experiments show that the majority of the cars we used adopts a frequency band close to 433 MHz.

## 4 Equipment: Hardware, Software and Set-Up Configuration

Our system consists of 2 components: the **Jammer** and the code sequence **Logger**.

### 4.1 Jammer

We implemented a mobile jammer by connecting a Raspberry Pi v3 to a HackRF One and a power bank as depicted in Fig. 2.

**HackRF One:** HackRF One is an open source, half-duplex Software Defined Radio device developed by Great Scott Gadgets and has the capability to receive or transmit radio signals starting from 1 MHz to 6 GHz.

**ANT500 Antenna:** ANT500 is a general purpose, telescopic antenna developed by Great Scott Gadgets and is designed to operate in the range from 75 MHz up to 1 GHz. Its length is configurable starting from 20 cm up to 88 cm.

**Raspberry Pi v3:** We installed GNU Radio on the RPiv3 and exploited the Python SDK to control the Hack RF One. The result is a script to transmit white Gaussian noise on a target frequency.

**Power-bank:** We adopted a generic power bank of 5000 mA guaranteeing a long lasting life to our system (about half a day).

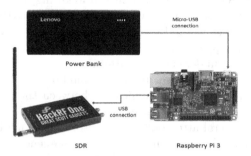

**Fig. 2.** The Jammer: An RPiv3 controls the HackRF One transmitting white Gaussian noise at the frequency of 434 MHz. The power bank guarantees half a day of jamming activity.

We exploited the embedded WiFi in the RPiv3 to access it through SSH, changing the various jamming parameters and switching it on and off. We observe that the jamming frequency (433 MHz) is far away from that one used by the WiFi (2.4 GHz), and therefore, the jammer can be remotely controlled. We set all the gains for the HackRF One platform to 40 dB, i.e., radio band (RF), intermediate band (IF) and base band (BB) gain. Finally, we set the sampling rate (sps) to 2M as an empirical trade-off to jam the fob-car communication without disturbing any other communications in the neighborhood.

### 4.2 Logger

The logger is mainly constituted by a mobile platform able to log the code sequence transmitted by the fob to the car. We adopted the following set-up:
**Laptop:** We configured a laptop with a Linux Ubuntu distribution and GNU Radio Companion.
**HackRF One and ANT500 Antenna:** A HackRF One has been connected to the above laptop to record all the code signals transmitted in the neighborhood.

Figure 3 resumes our logger setup and the main connections.

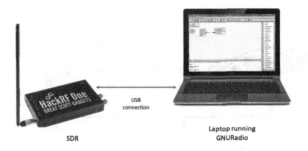

**Fig. 3.** The Logger: a laptop equipped with Ubuntu and GNURadio Companion is used to receive and log the code sequence transmitted by the fob.

We considered the following configuration for the SDR: frequency 434 MHz, sampling rate 2M (sps), RF Gain 10 dB, IF Gain 20 dB, and BB Gain 20 dB. We observe that the gains figures adopted by the logger are significantly different from that one used by the jammer. Indeed, the logger has to mitigate the noise power from the jammer in order to decode the code sequence transmitted by the fob. The above values are the result of several trials and they take also into account the relative distances between the jammer, the fob and the logger.

## 5   Measurement Results

We performed several measurements in the parking of our university (College of Science and Engineering - Hamad Bin Khalifa University, Doha, Qatar) during the week-end when the parking was empty, not to interfere with other users. The first step of our attack consists in identifying the communication frequency used by the fob-car communication link. Although different car brands might use different frequencies, there are mainly two different frequencies adopted world-wide [2]: 315 MHz for North America for 433.92 MHz for Europe and Asia. Therefore, an adversary can easily detect which frequency band is used in a couple of consecutive trials. Other unknown parameters such as the modulation scheme (ASK, FSK, PSK) can be easily detected as well by using simple Linux tools such as gqrx [1].

We tested the attack on six different cars: Škoda Yeti (2016), Škoda Octavia (2009), Mazda 6 (2009), Toyota Rav4 (2014), Mitsubishi Pajero (2015) and Nissan Sunny (2014). Another minor challenge introduced by our attack is to find the most effective position for the jammer in the car. Of course, the best position is close to the car signal receiver, which unfortunately is unknown to the adversary. We tried several positions all around the target car taking into account that the jammer should remain hidden to the user and an optimal position turned out to be in the back of the car (for all the car models).

Our measurement scenario is constituted by the target car, the user with the fob and the logger displaced as in Fig. 4.

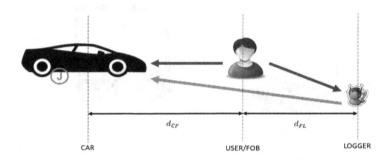

**Fig. 4.** Measurement scenario: the distance between the car and the user is $d_{CF}$ while the distance between the user and the logger is $d_{FR}$.

### 5.1    Results and Discussion

We considered 6 different displacements, i.e., $d_{CF} \in \{5, 10\}$ and $d_{FL} \in \{1, 2, 3, 4\}$, while each configuration has been run 20 times as depicted in Table 1. Firstly, we observe that the chances of the attack being successful get reduced when the distance between the logger and the fob ($d_{FL}$) increases. Moreover, we highlight that the presence of the jammer itself partially prevents the logger to eavesdrop the code sequence. Indeed, this is proved by the fact that when the distance between the jammer/car and the fob ($d_{CF}$) gets larger, the logger can record a good code sequence at 3 m from the fob (that distance is reduced to only 1 m when the fob is 5 m away from the jammer).

**Comparison with [11].** The attack proposed in [11] exploits the combination of both a logger and a jammer as well. Nevertheless, there are significant differences

**Table 1.** Measurement results.

| $d_{CF}$ (m) | $d_{FL}$ (m) | Successful attack frequency |
|---|---|---|
| 5 | 1 | 1 |
| 5 | 2 | 0.4 |
| 5 | 3 | 0.05 |
| 10 | 2 | 1 |
| 10 | 3 | 1 |
| 10 | 4 | 0.1 |

that make our attack scenario even more effective. Firstly, the attack proposed in [11] involves a precisely tuned jammer in order to prevent the self-jamming phenomena, i.e., the jammer on the car prevents the logger to collect a clean code sequence. Our measurements show that the self-jamming phenomena does not happen if the logger is close to the fob (1 m); moreover, if the distance between the user and the car is about 10 m, the adversary has a wider range of action (up to 3 m) having more chances to be hidden to the user. Secondly, our attack is much more flexible. Adopting a fully portable, and remotely controllable jammer, allows us to install the jammer on the car, preventing all the fob-car communications and intrinsically, having more chances to collect and log more code sequences. Finally, there is another significant difference with [11]: Kamkar et al. propose to collect two rolling codes: one for opening the car, while the second one for the future hijacking of the car. This approach might eventually turn out to be very difficult to implement. Indeed, every time the user clicks on the fob's button invalidates the previous codes (assuming the deployed RKS adopts the rolling code strategy). The user might keep trying to open and close the car, even after the car has been opened by the code sequence sent by the adversary. Unfortunately, this makes the solution proposed in [11] very dependent of the user's behaviour and consequently, the attack has to be strictly supervised by the adversary. Conversely, our attack scenario is more effective, since it prevents all the communications between the fob and the car, forcing the user to eventually use the mechanical key to enter the car.

**Discussion.** The proposed attack is very difficult to mitigate. An early strategy has been proposed in [11] involving a jammer detector. Although this strategy might detect an ongoing attack and raise an alarm to the user, it cannot be used to improve the robustness of the keyless communication system. This is mainly due to the intrinsic difficulty of dealing with jamming mitigation [6–9]. Moreover, depending on how "smart" is the car, the jammer might prevent other on-board communications such as the authentication of the key itself, and therefore, preventing the engine to switch on.

# 6  Conclusion

We have proposed a novel scenario attack for remote keyless entry systems involving a new jamming strategy and a remote controlled signal recorder. We tested the attack against six different car models considering different deployment strategies. The cheap HW employed, the easiness of attack deployment, and its effectiveness—always successful, even for a wide range of system parameters—show that RKS are still not secure and that further research by both industry and academia is needed.

# References

1. Gqrx SDR. http://gqrx.dk. Accessed 26 June 2018
2. Remote Keyless Systems. https://en.wikipedia.org/wiki/Remote_keyless_system. Accessed 26 June 2018
3. Alrabady, A.I., Mahmud, S.M.: Some attacks against vehicles' passive entry security systems and their solutions. IEEE Trans. Veh. Technol. **52**(2), 431–439 (2003)
4. van de Beek, S., Leferink, F.: Vulnerability of remote keyless-entry systems against pulsed electromagnetic interference and possible improvements. IEEE Trans. Electromagnet. Compat. **58**(4), 1259–1265 (2016)
5. van de Beek, S., Vogt-Ardatjew, R., Leferink, F.: Robustness of remote keyless entry systems to intentional electromagnetic interference. In: 2014 International Symposium on Electromagnetic Compatibility, pp. 1242–1245, September 2014
6. Di Pietro, R., Oligeri, G.: Jamming mitigation in cognitive radio networks. IEEE Netw. **27**(3), 10–15 (2013)
7. Di Pietro, R., Oligeri, G.: Freedom of speech: thwarting jammers via a probabilistic approach. In: Proceedings of the 8th ACM Conference on Security & Privacy in Wireless and Mobile Networks, WiSec 2015, pp. 4:1–4:6. ACM, New York (2015)
8. Di Pietro, R., Oligeri, G.: Silence is golden: exploiting jamming and radio silence to communicate. ACM Trans. Inf. Syst. Secur. **17**(3), 9:1–9:24 (2015)
9. Di Pietro, R., Oligeri, G.: Enabling broadcast communications in presence of jamming via probabilistic pairing. Comput. Netw. **116**, 33–46 (2017)
10. Francillon, A., Danev, B., Capkun, S.: Relay attacks on passive keyless entry and start systems in modern cars. In: Proceedings of the Network and Distributed System Security Symposium (NDSS). Eidgenössische Technische Hochschule Zürich, Department of Computer Science (2011)
11. Kamkar, S.: Drive it like you hacked it: new attacks and tools to wirelessly steal cars. In: DEFCON 23 (2015)
12. Wang, X., Hou, X., Rios, R., Hallgren, P., Tippenhauer, N.O., Ochoa, M.: Location proximity attacks against mobile targets: analytical bounds and attacker strategies. In: Proceedings of the European Symposium on Research in Computer Security (ESORICS), September 2018

# Aviation Security

# Surveying Aviation Professionals on the Security of the Air Traffic Control System

Martin Strohmeier[1]([✉]), Anna K. Niedbala[1], Matthias Schäfer[2],
Vincent Lenders[3], and Ivan Martinovic[1]

[1] University of Oxford, Oxford, UK
martin.strohmeier@cs.ox.ac.uk
[2] University of Kaiserslautern, Kaiserslautern, Germany
[3] armasuisse, Thun, Switzerland

**Abstract.** In this paper, we report findings from an exploratory study concerning the security of 15 different wireless technologies used in aviation. 242 aviation professionals and experts from 24 different countries completed an on-line questionnaire about their use and perceptions of each of these technologies. We examine the respondents' familiarity with and reliance on each technology, with particular regard to their security. Furthermore, we analyse respondents' perceptions of the possible impact of a wireless attack on the air traffic control system, from both a safety and a business point of view. We deepen these insights with statistical analysis comparing five different stakeholder groups: pilots, air traffic controllers, aviation authorities, aviation engineers, and private pilots.

**Keywords:** Aviation security · Air traffic control · Survey ·
Transportation systems

## 1 Introduction

Over the past decade, the (cyber) security of wireless aviation technologies has gained increasing attention. With both hackers [5] and academic researchers [3] detailing flaws in the fundamentally insecure protocols, awareness of the issue has risen, particularly with regards to the newest, 'next generation' technologies such as the Automatic Dependent Surveillance–Broadcast (ADS–B) protocol [9].

Attempting to fix these security problems requires broad awareness, agreement, and potentially also education across the different stakeholder groups found in aviation. To create the necessary momentum for implementing such changes in a system as slow-moving, safety-focused, and globalised as aviation, a sufficiently large number of people must be familiar with the security problems, their potential impact, and possible solutions. To assess the current level of such awareness, we conducted a survey across all aviation circles. This survey is the first to address these issues publicly, and we are thankful to all involved aviation authorities and air navigation service providers (ANSPs) for their help.

B. Hamid et al. (Eds.): ISSA 2018/CSITS 2018, LNCS 11552, pp. 135–152, 2019.
https://doi.org/10.1007/978-3-030-16874-2_10

We focus on two specific areas within our research. First, we examine the survey respondents' familiarity and knowledge of 15 different wireless technologies, in particular with regards to their security. Second, we examine the respondents' views of the potential impact of wireless attacks on each technology from a safety and business point of view, respectively. We deepen our analysis by comparing the perceptions of the different stakeholder groups.

It is important to note that our goal was not to survey those members of the aviation community with specialist knowledge of computer and systems security. Rather, we attempt to capture the realistic perceptions of typical aviation stakeholders, as we believe these views are more representative, and thus more crucial to influencing key decision making processes.

Some findings from this survey—concretely, an assessment of threat scenarios—have previously been reported in [9]. In the present paper, we focus instead on new quantitative and qualitative data from previously unreported questions and comments, providing novel results and insights through comprehensive statistical analysis. Further, we detail our experiences while conducting this survey and relate these to prevalent attitudes in aviation.

The concrete contributions we make in this work are the following:

- We report insights from an exploratory study with 242 aviation professionals regarding the security of the wireless technologies on which they rely.
- We present previously unreported data on the technological familiarity and dependency of different stakeholder groups found in aviation.
- We analyze the perceptions of flight safety and business impact through attacks on different key technologies and how they vary between stakeholders.

The remainder of this work is organized as follows: Sect. 2 provides the necessary background on the air traffic control technologies examined. Section 3 describes the design of the survey, Sect. 4 its results and Sect. 5 the possible limitations. The related work is outlined in Sect. 6. Section 7 discusses potential implications, and finally, Sect. 8 concludes this paper.

## 2    Air Traffic Surveillance Technologies

We provide a very brief overview of the type of technologies that we surveyed. For a full description of the specific aviation technologies and a review of the related technical work concerning their security, we refer the reader to [9].

Table 1 lists the full name of the technologies that were given to the aviation professionals in our survey. We systematize them into four different categories, illustrated in Fig. 1:

- **Air Traffic Control:** These technologies serve to establish the surveillance picture of the airspace. **VHF**, or voice communication, is the primary means of surveillance for most purposes. **Primary** and **Secondary Surveillance Radar** are the traditional means of locating aircraft's positions, altitude, and identities and providing them to the controller. **ADS-B** and **Multilateration**, on the other hand, are the 'next generation' approach, providing a more accurate surveillance picture with enhanced information.

**Table 1.** Overview of the surveyed technologies.

| Abb. | Technology |
|------|------------|
| *Air Traffic Control* | |
| VHF | Voice (Very High Frequency) |
| PSR | Primary Surveillance Radar |
| SSR | Secondary Surveillance Radar (Modes A, C and S) |
| ADS-B | Automatic Dependent Surveillance-Broadcast |
| MLAT | Multilateration |
| *General Purpose Data Links* | |
| CPDLC | Controller-Pilot Data Link Communication |
| ACARS | Aircraft Communications Addressing and Reporting System |
| *Special Information Services* | |
| TCAS | Traffic Alert and Collision Avoidance System |
| FIS-B | Flight Information System-Broadcast |
| TIS-B | Traffic Information System-Broadcast |
| *Navigation Aids* | |
| GPS | Global Positioning System |
| VOR | VHF Omnidirectional Radio Range |
| ILS | Instrument Landing System |
| NDB | Non-directional Beacon |
| DME | Distance-measuring Equipment |

- **General Purpose Data Links: ACARS** and **CPDLC** are data links that can be used to transmit arbitrary data, from clearances over weather reports and maintenance data to free text. Apart from direct line of sight communication, they also offer High Frequency (HF) and satellite options.
- **Special Information Services:** Contrary to the last group, these technologies provide specialized information: **TCAS** uses SSR and ADS-B to deliver collision avoidance to pilots, **TIS-B** provides traffic information, and **FIS-B** delivers well-defined services such as weather and other flight information. Both TIS-B and FIS-B are ground-based, and are provided by the FAA for general aviation; thus, they are currently only available in the US.
- **Navigation Aids:** The remaining five technologies help pilots navigate. **GPS** provides satellite positioning, while **VOR, NDB,** and **DME** are ground-based systems, delivering directions and distances. Finally, **ILS** provides the pilot with an acoustic indication of the correct glide slope for landing.

## 3  Survey Design

We planned and conducted our survey with the help of private pilots and a full-time professional ATCO. They advised us on the appropriate question language with relation to aviation subject terms. Furthermore, they provided us with the necessary aviation expertise and background at every stage during the design, implementation, and execution of this survey. We report the questions and answer options in Appendix A, and the comments in Appendix B.

Our survey was conducted fully anonymously over the internet, in order to protect respondents from potential repercussions when speaking freely about the security of ATC systems or disclosing potential safety problems. We designed and distributed the questionnaire using SurveyMonkey,[1] without storing participants' IP addresses or other metadata. Thus, no inferences about location or employer could be made from the responses. The study was approved by the University of Oxford Social Sciences & Humanities Inter-Divisional Research Ethics Committee (IDREC) under the reference SSD/CUREC1A/15-033.

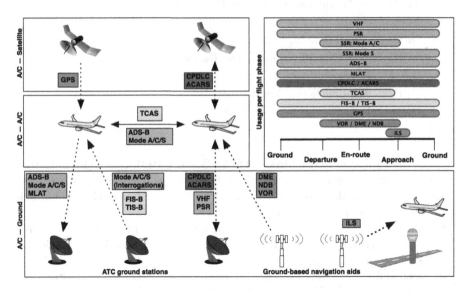

**Fig. 1.** Overview of wireless communication between ground stations, aircraft and satellites. Colours indicate groups, arrows the communication direction. (Color figure online)

### 3.1  Recruitment

We recruited participants through two channels: controlled dissemination (CD) and open dissemination (OD). In the CD phase, we sent our survey to about

---

[1] https://www.surveymonkey.com.

20 air navigation service providers, airlines, and other aviation-related organisations across Europe and the United States. We asked these institutions to post our recruitment page on their mailing list and disseminate it further to other interested entities. This phase lasted from 27 March until 23 June 2015.

In the OD phase, we distributed the questionnaire link in eight large but closely-moderated aviation forums. Two of these forums, focussed mainly on private pilots, agreed to post our survey. This second phase was significantly shorter, owing to the limited time our dissemination link was seen widely in these forums. It lasted from until 21 April until 29 April 2015.

A total of 242 participants completed the survey: 110, or 45.5% in the CD phase, and 132, or 54.5%, in the OD phase. We analyse the responses as a whole. The average response time length was 31 min 10 s.

**Table 2.** Overview of occupations and self-assessed technical comms knowledge.

| Occupation | Group | Number | Share [%] | Avg. Knowl. |
|---|---|---|---|---|
| Pilot | Private | 79 | 32.6 | 3.51 |
| | Commercial | 64 | 26.4 | 3.92 |
| | Military | 5 | 2.1 | 3 |
| Air Traffic Control (ATCO) | Civil | 39 | 16.1 | 4.13 |
| | Military | 4 | 1.7 | 3.25 |
| Aviation Engineer (AE) | - | 19 | 7.9 | 4.11 |
| Aviation Authority (AA) | - | 11 | 4.5 | 4.18 |
| Other | - | 21 | 8.7 | 3.29 |

*Recruitment Experiences.* Anecdotally, the attitudes of the aviation stakeholders contacted via email proved to be positive, interested, and encouraging (where informal feedback was provided). This may naturally be influenced by the fact that the contact persons knew someone in the recruiting team with one or two degrees of separation and were acting in their professional capacity.

The response in the pseudonymous aviation forums was very different. The two that posted the survey, only did so after thorough vetting of our 'bona fides'. Several negative questions about the intent of the research were posed, reflecting on aviation as a highly guarded community. This sentiment was multiplied in the other six forums, which were not willing to post our survey. Four did not give a reason for declining our request, *i.e.*, they did not allow publication of our recruitment page or deleted it shortly after posting. Two stated that they were explicitly concerned with potential negative publicity for the aviation sector as a whole, presumably because negative media headlines about the security of aviation systems are perceived to be either unfair, uninformed and/or unduly hurting the community, which is best poised to fix these problems without outside help.[2]

---

[2] This was epitomized by the well-known 'It's a trap' meme among the forum replies, which aimed to deter other users from answering the survey.

### 3.2 Demographics

Illustrated in Table 2 is the response to Question 1 about the respondents' occupation. A majority were private (33%) or commercial pilots (26%) followed by civil ATCOs (16%) and aviation engineers (8%). Among the respondents who chose 'Other', the professions ranged from software developers in aviation to Flight Information Service Officers. A slight majority (56%) of all OD respondents were private pilots, compared to less than 4% of CD respondents.

The participants' aviation (work) experience (Q2) was distributed fairly evenly, with 32% having 20 years or more, and about 22% offering an expertise of less than 5 years, 5–10 years, and 10–20 years, respectively.

The top working countries (Q3) were the UK (89 respondents) and the US (55). A further 86 worked in Continental Europe, with Germany (21), Estonia (15), Switzerland (10), Spain (7), Norway (7) making up the majority. Six respondents work in countries around the world (Indonesia, Hong Kong, Canada, UAE, Greenland, Armenia), six did not answer this question.

### 3.3 Self-assessed General Knowledge and Work Environment

We asked the pilots which aircraft type(s) they were most familiar with (Q4). Among the commercial pilots, the most named model was the A320 (31 times), followed by the B737 (21). Airbus models overall were mentioned 41 times, Boeing 36 times, and Embraer 11 times. The most named single-engine piston was the Piper PA28 (35), followed by several Cessna models (22).

The respondents estimated their general knowledge about aviation comms (Q5) with a mean of 3.76 out of a symmetric, equidistant 5-point Likert-type scale, where 1 is 'very bad' and 5 is 'very good'. Table 2 illustrates small differences between the stakeholders on this general self-assessment.

## 4  Survey Results

In this section, we present the results of our survey. We report the answers to six questions: two regarding the familiarity of the respondents with the 15 technologies, two concerning trust and security issues, and two in which the respondents were asked to assess the impact of any potential attacks. The full details on these questions are included in Appendix A.

We group the respondents into six different stakeholder types: professional pilots (commercial and military), air traffic controllers (civil and military), employees of aviation authorities, aviation engineers, private pilots, and others not fitting into any of the previous groups (e.g., software engineers and consultants).

Statistical analyses were completed using cumulative link mixed models, a type of ordinal logistic regression that estimates both fixed (predictors) and random (variance groups) effects for ordinal dependent variables. Unless otherwise noted, random intercepts for years of experience (Q2) and country (Q3) were included in each model to account for variance arising from these factors. Responses were coded as ordered factors with the same labels used in the survey (*e.g.* 'Very Unlikely'–'Very Likely'), and factor level contrasts were computed by re-parametrising the fitted model with different contrast codes and reference levels. All analyses were completed using the *ordinal* package in *R* [2,6]. It is important to note that this study was exploratory, thus any effects reported here require further research and confirmatory analysis.

### 4.1   Self-assessment of Technical Familiarity and Dependence

First, we wanted to know which technologies were used by the respondents and how this varied across the different stakeholder groups. Respondents were asked to rate how familiar they were with the 15 technologies (Q6) and how much they relied on each one in their work (Q7). The answers were given on 5-point Likert-type Scales with a separate 'Not heard of this technology' option for these and all following questions. Figure 2 shows the results.

The technologies that respondents across all groups considered themselves most familiar with are VHF and SSR, followed by navigation aids, in particular GPS. This is explained by the prevalence and importance of these technologies in current aviation processes: SSR and VHF are also the most relied upon

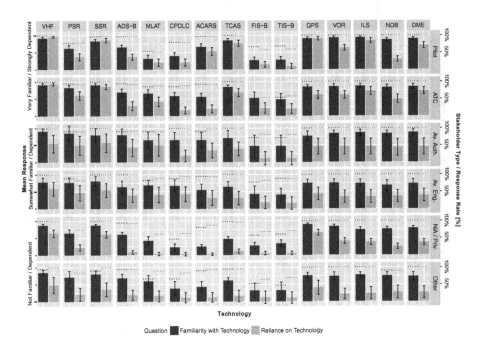

**Fig. 2.** Mean response values for familiarity with and reliance on all technologies by different stakeholders with 95% confidence intervals. The dotted lines illustrate the response rate for each stakeholder and technology.

technologies, followed by navigation aids. As is to be expected, there are differences between the different stakeholder groups. While commercial pilots and ATCOs are both familiar with and reliant on TCAS and ILS, this is not the case for private pilots, who do not usually have these technologies available to them. Respondents familiar with flying under instrument flight rules are unsurprisingly more likely to depend on all technologies, as they feed these instruments. This is in contrast to private pilots, who typically fly under visual flight rules.

At the end of the scale, we can find TIS-B and FIS-B, which are services that are currently only offered to general aviation in the United States; thus, a significant part of our sample would not be familiar with these technologies or use them in their work/aviation experience. Similarly, CPDLC is only being deployed slowly and for few IFR airspaces. Very interestingly, however, more than 50% of all respondents answered that they already rely on ADS-B to some extent, despite the protocol not being operational in most airspaces until 2020.

## 4.2    Assessment of Trust and Security Issues

Second, we examine the perceived attack likelihood and trustworthiness of each technology, again broken down by different stakeholder groups. Figure 3 shows the results for Q8 (*How would you rate the trustworthiness of information derived from these technologies against intentional manipulation by a malicious party?*)

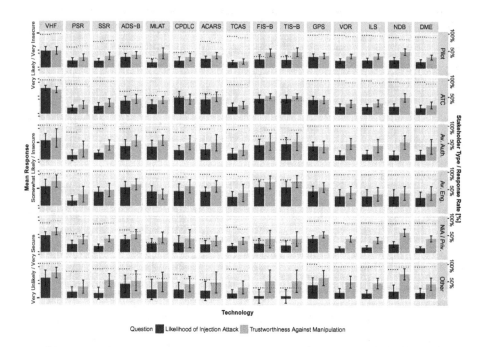

**Fig. 3.** Mean response values for attack likelihood (dark colour) and trustworthiness (light colour) of all technologies as seen by different stakeholders.

and Q9 (*How do you rate the likelihood that a malicious party injects false information into these technologies?*).

The most obvious result is the fact that the likelihood of injection attacks is considered relatively low across almost all technologies and stakeholders. With the (very notable) exception of VHF, which was rated as significantly less trustworthy (average $z = -5.39 \pm 1.9$, all $ps < 0.001$) and significantly more likely to be attacked (average $z = -3.43 \pm 2.25$, all $ps < 0.01$), than all other technologies when controlling for stakeholder type, the remaining technologies average a moderate or lower likelihood. As suggested by several comments (see Sect. 4.4), this is likely due to first- or second-hand experience with VHF interference. Such experiences may also explain the high likelihood rating of GPS. The technologies least likely to be attacked using wireless injection were also analog: DME and VOR, followed by PSR. We further note that while there is a correlation between attack likelihood and trust assessments (Spearman's $\rho = 0.324$), the values for the latter question were generally more similar across technologies, clustering around 'Moderately Secure'.

There were also differences in views between the different stakeholder groups. ATCOs found VHF by far the least trustworthy and most likely to be attacked compared to the other groups, in significant or marginally significant contrast to Pilots (commercial and military; trust $z = -1.95, p = 0.051$, attack likelihood $z = -3.76, p < 0.001$). Similarly to the previous set of questions, fewer pilots answered questions about MLAT (25%, compared to over 50% of ATCOs and over 90% of AEs), but those that did answer believed it to be significantly less likely to be attacked compared to the ATCOs ($z = -2.55, p = 0.011$) and engineers ($z = -2.76, p = 0.006$). Lastly, the private pilots judged a significantly lower attack likelihood across all technologies compared to ATCOs ($z = 3.79, p < 0.001$), AAs ($z = 2.01, p = 0.044$), and AEs ($z = 3.97, p < 0.001$), while their trust ratings across all technologies trended towards a significant difference compared to AEs and Others ($z = 1.75, p = 0.081$ and $z = 1.72, P = 0.085$, respectively).

### 4.3   Assessment of Attack Impact

Finally, we examine the perceived impact of attacks on flight safety as judged by the respondents, and how this contrasts with indirect impact on the business side (*i.e.*, not through effects on safety, but *e.g.*, through causing delays). Figure 4 shows the full results for Q10 (*How would you rate the impact on flight safety by false information injected by a malicious party into each of these technologies?*) and Q11 (*How would you rate the business or monetary consequences of false information injected by a malicious party into each of these technologies? Assume no direct safety incidents.*)

First, it is notable that the flight safety impact is considered higher than the business impact across all technologies and stakeholders: a one-point increase in safety impact rating (*e.g.* from 'Mod. Severe' to 'Severe') predicted an approximately 56% increase in business impact ratings, controlling for technology type and the respondent's familiarity with it (Q6). It is difficult to estimate the reasons for this; the respondents may hold an overall bias towards safety. There

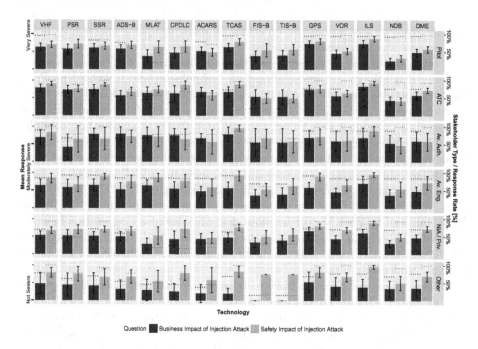

**Fig. 4.** Mean response values for business impact and safety impact of attacks on each technologies as considered by different stakeholders.

are some exceptions, however: respondents working for AAs judged the business impact of some technologies (SSR, ADS-B, MLAT, CPDLC, ACARS) as equally severe or more severe than their safety impact, while ATCOs did the same for data links (CPDLC, ACARS) and special information services (FIS-B, TIS-B).

Across technologies, the highest safety impact values are found for ILS, TCAS, and VHF. This reflects their status as directly safety-critical technologies. TCAS features the largest difference between potential safety and business impact, indicating that other technologies may be more easily used to force *e.g.* unnecessary turnarounds or other flight-prolonging manoeuvres. In general, we find the highest impact ratings among the ATC and navigation aids and the lowest for general and specialized data links, with the notable exception of TCAS.

Stakeholders' judgements of safety impact depended strongly on the different groups' usage and familiarity. Responses to Question 6 (Familiarity) significantly predicted severity ratings of safety and business impact ($z = -2.67, p = 0.008$ and $z = -3.35, p < 0.001$, respectively), with a 13% likelihood of increasing severity ratings for safety impact and 18% for business impact across all technologies and stakeholder groups. This varied significantly by stakeholder group, however. Controlling for familiarity, ATCOs were 40% more likely to judge the safety impact as higher and 63% more likely to judge the business impact as higher than were pilots across all technologies ($z = 3.16, p = 0.002$ and $z = 1$, respectively). We speculate that this is due to a different view on the aviation system in general, *i.e.*, the importance of the communication technologies as compared to the importance of the pilot. This is also illustrated by the differences in judging MLAT's impact in particular. MLAT is a passive localization technology that pilots do not normally come into direct contact with. Here, pilots' business impact ratings are as low as $2.1 \pm 1.2$ for private pilots ($2.5 \pm 1.2$ for commercial pilots) but average around $3.7 \pm 1$ for ATCOs, AAs, and AEs. Overall, ATCOs and AAs were 61% more likely to rate an attack on MLAT as having a severe business impact ($z = 5.65$ and $3.75$, both $ps < 0.001$; AEs were 24% more likely, but this contrast did not reach statistical significance, $p > 0.1$).

### 4.4   Qualitative Analysis

In addition to quantitatively-scaled questions, participants had the option to provide comments and additional thoughts in two free-response questions. All of these responses are enumerated in Appendix B. While some participants conflated both questions, we received 33 comments overall, with three main themes:

- **Direct feedback on the survey:** The largest group consisted of feedback on the survey, both about its design and perceived impact. On the design, this included positive (12, 14, 31) and negative comments (4, 8, 15, 16, 21, 24, 28, 29). Notably, none of the latter pointed out any concrete flaws but stayed very general. Several others pointed out that as private pilots they may not be able to answer all questions fully (7, 30, 32), which was the intended outcome.
- **Personal anecdotes about cybersecurity incidents:** Several comments (1, 3, 6, 10, 11, 17, 29) mentioned personal experiences of wireless interference, mostly on VHF but also SSR and GPS. Some of these were seen as malicious, in particular on VHF, where detection is straightforward. Two comments (25, 27) discussed potential countermeasures, suggesting the use of independent penetration testing or identity-based encryption for ADS-B.
- **Comments on the importance of security research:** Five respondents (3, 5, 13, 14, 19) emphasized the lack of current security research and hoped for increased activity in this area. One (22) hoped that legal threats will prevent any attacks, another suggested that digitalization may be the entirely wrong direction for aviation, in preventing future accidents. Finally, three comments (2, 9, 20) related to the fact that drones/Unmanned Aerial Vehicles (UAV) may be a bigger and more urgent problem to aviation than cyber security at this point in time.

## 5   Limitations

While we tried to carefully design our survey, limitations exist. Some of the more impactful ones are caused by characteristics inherent in the underlying aviation technology others by our design. We discuss all in the following:

- **Exploratory study design:** Participants are likely to have varying grasp of the technical security terms 'authentication' or 'integrity', which is difficult to mitigate without extensive briefing and instruction—something unlikely to be completed by most respondents. Thus, we had to focus on the *relative* differences, *i.e.*, between groups and technologies. Since this was an exploratory study, there were no *a-priori* hypotheses to examine, and thus some significant differences are possibly due to random chance, given the large number of comparisons. However, all significant reported p-values survive a Holm-Bonferroni correction for multiple comparisons.

- **Participant selection:** Our survey cannot necessarily be considered fully representative of the aviation community and its different subgroups. While the sample size is large, there are certainly concerns regarding distribution and potential self-selection. However, we have good reason to believe in the general validity of the results, as they fit in well not only with the existing literature but also with our own extensive experiences in this space as well as the reports of experts we have consulted during this and previous studies.
- **Design:** Because of the varying labels assigned to each survey question (*e.g.* 'Severe', 'Likely', 'Familiar'), the Likert-type scale items cannot be assumed to be equidistant, and thus, it is possible that some scales are slightly imbalanced. This was corrected for in the statistical models. Also, as only one question was posed for each construct we measured, the reliability and validity of the questions cannot be ascertained. Rather, this survey provides a snapshot of individuals' attitudes that can inform future research.
- **Proprietary technology:** Many of the surveyed technologies are implemented by different companies, following open standards that are comparably loose, or even non-existent, as in the case of MLAT. Even some of the very widely used protocols (*e.g.*, ACARS or CPDLC) have proprietary elements that are not freely available. Thus, we were more interested in the participants' general assessment and experiences with the abstract systems, no matter the exact implementation.
- **Fragmentation:** Likewise, there is a forest of different systems, regulations, and processes in aviation. Depending on the airspace, the availability, knowledge, and usage of the discussed protocols differs. However, we mitigated this problem by surveying experts from many countries, making sure their judgement of security in aviation technologies did not vary significantly.

## 6    Related Work

Survey-based analysis is an accepted tool in aviation research, in particular when it comes to examining opinions on and perceptions of safety. For example, a recent article [7] recently used it to analyse the safety of the ADS-B In technology (including the related FIS-B and TIS-B, also covered in our survey). The authors report that almost two thirds of the respondents who used ADS-B-based services felt that they have helped them to visually acquire traffic; more than 40% even believed the information provided aided in the prevention of mid-air collisions. The results clearly illustrate the safety-related benefits of these technologies.

Following recent headlines and increased awareness on security, at least in the academic community, there have been some attempts at extracting the opinions of aviation professionals on this matter. Besides our own survey, the authors in [10] complement our mostly quantitative approach on aviation security perceptions with a number of expert interviews specifically on ADS-B security. Their findings indicate which concrete cyber attack classes are more likely to seriously impact the work of pilots and controllers.

Finally, there have been similar attempts recently to capture the cyber security perceptions of professionals working in the maritime sector, an industry suffering from the same problems as aviation [8].

## 7    Discussion

Our overall results suggest that knowledge about security issues in ATC technology is limited, experience-dependent, and varies strongly across different stakeholder groups. However, while this indicates that the state of cybersecurity in aviation leaves much to be desired—both in knowledge about and awareness of the problem among key stakeholders—there is a slow and steady change in the right direction. In recent years, many regulators and authorities have finally put security higher on the agenda. There are concrete new efforts with regards to information sharing, including the European Centre for Cyber Security in Aviation (ECCSA), which is currently being developed by the European Air Safety Agency (EASA). Along similar lines, a Cyber Air Act has been discussed in the US [1]. We hope that our survey can help to additionally inform these initiatives.

Related to the previous point, we further suggest a reassessment of the wider industry's approach to security and obscurity. The current state of defensiveness and secrecy encountered on security issues in aviation (not only during the implementation of this survey) is notably reminiscent of the behaviour of large software companies in the 1990s, which often preferred to take legal measures against independent security researchers instead of working closely with them as they do today. This has been reflected in our experiences during the recruitment phase of this survey. However, we also found many helpful individuals, typically aided by pre-existing relationships, in particular when established on the personal rather than the institutional level.

It is clear that the fast pace of emerging cybersecurity threats clashes with the time that it takes for new aviation standards and technologies to be conceived, deployed, and finally used operationally on a global scale. This conservative approach has worked well to improve aviation's safety record by minimizing software bugs and hardware problems. However, with regards to wireless security vulnerabilities, aviation has moved at a pace much slower than seen in other, less safety-oriented industries, and it is quickly running out of time.[3]

---

[3] In Feb. 2018, the US Government Accountability Office stressed this point: "Given the amount of time that has transpired since DOD initially raised security concerns in 2008 and the amount of time it will take to formalize, operationalize, and train employees to implement any agreements prior to the January 1, 2020, deadline, it is critical that both DOD and FAA make this a high priority." [4].

We do not discuss any concrete security countermeasures, technical or procedural, as they are out of the scope of this paper. We argue that educating those stakeholders that use the affected systems regarding their security and and working closely with them may be one clear avenue to improve the current state of the art. Due to space limitations, we also do not analyze the accuracy of the perceptions individually; it is trivially obvious that all technologies are inherently insecure as security was never part of their design phase, despite some differences in the ease of exploitation. For an extensive overview of the technical possibilities, the reader is referred to [9].

## 8    Conclusion

In this paper, we reported from a survey about the security of wireless technologies used in aviation. We captured and analysed the knowledge and perceptions of almost 250 aviation professionals and experts, from pilots over air traffic controllers to aviation engineers. As seen during the survey dissemination and the quantitative and qualitative analysis of our findings, there are very different attitudes concerning the topic of security, ranging from ignorance and complacency to hyper-awareness and anxiety.

In summary, we believe that increased awareness by *all* aviation stakeholders can provide the necessary basis for a change in the aviation community's approach to cybersecurity issues. Without all parties on board, crucial regulatory, educational and technical changes are unlikely to be implemented within reasonable time frames.

**Acknowledgements.** We thank Rui Pinheiro for his input on the survey design and all things air traffic control and Kasper B. Rasmussen for his point of view as a private pilot.

## Appendix

## A    Survey Questions

**Question 1:** What is your current line of work?
*Answer options:* Commercial Pilot, Civil Air Traffic Controller, Military Air Traffic Controller, Aviation Engineer, Military Pilot, Aviation Authority, Airline Operator, Not working in aviation; Private Pilot, Other (please specify)
**Question 2:** How long have you been in your current line of work?
*Answer options:* <5 years, 5–10 years, 10–20 years, >20 years
**Question 3:** In what country is your current work based?
*Answer options:* 249 global countries.
**Question 4:** What aircraft type(s) are you most familiar with?
*Answer options:* Free text.
**Question 5:** In general, how would you judge your knowledge of air traffic comm. technologies?

*Answer options:* 5-point Likert scale, 1 = Very bad, 5 = Very good.

**Question 6:** Which of these specific air traffic communication technologies are you familiar with?

*Answer options:* List of all 15 technologies, 5-point Likert scale, 1 = Very familiar, 5 = Not familiar (but heard of it). Separate option 'Not heard of this technology', also covering all following questions.

**Question 7:** Which of those technologies do you rely on in your work?

*Answer options:* 5-point Likert scale, 1 = Very bad, 5 = Very good.

**Question 8:** How would you rate the trustworthiness of information derived from these technologies against intentional manipulation by a malicious party?

*Answer options:* 5-point Likert scale, 1 = Very insecure, 5 = Very secure.

**Question 9:** How do you rate the likelihood that a malicious party injects false information into these technologies?

*Answer options:* 5-point Likert scale, 1 = Very unlikely, 5 = Very likely.

**Question 10:** How would you rate the impact on flight safety by false information injected by a malicious party into each of these technologies?

*Answer options:* 5-point Likert scale, 1 = Not severe, 5 = Very severe.

**Question 11:** How would you rate the business or monetary consequences of false information injected by a malicious party into each of these technologies? Assume no direct safety incidents.

*Answer options:* 5-point Likert scale, 1 = Not severe, 5 = Very severe.

# B    Survey Comments

**Comment 1:** Have experienced external parties checking in and disturbing on actual air traffic control frequencies, fortunately without any serious consequence.

**Comment 2:** New RPAS/UAV threat could ease both jamming ATC to pilots communication, and spoofing ATC instructions. Mechanisms to authentify (and encrypt) controllers-pilots communication will become necessary.

**Comment 3:** I do research in Mode S based systems. I think they are by far too easy to attack. Problem is that my company [an ANSP] is very closed-minded and not open for any help or suggestions to improve their systems. Existing problems are not recognized (missing Know-How) or are ignored intentionally. Actions are taken AFTER regulations are released by authorities (ex: Eurocontrol). I think, a lot of huge companies behave this way to save costs. EU is very strict in expecting air traffic service providers to reduce costs. So the main target of this research should be informing these authorities about the problems (not directly industry or air traffic service provider) to put them in a position being able to release necessary regulations to improve mentioned systems.

**Comment 4:** This survey is grossly misleading and the construction of the questions pay scant regard to the real world. There are many examples of these episodes occurring, and having been involved with some of them, this survey misses the mark totally.

**Comment 5:** Security is often considered as "just existing" investment is often stopped because management finds everything safe and above mentioned scenarios as too far fetched history states it different (9/11).

**Comment 6:** VHF is an increasingly common comms signal to be maliciously emulated by non involved parties. Particularly on tower frequencies. Anyone can buy a transceiver without licence.

**Comment 7:** I am a CPL working as a Flying Instructor on light aircraft. Consequently the impact of many of the technologies mentioned is limited for me.

**Comment 8:** You need to talk to Air Traffic Controllers face to face if you genuinely wish to formulate meaningful questions; you must also understand the if an aircraft does not carry a transponder, it will not show on TCAS hence your questions are irrelevant.

**Comment 9:** Commercially available drones are becoming more of a problem to general aviation. Those in control of the drones could deliberately endanger aircraft. Also the comms controlling the drones are susceptible to interference from terrorists. A potential development for airliners is the onboard systems overruling pilots thought to be deliberately trying to crash into mountains. If that is done by some remote override, the system needs to be robust against terrorists using that system and/or spoofing other navigation system information to remotely crash the airliner! I still prefer the pilot to be in ultimate control of where the plane is going.

**Comment 10:** There are plenty of known occurrences in Europe where things go wrong on 1030/1090 MHz. In most cases, it is not an intentional issue, but the effects are there.

**Comment 11:** I am not aware of any, other than spurious GPS during recent jamming exercises that were carried out, but this did not affect me directly.

**Comment 12:** Interesting survey which hopefully will contribute to form basis for future contingency policy on Aviation/ATM Security.

**Comment 13:** ADS-B has to be secured in case it becomes the primary means (and it will!).

**Comment 14:** In my point of view this study, is a very important area of research as a malicious attack on Aviation Technology can cause severe damage, and the entire aviation community should work together to enhance Security in aviation. Congratulations! Well done.

**Comment 15:** From the way you asked your questions and what you asked you should not expect to draw scientifically sound conclusions from the questionnaire.

**Comment 16:** As a human factors and system safety researcher, if a student of mine proposed a questionnaire such as this, there would be discussion about its limitations and council not to field as is. I can see not valid data being generated – it will lacks authority and credibility.

**Comment 17:** Updates on navigational aids e.g. running SkyDemon on an iPad using an external GPS. I recently carried out the iOS update on my iPad which had bugs which then did not allow SkyDemon to recognise location date being transmitted by the external GPS. All flights then were solely carried out using traditional charts!!!

**Comment 18:** That government which governs least, governs best. That ATC system that controls least, controls best. And is the most secure. More see and avoid, not more computerize and avoid, is not only safer, it is more secure. The enemy can outmaneuver us better if we are not looking. Patrol vigorously, less reliance on gadgets. I have been to many airports that lock pilots out of the ramp but don't even have a fence to keep a terrorist to set up on the end of the runway with a Stinger.

**Comment 19:** A general lack of appreciation, ignorance and complacency surrounds the vulnerability of civil aviation comms.

**Comment 20:** RC comms with multirotor RC aircraft seem a more likely route to attack than aviation specific comms.

**Comment 21:** Sorry, but the questions are phrased rather badly. Are you pilots?

**Comment 22:** I'm amazed that we still rely on the systems that we do. Even simple things like VHF. They're not secure, but they work and the cost to improve them is likely unmanageable. Hopefully laws will continue to work in preventing nasties.

**Comment 23:** Impact on automated operations is different - all the systems today are human mediated.

**Comment 24:** Well that survey isn't leading the answers in any way at all...

**Comment 25:** Need to make portable ADS-B out units assigned to a specific pilot with a encoded id an option for small private aircraft for a reasonable cost.

**Comment 26:** Silly survey questions. Adapted from a internet-like cyber security. Remember aviation is behind by 30 years!

**Comment 27:** Similar to pen testing in my industry (IT Security), can it be attempted to prove that hacking into the on-board system will not mean access to the primary flight controls (A/P). It would calm the travelling public, if that be undertaken by an independent/academic institute.

**Comment 28:** The writer needs to understand aviation technology a little better before embarking on a piece of work like this.

**Comment 29:** Some of the questions might have been worded better....perhaps should have run them past a pilot or controller first, or maybe even used some risk analysis from an aviation SMS. Just a thought. Quite interesting possible concepts though...the only time we really experience malicious interference is on VHF, and that, thankfully, is rare where we operate.

**Comment 30:** Many questions not comprehensible to simple private pilot.

**Comment 31:** Hope it's not too boring compiling this survey. Thank you for your good work. I'm sure the pub beckons soon...

**Comment 32:** Not so sure as a private pilot if I help in this survey, perhaps those with an IR and above [are] more helpful.

**Comment 33:** You are missing FPL comms.

# References

1. Avionics, P.: What are the Biggest Threats to Airlines? January 2018. https://up. panasonic.aero/2018/01/18/cybersecurity-biggest-threats-airlines
2. Christensen, R.H.B.: Ordinal: Regression Models for Ordinal Data (2018). R package version 2018.4-19: https://CRAN.R-project.org/package=ordinal
3. Costin, A., Francillon, A.: Ghost is in the air(traffic): on insecurity of ADS-B protocol and practical attacks on ADS-B devices. In: Black Hat USA, pp. 1–12, July 2012
4. Kirschbaum, J.: Urgent need for DOD and FAA to address risks and improve planning for technology that tracks military aircraft. Technical report GAO-18-177, US Government Accountability Office, January 2018
5. Polstra, P., Polly, C.: Cyber-hijacking airplanes: truth or fiction? Presented at DEFCON 22, Las Vegas, USA, August 2014
6. R Core Team: R: A Language and Environment for Statistical Computing. R Foundation for Statistical Computing. Vienna (2017). https://www.R-project.org/
7. Silva, S.S., Jensen, L., Hansman Jr., R.J.: Safety benefit of automatic dependent surveillance-broadcast traffic and weather uplink services. J. Aerosp. Inf. Syst. **12**(8), 579–586 (2015)
8. Skoglund, R.: Perceived information security in the maritime sector. Master's thesis, Norwegian University of Science and Technology (2017)
9. Strohmeier, M., Schäfer, M., Pinheiro, R., Lenders, V., Martinovic, I.: On perception and reality in wireless air traffic communication security. IEEE Trans. Intell. Transp. Syst. **18**(6), 1338–1357 (2017)
10. Viveros, C.A.P.: Analysis of the cyber attacks against ADS-B perspective of aviation experts. Master's thesis, University of Tartu (2016)

# On the Security of MIL-STD-1553 Communication Bus

Orly Stan[✉], Adi Cohen, Yuval Elovici[✉], and Asaf Shabtai[✉]

Department of Software and Information Systems Engineering,
Ben-Gurion University of the Negev, Beersheba, Israel
stan@post.bgu.ac.il, {elovici,shabtaia}@bgu.ac.il

**Abstract.** MIL-STD-1553 is a military standard that defines the physical and logical layers, and a command/response time division multiplexing of a communication bus used in military and aerospace avionic platforms for more than 40 years. As a legacy platform, MIL-STD-1553 was designed for high level of fault tolerance while less attention was taken with regard to security. Recent studies already addressed the impact of successful cyber-attacks on aerospace vehicles that are implementing MIL-STD-1553. In this work we present a security analysis of MIL-STD-1553, which enumerates the assets and threats to the communication bus, as well as defines the attacker's profile.

**Keywords:** MIL-STD-1553 · Anomaly detection ·
Communication bus security

## 1 Introduction

MIL-STD-1553 is a military standard developed by the US Department of Defense (DoD) for the purpose of military platform integration [2] which has served as the backbone of military and aerospace avionic platforms (e.g., F-15, AH-64 Apache, F-16, V-22, X-45A, F-35) for more than 40 years. It is primarily used for mission-critical systems that require a high level of fault tolerance, since it is deterministic and dual redundant; it also uses a reduced cable topology, connecting all devices on a single bus in a multipoint topology, as opposed to point-to-point topologies.

MIL-STD-1553 is considered deterministic, because it is based on a master/slave methodology in which the master issues messages based on a predefined order and timing. Although other modern, reliable and deterministic data buses have been introduced [3,9,13,15], MIL-STD-1553 remains the most widely used standard in military aviation as it has been for the last 40 years, and is expected to be used in the future. The main reason that alternative deterministic communication buses are not used in existing platforms is the difficulty of modifying an entire operational platform and replacing the main data transmission topology. Moreover, subsequent standards are based on the communication protocol defined by MIL-STD-1553, or contains original MIL-STD-1553 components in

B. Hamid et al. (Eds.): ISSA 2018/CSITS 2018, LNCS 11552, pp. 153–171, 2019.
https://doi.org/10.1007/978-3-030-16874-2_11

order to preserve high reliability [13]. For these reasons, MIL-STD-1553 will likely be an integral component of critical military platforms for many more years to come.

MIL-STD-1553 was developed long before the notion of cyber security was familiar and even basic cyber-attacks, such as denial-of-service (DoS) attacks [4], had not yet been introduced. Research regarding DoS attacks initially reported in the early 1980s, several years after the release of the most recent version of MIL-STD-1553 in 1978, and focused mainly on DoS in operating systems, rather than computer networks [4]. The Designer's Notes for MIL-STD-1553 include a chapter discussing several aspects of network system security which should be addressed when implementing a 1553 communication bus [2]:

- system security policy: defines the classification levels of the system, data, and personnel that are related to the communication bus;
- system security architecture – specifies four approaches for designing systems that process classified plain text data and unclassified data;
- Tempest: states that all components processing unencrypted classified data should be protected against compromising emanation;
- Encryption: should be used in order to isolate components with different classification levels from classified data;
- Trusted message routing and control design: maintaining low bit error rate, parity coding of control words, and monitoring the bus controller can help in detecting errors in messages or in their routing.

Although the Designer's Notes provide references to security aspects, they only contain general guidelines, including references to standards that might not be appropriate for all MIL-STD-1553-based systems (e.g., military vessels developed by other countries might have different or additional compliance requirements than those defined in MIL-STD-1553). Moreover, because the standard is defined for military purposes, more specific guidelines cannot be provided due to confidentiality requirements. Finally, the standard is implemented by various types of systems with diverse objectives, which makes it extremely complicated to provide more specific requirements will suite all existing systems.

Therefore, despite the attention paid to security issues in the Designer's Notes, MIL-STD-1553 still contains vulnerabilities that expose the platforms implementing it to cyber-attacks. Moreover, as presented in Sect. 4, there are modern attacks that are not addressed in the Designer's Notes.

As cyber-attacks play a major role in modern warfare and since military platforms are likely to be attractive targets for attackers [7,11], it has become clear that systems implementing the MIL-STD-1553 standard require improved protection. Recent studies have already addressed the impact of successful cyber-attacks on aerospace vehicles that implement MIL-STD-1553 [10,14]. In [14] the author presents some of the associated vulnerabilities and suggests theoretical methods for creating covert channels over the communication bus. The authors in [10] illustrated the physical impact of simulated cyber-attack on an aerospace vehicle. However, none of them proposed a solution for detect and/or prevent such attacks.

The following sections provide: an overview of the MIL-STD-1553 architecture and communication protocol (Sect. 2); a review of related works regarding the security of systems implementing MIL-STD-1553 and other communication bus technologies (Sect. 3); a security analysis of MIL-STD-1553 (Sect. 4); a conclusion of the paper and a suggestion towards an IDS architecture for identifying attacks on a MIL-STD-1553 communication bus (Sect. 5).

## 2    1553 Communication Bus - Background

MIL-STD-1553 defines a dual redundant serial communication bus used for transmitting data between a bus controller and remote terminals using a multipoint, master-slave bus topology. It was first published in 1973 and the latest version, MIL-STD-1553B, published in 1978, is still used in many military and aerospace systems to this day. MIL-STD-1553 defines the physical layer of the communication bus as well as the logical layer and a command/response time division multiplexing methodology using a 1 Mbps transfer rate data bus, while specifying the transmission timings.

### 2.1    Bus Architecture

The 1553 communication bus includes five key elements: Remote terminal (RT), bus controller (BC), bus monitor (BM), coupler, and the bus itself (illustrated in Fig. 1). The bus is redundant – if a message cannot be transmitted on the main channel it will be retransmitted on the backup channel. Although there are redundant channels, only one element can transmit data over the bus at a time. All elements connected to the bus are continuously exposed to the data transmitted, even if not designated for them. The communication is managed by the BC, and all other elements follow its commands. The bus can support up to 31 connected remote terminals.

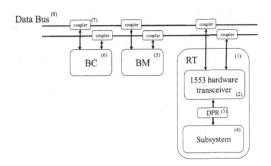

**Fig. 1.** The MIL-STD-1553 bus architecture and its primary components.

**Remote Terminal (RT):** consists of three components. The hardware transceiver is responsible for data transfer between the bus and the subsystem.

It is connected directly to the bus and exchanges data with the subsystem via a dual port RAM (DPR). In addition, it must be able to decode and buffer messages, detect transmission errors, and perform data validation tests. Invalid data should be discarded. The DPR is shared memory which enables data transfer between the transceiver and the subsystem. Both the transceiver and subsystem have read and write permission to this memory. The subsystem is the computational unit (platform computer) of the RT. The subsystem is responsible for all data processing and calculations required for the system to function.

**Bus Controller (BC):** responsible for managing the communication between the RTs connected to the bus using command/response messages. It is the only component that initiates data transfers on the bus to/from RTs or between two RTs. There may be several terminals with BC capabilities connected to the same bus for backup, but only one of them can function as the active BC at a given time. The BC initiates commands to the RTs based on a predefined order and timing.

**Bus Monitor (BM):** responsible for listening and collecting data from the bus in order to observe the state and operational mode of the system and subsystems. The BM is a passive device and does not send any messages, and therefore cannot provide a status report on the data transferred over the bus.

**Coupler:** a physical component used to isolate the components connected to the bus from one another and eliminate the possibility of damage to the bus in case one of the components malfunctions.

**Data Bus:** the transmission medium that physically enables all communication between the components connected to it.

## 2.2   Communication Protocol

Words are the data structure used for transmitting commands, data, and status over the bus. A collection of words defines a message used for receiving or transmitting data. Messages can be periodic or aperiodic. Periodic messages are sent at fixed time intervals (i.e., time cycles). A major frame is a predefined time frame in which all periodic messages are transmitted at least once (derived from the periodic message with the longest time cycle). Aperiodic messages are event-driven and therefore are not sent in fixed time cycles. However, they have a fixed time slot in the major frame.

The standard defines three types of words: command, data, and status (illustrated in Fig. 2). All words are 20 bits long, starting with three bits of synchronization and ending with a parity bit.

**Command Word:** initiated by the BC and designated to an RT. The command specifies the action that the RT should perform: whether to receive or transmit data. The remaining 16 bits are defined as follows:

– Terminal address (TA): a five bit field containing the address of the RT that the command is designated for. It can contain up to 31 RT addresses (00000B

Command Word

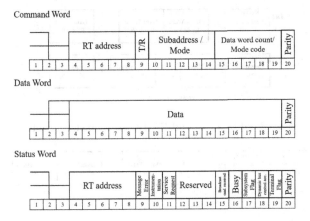

Fig. 2. Communication protocol words structure.

to 11110B), since the terminal address 11111B is reserved for broadcast command.

– T/R bit: a single bit that indicates the direction of the required data transfer. Logic 1 indicates that the RT should transmit data, and logic 0 indicates that the RT should receive data.
– Subaddress/Mode: a five bit field indicating the subaddress of the RT to receive/transmit the data, or that this command is a mode code (in this case it is set to 00000B or 11111B). Mode codes are special commands used to change the operation mode of the RTs such as: timing synchronization, RT transmitter shut down, and request to initiate self-test.
– Data word count/mode code: a five bit field which contains the number of data words to be received/transmitted. If a mode code is set, these five bits indicate the mode code.

**Data Word:** Contains the actual data being transferred on the bus. There is no predefined structure for data words.

**Status Word:** Sent by the RT to the BC upon receiving a valid message, in order to report its status to the BC. It contains different flags indicating different types of errors, such as received data error, data processing error, and circuitry error. It also allows the RT to request a service from the BC.

### 2.3 Communication Formats

There are four types of communication between elements over the bus, all of which are initiated by the BC. The communication formats are designed to maintain high reliability of the protocol by acknowledging every message sent on the bus and flagging for errors and validation of the messages (using status words).

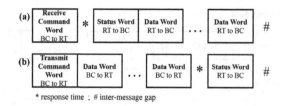

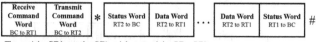

**Fig. 3.** BC-RT (a) and RT-BC (b) transfer format.

The receiving RT is noted as RT1 and the transmitting RT as RT2.
* response time ; # inter-message gap

**Fig. 4.** RT-RT transfer format.

**BC-RT/RT-BC Data Transfer:** the communication between the BC and an RT has two formats: 'receive' (BC-RT) and 'transmit' (RT-BC). In order to initiate a BC-RT communication (Fig. 3(a)), the BC issues a 'receive' command to the RT, and immediately transmits the data words. The RT receives and validates the data, and responds with a status word. In order to start a RT-BC communication (Fig. 3(b)), the BC issues a 'transmit' command to the RT. The RT receives the command and responds with a status word, which is immediately followed by the data words it should transmit.

**RT-RT Data Transfer:** in RT-RT communication (Fig. 4), one RT transmits data to another RT. The BC starts the communication by issuing a 'receive' command to the receiving RT, which is immediately followed by sending a 'transmit' command to the transmitting RT. The transmitting RT responds with a status word and transmits its data words. Upon receiving the data, the receiving RT responds with a status word.

**Mode Code Transfer:** the BC can send a mode command by setting the subaddress/mode field to 00000B or 11111B. In this case the word count field defines which mode code should be performed. A mode command can be sent to a specific RT or to all RTs. A mode command can be associated with up to one data word.

**Broadcast Transfer:** the standard also supports broadcast messages. Broadcast can be used with messages in which only the BC is transmitting data and all others are receiving. The broadcast message format is similar to the non-broadcast messages, with two exceptions: the terminal address field is set to 11111B, and all receiving RTs suppress their status word transmission.

# 3   Related Work

Although MIL-STD-1553 is the basis for many mission-critical platforms, there has been very little research conducted regarding its security. The security of mission-critical and embedded systems was discussed in [1,5,16]. In 2005, Chong et al. [1] suggested design principles and guidelines for a survivability system architecture and applied it to a DoD information system. In 2016, Vai et al. [16] developed a methodology for designing a general mission-critical embedded system that considers cyber security aspects. The authors suggest a modular system architecture that contains cyber security features (e.g., cryptographic components and a separation kernel), and monitoring and recovering services.

These kind of security measures are suitable for systems that are in their design phase, in which different security features and principles can be considered and integrated correctly; however, they are not suitable for enhancing the security of existing 1553 bus implementations, because changing components of the 1553 communication bus is cost prohibitive due to its extensive deployment in wide range of aircrafts and vehicles.

In the context MIL-STD-1553, in 2014, McGraw et al. [10] explored the impact of malicious actions on a satellite that uses a 1553 communication bus for intercommunication between its subsystems. The communication bus was modeled using SimPy (a simulation framework written in Python), and consists of a BC, BM, and 10 RTs. In addition, STK SOLIS (a simulation environment for spacecraft) was used for generating a high fidelity model and data exchange between the simulated subsystems. In order to explore malicious actions, McGraw et al. [10] characterized the normal behavior of a space asset and used it to detect perturbations which may indicate the presence of a malware. Two scenarios of abnormal behavior were simulated: the presence of solar flares or ionization activity, and the presence of a malware. These abnormal scenarios were simulated by injecting noises (of different magnitudes) into the sensors' models. Manual analysis of the results indicated that it is possible to detect the anomalous events. Moreover, the authors were able to distinguish between events that might be caused by ionization and those that might be caused by a malware. The authors also observed a significant change in the satellite physical position in the presence of malware.

In 2015, Nguyen [14] introduced several methods for creating covert channels over a 1553 communication bus, in order to leak data from high security level subsystems to lower subsystems. The suggested attacks utilize different features and behavioral characteristics of the communication protocol defined by the standard, in order to establish a signaling mechanism between two cooperating subsystems connected to the same communication bus. Nguyen presented three attack scenarios and categorized them into two types: timing and storage attacks. Timing attacks utilize time delays between messages defined by MIL-STD-1553, while storage attacks utilize word structure and programmer-defined features. More specifically, the storage attacks utilize the 'command illegalization' implementation (which is a programmer defined feature), and the Service Request (SR) feature defined by the standard which enables an RT to notify the BC that it needs to transmit or receive data. The suggested attack scenarios are merely theoretical and were not empirically tested. In addition, the suggested attacks rely on assumptions which are not necessarily correct or applicable for all 1533 communication buses and are inefficient. For example, if the RT that executes a timing attack is able to control its response delays to the granularity of one microsecond, it can leak up to three bits per message. Covert channel attacks were taken into consideration in the security analysis we present in Sect. 4.

## 4 Security Analysis of the 1553 Communication Protocol

In this section we present a comprehensive security analysis of the MIL-STD-1553 communication protocol which consists of the following elements.

**Asset:** an element, which is part of the 1553 communication bus, that (1) an attacker might be interested in, and (2) has the potential to disrupt the system's operation or leak information when compromised. An asset might be a physical component (e.g., a subsystem), or data present in the system (e.g., transmitted messages, data stored in a subsystem).

**Attacker Profile:** an individual, group, organization, or government that have interest in attacking the system's assets and attempt to access them via attack vectors.

**Attack Vector:** indicating various methods used by an attacker to penetrate the system in order to perform the malicious activity.

**Threat Agent:** an entity (individual, software, hardware), internal or external to the system, that uses its privileges in order to execute the attack.

**Attack Method:** the actions that an attacker should perform in order to execute an attack.

### 4.1 Assets

The identified assets that are part of a MIL-STD-1553 communication bus and might have value to a potential attacker are can be categorized as follows.

**Connectivity Assets:** the physical components responsible for data transfer between the different components at different levels:

- Transmission medium (the bus itself) (component 8 in Fig. 1): the physical wires that connect the RTs and enable all communication and data transmission.
- Transceiver (component 2 in Fig. 1): responsible for decoding the analog signals into digital data which is comprehensible to the subsystem (and vice versa) and thus enables data transfer between the bus and the subsystem.
- Coupler (component 7 in Fig. 1): an electrical unit that isolates the bus from an RT and connects the transceivers to the transmission medium.

Damage to one of these components might harm the availability of a part, or the entire, system. Denying a critical subsystem to transmit data (by sabotaging its connectivity assets for example) prevents inputs for other component that might fail in performing their tasks, potentially leading to disconnection between components. Since these components are physical, they are capable for compromising emanation, which harms the confidentiality of the system. The integrity of the system is also threatened by these assets, since they have access to the inputs and outputs of each component, and once compromised, they can manipulate these data.

**Data Assets:** the data stored in different parts of the system:

- DPR data (component 3 in Fig. 1): the data stored in the shared memory of the transceiver and the subsystem (DPR).
- Subsystem data (component 4 in Fig. 1): the data that is stored in the memory of the subsystem and consumed by the subsystem in order to perform its tasks (e.g., geographical location).
- Data in motion (components 8 in Fig. 1): the current signals (data) transmitted over the bus.

Any damage or changes made to these assets violates the integrity of the system. Moreover, as previously described, manipulation of the inputs and outputs of subsystems can damage the system's availability. Moreover, lack of data encryption breaks the system's confidentiality once leaked outside.

**Computational Units:** the subsystem (component 4 in Fig. 1) consists of physical components (e.g., CPU, memory, sensors) and the software responsible for performing the subsystem's tasks (e.g., reporting the current position, calculating distance from objects).

Compromised subsystems can manipulate or generate false outputs and break the system's integrity, stop communication with other subsystems and damage its availability, or abuse access to other devices in order to leak data and violate the system's confidentiality.

The table in Appendix A provides more detailed description of each asset and the security concerns (i.e., potential consequences) related to it, categorized by integrity, confidentiality, and availability.

## 4.2   Attacker Profile

Since MIL-STD-1553 is mainly implemented in military platforms, most of the attack vectors require physical access to the system (e.g., change components' code, eavesdropping), or access to external devices that interact with the system (such as USB devices or CDs) or sensors (such as GPS or RADAR). This kind of access requires highly skilled attacker such as a state actor.

The attack vectors can be categorized into three main groups: code injection and manipulation, data injection, and physical tampering. The attacker is assumed to have the ability to execute at least one of these attack vectors during the life cycle of the system (e.g., development, supply chain, deployment, or maintenance stages). These individuals can abuse their access rights in order to sabotage various components.

Once the attacker gained access to the system he/she executes the attack via a component connected to the system or an individual that have physical access to it, which are referred to as *threat agents*.

### Attack Vectors

**Code Injection and Manipulation:** this attack vector refers to the ability to inject or manipulate the code of the system's components in order to perform the attack. This includes the program coded in the transceiver, as well as the operating system or software of a subsystem. Malicious code can be injected during the main phases of the component's life cycle: development, supply chain, and deployment and maintenance.

The development phase includes all processes that take place before delivering the product to the client: hardware manufacturing, code writing, integration, and testing. During the development phase, malicious individuals can exploit their access to the components and insert erroneous or malicious code, or physically tampering with components. Though components are tested before they are delivered to clients, a sophisticated attacker can inject code that is programmed to operate within a specific context and can identify when it is in the real environment, thereby evading detection tools.

During the deployment and maintenance phase various procedures performed may expose the system to malicious code injection. These procedures include: operating system and software updates, bug fixes, system configuration, and data loading. Such maintenance activities may be performed via wireless communication or physically via CD/DVD, USB connection, or through a computer that is connected to the bus. In this phase, code injection and manipulation may also be performed by another component that was previously compromised and is connected to the bus.

**False Data Injection:** data injection refers to false data provided by sensors, such as Global Positioning System (GPS) or Radio Detection And Ranging (RADAR) systems, or an external device (e.g., magnetic tape, CD/DVD, or computer). In recent years extensive research has been conducted regarding false data injection attacks on control systems, mainly on electrical power grids [8,12]. In this type of attack, the attacker injects crafted data into the system through sensors (or other input devices) that alter the normal behavior of the system and might lead to failures and even the execution of malicious code. Note, however, that in order to perform a successful data injection attack without detection, the attacker must have in depth knowledge of the system and its vulnerabilities.

**Physical Tampering:** every electronic device emits electromagnetic radiation. By eavesdropping on the device and analyze its electromagnetic emanations, an attacker can reveal information regarding the device's operation. This type of attack is called tempest [6], and it is addressed in the Designer's Notes for MIL-STD-1553. However, a malicious individual who has physical access to the system can make subtle changes to the system, such as adding computational capabilities to a coupler, manipulating wiring or the coupler's grounding. Such modifications may not change the component's behavior significantly, but does create some type of side effect (such as amplified electromagnetic radiation), which may also go undetected if the system is not specifically tested for those specific side effects.

### Threat Agents

After the attacker managed to gain access to the system, he/she can use one of the following threat agents in order to execute an attack: a component connected to the bus or a malicious individual (human) possessing access permissions to the system.

**Component (RT and BC):** we distinguish between two types – a compromised component and a fake component. A compromised component is a component which was originally part of the system and was manipulated by the attacker. This may include components that are not constantly connected to the bus and are connected on demand (e.g., for uploading configurations, downloading logs, and maintenance). A fake component was not part of the system and was connected to it illegitimately. Once connected, the fake component becomes part of the system and can transmit data and listen to all communications. We also distinguish between BC and RT components, since the functionality of the BC is more extensive than the functionality of the RT, and hence has greater capabilities for executing attacks.

**Malicious Individual:** an individual (human) that cooperates with the attacker (or the attacker himself) and has access to the system, who can tamper with its components physically (by sabotaging their circuitry, for instance), or logically (e.g., by inserting errors in a component's code).

### 4.3   Attack Methods and Consequences

This section describes the threats to the MIL-STD-1553 communication protocol, which are categorized by their consequence: denial of service, data leakage and data integrity violation. The following subsections elaborate on the different threats to the 1553 communication bus and provide methods to execute them. Appendix B provides more detailed description of each attack method, categorized by message manipulation and behavior manipulation. Message manipulation refers to modification of legitimate words (command, data, or status) transmitted over the bus. Behavior manipulation refers to altering the behavior of the compromised component, for example, transmitting fake (malicious) messages in unusual timing or order.

**Denial of Service (DoS).** DoS can be achieved by damaging physically or logically the system's assets, and will usually require only one threat agent. Physical damage to a component can harm its ability to perform operations, produce outputs, or transmit them over the bus. In particular, if the damaged component is the bus itself, there could be a complete disconnection between all of the components connected to it.

Logical damage refers to exceptions occurred during component's normal operation, component's incorrect operation, or data manipulation and corruption. These scenarios result in corrupted output or lack of response, which can lead to denying the operation of one or more components. Following a description of possible methods to achieve DoS to an 1553 communication bus.

**Message Manipulation:** compromised components with BC capabilities can change fields of a command word (e.g. WC, T/R, and TA) to control data routing and cause collisions. For example: denying a 'transmit' command from reaching the GPS by changing its TA field will cause other subsystems (e.g. navigation, artillery, etc.) rely on outdated data, which can have severe outcomes. Manipulating status words by a threat agent to falsely indicate on errors in the target RT might lead to termination of the communication with it, although it operates correctly. Data words can be easily corrupted by different threat agents, by causing collisions or manipulating them at the subsystem's level. Lack of sufficient input validation by the component can lead to an incorrect operation and even crash it.

**Behavior Manipulation:** compromised components that can control their response delays and transmission times or behave differently than the command specifies can also cause collisions and failures to other component, thus lead to DoS.

**Possible Operational Consequences:** DoS to the 1553 communication bus can have devastating results, especially because it is used for mission critical systems. The attack can be executed upon detection of some operation in order to intercept it. For example, an attacker that listens to the bus can identify that the system entered a certain geographic zone and deny location data from updating the navigation system, or identify that the system is aiming to fire at a target and deny the firing command from reaching the relevant components (as illustrated in Fig. 5(a)).

**Data Leakage.** Data leakage in the context of the MIL-STD-1553 communication bus is the result of unauthorized data transmission between components (i.e. components of different security levels) or outside the system.

**Message Manipulation:** by changing the WC or TA fields in a command word, a threat agent can instruct a component to transmit exceeding data words, or to transmit data words to another component (that may have lower security level). Data can also be leaked using the reserved bits of a status word, or by modulating additional payload on legitimate data words.

**Behavior Manipulation:** threat agents that can control their behaviors are capable of creating a covert channels in order to leak data as presented by Neugen in [14]. If the threat agent has BC capabilities it can also utilize idle time on the bus and initiate unauthorized data transfers. Moreover, if the threat agent has an access to an external device or removable hardware it can utilize it to leak data outside the system. Data can also be leaked physically by eavesdropping the electromagnetic emanations of components.

**Possible Operational Consequences:** leaked data can help the attacker conclude information about the operation of the system. Usually vehicle have service ports (e.g. USB) that are easily accessible to maintenance crew for debugging and investigating the vehicle's performance. A malicious crew member can extract logs and traffic traces from the system and pass them to the attacker. Sensitive information, such as: current vehicle location, targets, and destinations, can be leaked by a compromised component outsize the vehicle by using legitimate external communication channels (e.g., radio).

**Violation of Data Integrity.** Violation of data integrity refers to invalid or incorrect data that flows inside the system and causes other component to fail or operate incorrectly. Incorrect data can get inside the system by a threat agent external to the system (see Sect. 4.2) or by an inside threat agent that can manipulate messages exchanged over the bus or send fake data in the behalf of another component (i.e., spoofing), and cause the system to behave abnormally.

**Possible Operational Consequences:** by altering the data words an attacker can cause the system to navigate to the wrong destination, fire at the wrong target, and even to no fire at all, or withhold/add objects from/to the vehicle's dashboards and deceive the crew aboard. Figure 5(b) illustrates an attack scenario in which the attacker provides fake object location by utilizing: (1) the transmission time gap between two legitimate messages; and (2) the refresh timing of the displays RT.

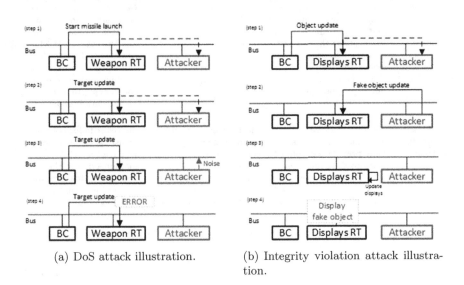

(a) DoS attack illustration.          (b) Integrity violation attack illustration.

**Fig. 5.** Attacks illustration.

# 5   Conclusions and Future Work

MIL-STD-1553 is a widely used standard in military avionics, which is vulnerable to cyber-attacks that potentially lead to devastating results. In this paper we present a security analysis of MIL-STD-1553 that enumerates the assets and threats to a MIL-STD-1553 communication bus, as well as defines the attacker's profile. To the best of our knowledge, there are no security solutions for identifying and/or preventing cyber-attacks on a MIL-STD-1553 communication bus. Thus, a security solution is required.

In future work, we plan to establish an operational testbed and implement the attacks described in this work. In addition, we plan to develop an intrusion detection system (IDS) which will monitor the bus continuously in order to identify malicious activities. The IDS will focus on the presented attack methods: (1) identifying data transmissions from illegitimate source (i.e. spoofing); (2) identifying anomalous message sequences (DoS and data leakage attacks); and (3) identifying anomalous data words (integrity violation attacks).

# A   Assets and Potential Consequences

| Asset | Integrity | Confidentiality | Availability |
|---|---|---|---|
| Transceiver | Compromised transceiver can provide corrupted data to the subsystem it connects to the bus or to other components connected to the bus which can lead to incorrect operation | | Compromised/corrupted transceiver can stop data transfer between the bus and the subsystem which can lead to DoS to the subsystem it connects to the bus, and/or to other components that depend on the data it should transmit |
| Transmission medium (the bus itself) | Shorts or failure of the transmission medium may provide corrupted data to the components connected to the bus which can further lead to incorrect operation of the system | Electromagnetic energy emanating from compromised transmission medium may be used to deduce the information transmitted on the bus and compromise the system's confidentiality | Shorts or failure of the transmission medium may lead to total disconnection of the communication over the bus and interrupt the system's operation |

(*continued*)

*(continued)*

| Asset | Integrity | Confidentiality | Availability |
|---|---|---|---|
| Coupler | Compromised coupler can provide corrupted data to the RT it connects to the bus, or to other components connected to the bus which can lead to incorrect operation | Electromagnetic energy emanating from a compromised coupler may be used to deduce the information transmitted on the bus and compromise the system's confidentiality | Unavailable coupler disconnects the RTs connected to the coupler from the bus. In some cases it can also cause DoS to other components connected to the bus |
| Subsystem | Compromised subsystem can provide corrupted data to other components and lead to incorrect operation. It can also spoof as another component by changing the TA field of a command | Compromised subsystem can abuse access to devices that have the ability to transmit data outside the system (i.e., radio transmitter) and leak sensitive information | Unavailable subsystem stops responding to commands and data transmission which might lead to DoS to other components depending on its outputs and possibly even to the entire system. Corrupted data sent by a compromised subsystem to other subsystems may also result in DoS |
| DPR data | Corrupted data provided to a component can lead to incorrect operation | Classified data that leaks outside the system in plain text can be abused by malicious individuals | Unavailable or corrupted data may lead to DoS to the components depending on it, and possibly even to the entire system |
| Subsystem data | Corrupted data provided to a component can lead to incorrect operation of the system | Classified data and/or operation logic that leaks outside the system in plain text can be abused by malicious individuals | Unavailable or corrupted data may lead to failure of the subsystem's operation and may also result in DoS to the components depending on its outputs and possibly even to the entire system |
| Data in motion | Corrupted data provided to a component can lead to incorrect operation of the system | Classified data and/or operation logic can be leaked outside the system by compromising emanation and can be abused by malicious individuals | Unavailable data might lead to DoS to the components depending on it and possibly even to the entire system |

# B    Threats and Attack Methods

| Category | DoS attack | Data leakage | Data integrity vaiolation |
|---|---|---|---|
| *Message manipulation* | | | |
| Command word | **WC field**<br>– Changing the WC field to a smaller number causes the target RT to receive or transmit partial data which can lead to an error in the target RT or other RTs depending on its output<br>– Changing the WC field to a larger number can also lead to an error due to collisions and corrupted data reception<br>**T/R bit**<br>– Flipping the T/R bit in a 'transmit' command causes the target RT to receive a 'receive' command that causes the target RT to respond with an error or wait for data to arrive (while no data is transmitted); furthermore the RT won't send the data it should to other RTs and they won't get their inputs<br>– Flipping the T/R bit in a 'receive' command causes the target RT to receive a 'transmit' command that can lead to an error or data transmission that causes collision (since the BC continues to transmit the data of the 'receive' command)<br>**TA field**<br>– Changing the TA field to another/unsupported RT address prevents the command from reaching its target RT and can cause a failure in the RT's operation or failure of other RTs depending on it | **WC field**<br>– By changing the WC field of a 'transmit' command to a larger number the threat agent might cause the target RT to transmit more data than it should. If the attacker is familiar with the memory map of the target RT, he/she can use this method to access restricted areas in the target RT's memory<br>**TA field**<br>– By changing the TA field in a 'transmit' command to another RT address the threat agent might obtain data from a subsystem that it is not authorized to hold<br>– By changing the TA field of a 'receive' command, the threat agent can force an RT to accept data that it might not be authorized to hold | A threat agent with BC capabilities can be used to tamper with the communication between the real BC and various RTs. The threat agent can corrupt the original command when it is transmitted over the bus, and send its own command to the target component instead. The target component will send its response without knowing that the command received is different than the original one, and the real BC will receive a response for a command it did not send |
| Status word | A compromised RT can impersonate as another and set the 'Busy', 'Terminal', or 'Subsystem' flags in its status word and provide a falsely indication to the BC regarding a malfunction or inability to handle messages and thus disrupt the communication with that RT. Similarly, a fake BC can respond on behalf of the target RT and signal the BC to stop sending commands to the target component | Leaking data via status words can be done by utilizing the 'reserved' bits (see Fig. 2) - three bits that are reserved for future development of the standard. The standard specifies that these bits should be unused and remain set to zero. A lack of status word monitoring enables cooperating threat agents to easily transfer any data without detection | Any threat agent connected to the bus (with BC or RT capabilities) can corrupt status words transmitted back to the real BC and send fake statuses as if is the transmitting RT |

*(continued)*

(*continued*)

| Asset | Integrity | Confidentiality | Availability |
|---|---|---|---|
| Data word | – A malicious BC or RT can alter legitimate data transmitted and cause failure in the target component (if the target component doesn't perform validation at the subsystem level)<br>– An attacker who has prior knowledge about the target component can generate and inject fake data that can cause failure, disrupt the normal operation, or impair the outputs of the target component | Any threat agent can use the data words it transmits in order to modulate additional payload. This type of attack requires a cooperating threat agent who is familiar with the modulation method and can then decode the additional payload | Threat agents can utilize idle times on the bus and resend fake commands to target components on behalf of legitimate components, in order to override the real data stored in the target components' memory. The target components will consider the fake data to be the real data received from the legitimate component |
| *Behavior manipulation* | | | |
| Command word | **Fake command**<br>Issuing fake commands (either defined by the standard or meaningless) that are not part of the system's normal operation may result in collisions, blocking all communication over the bus or affecting the proper system's operation (e.g. issuing shut-down commands or clock synchronizing at incorrect timings)<br>**WC field**<br>– Sending less data than specified by the WC field of a command causes the target component to receive incomplete data and may fail to operate<br>– Sending excessive amount of data can cause a collision if the target component responds with its status while the threat agent is still transmitting data | Neugen presented in [14] a storage attack method to create covert channel between two compromised components of different security levels over the 1553 bus, which requires a compromised BC and a compromised RT, and is based on the RT's specific 'command illegalization' implementation | |
| Status word | | Neugen presented in [14] a storage attack method to create covert channel between two compromised components of different security levels over the 1553 bus, which is based on the Service Request (SR) bit of a status word and requires a cooperating BC and RT | |

(*continued*)

| Asset | Integrity | Confidentiality | Availability |
|-------|-----------|-----------------|--------------|
| Transmission timings | – Threat agents that can control the timing of their transmissions can transmit messages at the time of choice. Sending unexpected messages to target components may result in failures.<br>– Threat agents that can control the timing of their transmissions can cause collisions that corrupt data transmitted over the bus (e.g., by transmitting at random timing) and can lead to error or incorrect operation of other components | – Neugen presented in [14] a timing attack method to create covert channel between two compromised components of different security levels over the 1553 bus, in which two cooperating RTs establish a signaling mechanism based on their response time delays that are interpreted into binary data<br>– Threat agent with BC capabilities can utilize idle time periods on the bus and initiate data transfer with any RT in order to extract data. If there is a cooperating threat agent connected to the bus, then the agent with BC capabilities can initiate RT-RT communication and transfer data from the target RT to the cooperating threat agent | |
| BM impersonation | | Any threat agent connected to the bus can act as a BM and record the data transmitted over the bus which is available to all components connected to the bus. This data may be further leaked to other components or external devices via removable hardware (e.g., USB, CD, or magnetic tape), an available connection to other networks, or covert channels | |
| Tempest | | Malicious individuals can eavesdrop and capture the electromagnetic emanations of components [6] (which can be enhanced by physically sabotaging the components), and analyze them in order to obtain information about the target component's operation that can imply on other operations and characteristics of the entire system and help the attacker better understand it | |

# References

1. Chong, J., Pal, P., Atigetchi, M., Rubel, P., Webber, F.: Survivability architecture of a mission critical system: the DPASA example. In: 21st Annual Computer Security Applications Conference (ACSAC 2005), December 2005, pp. 10, 504
2. Data Device Corporation: MIL-STD-1553 Designer's Guide (1998)
3. Gillen, A., Shelton, J.: Introduction of 3910 high speed data bus. In: Military Communications Conference, MILCOM 1992, Conference Record. Communications-Fusing Command, Control and Intelligence, pp. 956–960. IEEE (1992)
4. Gligor, V.D.: A note on the denial-of-service problem. In: IEEE Symposium on Security and Privacy, pp. 139–149 (1983)
5. Jiang, W., Guo, W., Sang, N.: Periodic real-time message scheduling for confidentiality-aware cyber-physical system in wireless networks. In: 2010 Fifth International Conference on Frontier of Computer Science and Technology, pp. 355–360, August 2010
6. Kuhn, M.G., Anderson, R.J.: Soft tempest: hidden data transmission using electromagnetic emanations. In: Aucsmith, D. (ed.) IH 1998. LNCS, vol. 1525, pp. 124–142. Springer, Heidelberg (1998). https://doi.org/10.1007/3-540-49380-8_10
7. Lindsay, J.R.: Stuxnet and the limits of cyber warfare. Secur. Stud. **22**(3), 365–404 (2013)
8. Liu, Y., Ning, P., Reiter, M.K.: False data injection attacks against state estimation in electric power grids. ACM Trans. Inf. Syst. Secur. (TISSEC) **14**(1), 13 (2011)
9. Mayoux, J.-J.: The data bus of the next generation European fighters. In: Proceedings of the IEEE 1993 National Aerospace and Electronics Conference, NAECON 1993, pp. 152–156. IEEE (1993)
10. McGraw, R.M., Fowler, M.J., Umphress, D., MacDonald, R.A.: Cyber threat impact assessment and analysis for space vehicle architectures. In: International Society for Optics and Photonics SPIE Defense+ Security, p. 90850K (2014)
11. Miller, B., Rowe, D.: A survey SCADA of and critical infrastructure incidents. In: Proceedings of the 1st Annual Conference on Research in Information Technology, RIIT 2012, pp. 51–56. ACM (2012)
12. Mo, Y., Sinopoli, B.: False data injection attacks in control systems. In: Preprints of the 1st Workshop on Secure Control Systems, pp. 1–6 (2010)
13. Murdock, J.K., Koenig, J.R.: Open systems avionics network to replace MIL-STD-1553. In: Proceedings of 19th Digital Avionics Systems Conference, 19th DASC (Cat. No. 00CH37126), vol. 1, pp. 4E5/1–4E5/6, October 2000
14. Nguyen, T.D.: Towards MIL-STD-1553B covert channel analysis. Technical report, Naval Postgraduate School, Monterey, California (2015)
15. US Department of Defense: Fiber Optics Mechanization of an Aircraft Internal Time Division Command/Response Multiplex Data Bus, May 1988
16. Vai, M., et al.: Systems design of cybersecurity in embedded systems. In: 2016 IEEE High Performance Extreme Computing Conference (HPEC), pp. 1–6, September 2016

# Author Index

Printed in the United States
By Bookmasters